COLOR
DRAWING

COLOR DRAWING

Design Drawing Skills and Techniques for Architects, Landscape Architects, and Interior Designers

SECOND EDITION

MICHAEL E. DOYLE
CommArts

JOHN WILEY & SONS, INC.
New York, Chichester, Weinheim, Brisbane, Singapore, Toronto

TO ELLEN

For your love, support, and ability to focus on what's important in life.

This book is printed on acid-free paper.

Copyright ©1999 by Michael E. Doyle. All rights reserved.

Published simultaneously in Canada.

No part of this publication may be reproduced, stored in a retrieval system or transmitted in any form or by any means, electronic, mechanical, photocopying, recording, scanning or otherwise, except as permitted under Sections 107 or 108 of the 1976 United States Copyright Act, without either the prior written permission of the Publisher, or authorization through payment of the appropriate per-copy fee to the Copyright Clearance Center, 222 Rosewood Drive, Danvers, MA 01923, (978) 750-8400, fax (978) 750-4744. Requests to the Publisher for permission should be addressed to the Permissions Department, John Wiley & Sons, Inc., 605 Third Avenue, New York, NY 10158-0012, (212) 850-6011, fax (212) 850-6008, E-Mail: PERMREQ @ WILEY.COM.

This publication is designed to provide accurate and authoritative information in regard to the subject matter covered. It is sold with the understanding that the publisher is not engaged in rendering professional services. If professional advice or other expert assistance is required, the services of a competent professional person should be sought.

Library of Congress Cataloging-in-Publication Data:

Doyle, Michael E.
      Color drawing : design drawing skills and techniques for architects,
    landscape architects, and interior designers /
    Michael E. Doyle. -- 2nd ed.
        p.   cm.
    Simultaneously published in Canada.
    Includes bibliographical references and index.
    ISBN 0-471-29245-1 (cloth : acid-free paper)
    1. Color drawing--Technique.   I. Title.
NC892.D69 1999
720' .28' 4--dc21   98-34054

Printed in the United States of America.

10 9 8

CONTENTS

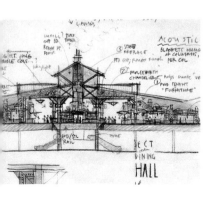

CONTENTS

PREFACE

Color Drawing was initially published in 1981. It was based on the premise that designers can use readily available dry color media, on papers used in everyday practice, to efficiently and effectively illustrate their ideas.

Since that time I have had the good fortune of working as a senior designer at CommArts, a multidisciplinary design firm whose work intersects the fields of architecture, urban design, landscape architecture, interior design, graphic design, and environmental graphic design. In addition to gaining further experience from the numerous and rewarding projects with which we have been involved, I have also come to know something of the state of professional design education, as a number of us regularly review graduate portfolios and interview prospective designers. The number of portfolios submitted by design graduates that exhibit effective drawing skills has diminished considerably in recent years. In fact, so few applicants have exhibited evidence of understanding the use of traditional design drawing that it seemed surely headed for extinction.

However, once hired, the large number of designers in our office who have graduated within the last five years have shown a voracious appetite for just these skills. Although their facility with the computer is unquestionably sophisticated, almost all of these designers have taken it upon themselves to learn and utilize traditional drawing skills in their everyday design process. They have been working in perspective, plan, and elevation with pencil and felt-tipped pens. They have been using markers, color pencils, and pastels to explore color and light and to represent architectural and plant materials, furnishings, and people. No one required them to work this way, so I was curious to find out why they have done so.

Their motivations vary, but fall under the general headings of speed, directness, and image quality. A number of them mentioned that they were able to express their ideas faster during the early parts of a project, with far fewer preliminary steps and distractions caused by requests for the input of objective information. In addition, with the real-world constraints of time and fee, the speed with which they can illustrate conceptual and schematic ideas, using these skills, holds wide appeal.

Others felt that their use of hand drawing allowed them a more direct connection with both their ideas and the result on the page. They appreciate the fact that they can physically touch the images they create through the application of line and color media, and that enables them to feel more in control of the project's design evolution.

Still other designers mentioned that the quality of the resultant design images was softer and more ambiguous than those generated entirely by computer. Of particular importance to them is the way these qualities seem to consistently indicate to the members of the various design teams with whom they work, and especially to clients, that the design process is not closed but is, in fact, ongoing and that their participation is still invited.

These New Designers work in an unprecedented way, moving easily between hand drawing and computer as they pursue design ideas. For instance, a designer may generate nascent ideas by hand, then delineate the more promising of those either by hand or, for more complex forms and spaces, by generating a wireframe view with a computer. She then overlays the wireframe with a sheet of tracing paper and uses traditional line and dry color media to explore and develop successively more detailed levels of information, including further articulation of forms and spaces, fenestration, lighting, color, furnishings, and architectural and plant materials. She may then either color photocopy the studies or she may scan the drawing back into the computer to add photographic imagery, when appropriate, or type for signing, words, and notes. The finished drawing is then printed by a color printer directly from the computer.

My ongoing interaction with these designers indicates that the early part of the design process may be destined to remain a hands-on component of the professions after all, despite enormous and persistent market pressures to the contrary. This book has been written and illustrated to assist students and young practitioners, as well as teachers, in allowing this component of their design education to flourish.

◆ ◆ ◆

This book would not have been accomplished without the presence of the many generous people in my life:

My sons, Devin and Trevor, who have been very patient with their dad's hermitic ways during this long writing process.

The partners of CommArts—Janet Martin, Richard Foy, and Henry Beer—whom I thank for their continued and enthusiastic support.

The many designers and staff at CommArts, who freely gave their assistance. Jason Howard, Jim Babinchak, Grady Huff, Nat Poomviset, Amy Schroeder, Aaron Howell, Dave Dute, Patty Van Hook, Gary Kushner, Keith Harley, Taku Shimizu, Meg Hansen, Kristin Reddington, Derek Friday, and John Bacus, who deserve special thanks for their help and advice. A special thank you to Doug Stelling for sharing his special approach to the use of pastel.

The Design Communication Association (DCA), especially William Kirby Lockard, FAIA, and Bill Stamm, AIA, of the University of Arizona, for its support of both traditional and new design communication education. The DCA has given us a wonderful way to exchange ideas about how to more effectively communicate our design ideas.

James R. DeTuerk of Pennsylvania State University and Thomas Kachel of Southwest Missouri State University, who took the time to kindly and carefully review and critique *Color Drawing*, Revised Edition.

Denise Bertoncino of University of Arkansas, Eric Strass of Brookdale Community College, and Mary Laham of Kendall College of Art and Design for reviewing and commenting on *Color Drawing*.

Frank M. Costantino, Douglas E. Jamieson, Ronald J. Love, Thomas W. Schaller, AIA, and Curtis J. Woodhouse for their generosity in allowing me to publish their professional illustrations. Their words of encouragement were much appreciated.

Paul Stevenson Oles, FAIA, for his gentle insistence, through his work and his words, that value is the key to effective color illustration.

Molly Gough and Aaron Hoffman for sharing their photographic equipment.

Kristin Schrepferman of Sanford Corporation for her help with Prismacolor pencils and markers.

Pat McLaughlin of Chartpak for her information on AD markers.

Elaine Tito of Macbeth for her help with the Munsell Color media.

Terry Stonich of the Department of Community Design, Planning and Development, City of Boulder, Colorado.

Douglas Ward of Art Hardware, Boulder.

Eight Days A Week Copy Center, Boulder.

Bradbury & Bradbury Art Wallpapers, Benicia, California.

Alex Price of Canon USA.

Clint Hoffman of Sony Electronics, Inc.

INTRODUCTION

The purpose of this book is to provide an approach to drawing in color during the early phases of your design process. As you become familiar with this approach, you will find your ability to draw in color considerably expanded and, as a result, you will be able to create your design studies more quickly and effectively. You will also find yourself selecting—and inventing—favorite ways of drawing in color. This is as it should be, as there is no one correct approach to creating these drawings. Rather, you will find that your approach keeps changing and adjusting, depending on the design communication task before you. Use the approach—or combination of approaches—that works best for each situation.

To keep this book a manageable size, you may notice, there is little discussion or illustration of perspective or shade and shadow techniques. Most of the step-by-step drawings in the book are in perspective, but begin with a completed line drawing. However, be assured that no amount of skill with color can help a drawing that has a poorly drawn underlying structure or one that demonstrates a lack of understanding of light, shade, and shadow. Perspective and shade and shadow are the universal language of design picture making. They form the link between you and those to whom you wish to communicate your conceptual ideas about form, space, and, ultimately, place.

If you are new to color design drawing, start at the beginning of the book, because it is organized in a way that builds skills one step at a time, with each succeeding chapter predicated on information supplied by those previous to it. On the other hand, if you are more familiar with this kind of drawing, you may wish to use the book more like a handbook, accessing materials, methods, and techniques as needed.

Part I is an overview of the basic phenomena, media, papers, and techniques that assist you in illustrating the various elements, materials, and finishes you propose to use to bring your ideas to life. You illustrate them to communicate them both to yourself and to others. Chapter 1 is an empirical introduction to the subject, presenting the phenomena of color and light that inform the effects and techniques used throughout the book. Chapter 2 discusses the media and papers that work best for color design drawing. New line media and color media—including pastels and alcohol-based markers— are introduced, as well as new recommended palettes of markers, color pencils, and pastels. Canson paper and bond paper have been added to the list of papers that are compatible with the color media described herein. Chapter 3 shows a variety of techniques used to apply color media and to create impressions of materials. The effects of light, including ways to create dusk views with the new "retrocolor" technique, are a particular focus. Chapter 4 uses these media, paper, and techniques to create an encyclopedia of step-by-step approaches to the illustration of elements, materials, and finishes that architects, landscape architects, and interior designers commonly use in practice. Most of these elements, materials and finishes are newly illustrated, using faster techniques, and an expanded section on interior materials is included in this chapter. Chapter 5 shows a way to draw scale elements in color, including unique approaches to drawing automobiles and a new section on drawing human figures.

Part II shows how the basic skills found in Part I can be used to create a range of drawings for presentation purposes. In addition to looking *into* a drawing for design information, as Part I implicitly encourages, the designer is introduced to ways of looking *at* his drawings as a graphic composition and how to provide his drawings with visual organization and impact.

Chapter 6, a new addition to the book, shows how to consider your color design drawings as compositions in their own right. Color relationships are discussed in terms of contrasts, and unity, balance, proportion, and rhythm are introduced as compositional principles to be used as tools to evaluate your drawings as you prepare them for presentation. Chapter 7 shows step by step how to utilize the material covered in the first six chapters to create a variety of kinds of color design drawings—from quick sketches to finished presentation drawings. The first part of the chapter covers new ways to plan your drawings, with an emphasis on value composition as a means to creating dramatic impact. New ways to use a black and white photocopier for quickly transferring line drawings to the paper of your choice—including white roll tracing paper—are also included. The rest of the chapter covers approaches for creating color design drawings on a variety of papers, including Bristol paper, bond paper, tracing paper, and toned papers such as Canson and diazo prints, using both traditional line drawings and different kinds of computer "setup" drawings. Additional layers of information found in design drawings are also discussed, including photography and various ways of applying notes. The chapter closes by showing a variety of ways to revise and repair color design drawings.

The technological development that has most dramatically affected the use of color drawing in the early part of the design process has not been the computer per se, but the advent of the high-quality color photocopier and printer. This allows designers not only to work freely in color at all stages of the design process, but also to draw at a much smaller scale. By drawing small, they can produce design imagery more quickly than they could even a few years ago, fully confident that the color photocopier not only will do the work of making their drawings large enough for presentation purposes, but can enhance the imagery through a variety of adjustments when necessary. Together with the flatbed scanner, it has opened an easy relationship between traditional drawing and the computer. Chapter 8 shows ways to utilize color photocopy and computer technology to present color design drawings in small-scale and large-scale presentations, as well as how to distribute them in an easily assembled take-along form called a "sketchpack." A new section, "How to Make Perfect Slides of Your Color Drawings," has been included, giving you a way to present your color design drawings in large-scale presentations, as well as a way to conveniently archive them.

Use what you can from this book as you develop your own approach to a drawing-based design process—one that will, it is hoped, allow you access to the deepest reaches of your abilities. Like any tool, this book is a means to an end. Its ultimate purpose is to enable you, the designer, to make our built surroundings better than we could ever have dreamed possible.

COMMUNICATION

I

"**A**lthough draftsmanship is no longer the price of admission to a design career, those who master the language of drawing are likely to see, to think, and to communicate with more sophistication than those who only master the computer. Aside from this competitive advantage, however, there's a deeper satisfaction to be derived from draftsmanship: the thrill of vanquishing a monster-sized, fire-breathing design problem with nothing more than a small, sharpened stick."

| *Marty Neumeier*

INITIAL CONSIDERATIONS

Those who design places for use by others—architects, landscape architects, and interior designers—engage in a specialized form of communication. They first create images of their ideas about the three-dimensional forms and spaces that make these places, but they create them on two-dimensional surfaces.

To do this effectively, a designer must understand the visual phenomena on which these kinds of images are based. For example, before she can create even a simple line drawing of a place idea, the designer must first understand the phenomena of perspective. Once she posesses this basic understanding, she is then in a position to learn the techniques necessary to recreate these phenomena on a sheet of paper. She can engage in a picture-based language, using lines, by which her ideas about places can be universally understood.

The same holds true for light and its natural consequence, color. When you begin learning an approach to drawing your design ideas in color, it is important that you observe the phenomena of light and color that surround you every day—and night. As you observe these phenomena, ask yourself, "How would I create this on paper?" This book attempts to help you answer that question.

As a designer, you will also find it necessary to express your ideas and observations about color in words. To this end, you should understand the three dimensions of color and how they are interrelated. The last part of this chapter introduces you to these basic color terms and the importance of their relationships.

PHENOMENA OF COLOR AND LIGHT

To successfully illustrate design ideas, it is instructive—and, more to the point, necessary—to observe the color phenomena that surround you in your everyday life. Ten such basic phenomena are briefly discussed and illustrated here. You will discover more, but these 10 should help you to understand the relationship between what you see around you and the techniques shown later in the book. It is hoped that they will also inspire you to use the power of your own unique observations.

Local Tone

Every object has an intrinsic lightness or darkness, regardless of its illumination. This phenomenon is known as *local tone,* a term coined by artist and teacher Nathan Goldstein (1977). A typical brick, for example, has a much darker local tone than a block of white marble. When both are exposed to sunlight, each will have lighter and darker sides, but the illuminated faces of the brick will still be darker than the shaded faces of the marble (1-1).

When you create color drawings that illustrate various forms, whether buildings, landscapes, or interiors, each form will possess a local tone owing to your choice of its material. Each form will have lighter and darker surfaces, as in the preceding example, depending on the location of the light sources. The degree of lightness or darkness of these surfaces will be in proportion to the lightness or darkness of the local tones of the forms.

Chiaroscuro

The term *chiaroscuro* refers to the light-to-dark shading of an illustrated form in order to make it appear three-dimensional. Its use has a long history in art. Leonardo da Vinci said of chiaroscuro that "he who excels all others in that part of the art, deserves the greatest praise" (Birren 1965, 77).

In a black-and-white drawing, these shadings and shadows may range, of course, from light gray to black. However, this is not the case in color drawing. Gray to black shadings and shadows in a color drawing (unless on a gray form) will appear dull and lifeless. Instead, as figure 1-1 illustrates, you can see that the color of a surface in shade or shadow usually remains the same color as its illuminated sides, only darker, and that the degree of darkness depends on the local tone of the form.

Fig. I-I

Fig. I-I **Notice the sunlit and shaded/shadowed surfaces of the pitcher, table, and floor. Each has shades or shadows whose degree of lightness or darkness corresponds to its local tone. For example, the side of the pitcher in shade is light, whereas the shadow of the pitcher on the table is quite dark. The medium-toned floor has a corresponding medium shadow.**

    Look closely at the colors of the shadows on the floor. They are not gray or black, but darker versions of the corresponding sunlit colors of the floor.

Color of Shade and Shadow

You can see, however, under certain conditions, that the shades and shadows on forms also take on subtle colorations other than only the darker versions of their illuminated surfaces.

This condition most commonly occurs when the shaded or shadowed surface faces a source of colored light. This source may be direct light, or it may be light reflected from a nearby form that is itself brightly illuminated. A common example of this phenomenon appears on the shaded surfaces of buildings on a clear day. These surfaces are illuminated by the bright blue "light source" of the sky, resulting in a surface that is a mixture of the building's surface material and the blue of the sky (1-2). The shaded face of a red brick building, for example, can have a purplish cast to it. This is because the resultant color falls somewhere on the color wheel between the red of the brick and the blue of the sky (see figure 1-12).

This effect is also readily apparent on neutral—white or gray—surfaces. Notice the colors of the shadows on snow, concrete, or worn (light gray) asphalt on a sunny day. The shadows on these surfaces appear bluish, so blue in fact that you can see yet another color phenomenon manifest itself. The sunlit portion of these surfaces will appear slightly "warm," or tinged with a pinkish orange. This effect, called *simultaneous contrast,* forms in our perception when we behold a color next to a neutral surface. We perceive the neutral surface as tinged with the color opposite on the color wheel, its *complementary color.* The more intense the color, the more it tends to tinge its neighbors with its complement. A red apple and its surrounding green leaves will appear particularly brilliant against one another.

Simultaneous contrast was written about as early as the sixteenth century. M. E. Chevreul was the first to study this effect in depth in the early nineteenth century, and the phenomenon was utilized extensively by the Impressionists in the late nineteenth and early twentieth centuries (Hope and Walch 1990). It is an established part of the visual language of artists and illustrators today. Color contrasts are discussed further in Chapter 6.

Fig. 1-2

Fig. 1-2 The surfaces in shade and shadow are alive with color. The pink stucco grades to purplish on the upper left-hand wall owing to its reflection of blue sky; the dark gray foreground floor and windowsill also reflect the blue sky. The right-hand wall takes on an orange cast, reflected from the sunlit floor tile. Notice the reflected colors on the shaded and shadowed surfaces in the space beyond.

Gradation

Have you ever noticed that very few flat surfaces in your surroundings actually appear uniformly colored or illuminated? Most appear uneven, graduating from one color to another and one level of lightness or darkness to another. This effect is particularly easy to notice on large surfaces like walls, floors, and ceilings but occurs on most all surfaces if you look carefully (1-3).

Continuous surfaces *gradate* in appearance because of their proximity to sources of direct light and because of the light and colors reflected onto them (and into them) from nearby objects and surfaces. These *gradations* usually appear gradual on matte surfaces and become sharper with the increasing specularity or "polish" of a surface. A concrete or drywall surface will host more even color and light gradations than one of, say, brushed stainless steel. Polished wood or glass will exhibit much sharper boundaries between changes in light and color.

You will find gradations a useful tool in color illustration. They make surfaces appear more realistic and result in illustrations that are far more dynamic. For example, in a technique used by fine arts painters called *forcing the shadow,* a shadow is graded darker toward its boundary with the illuminated portion of the surface. The illuminated portion is graded lighter toward this same boundary. The result is an unexpectedly brilliant effect of illumination. The same technique is often employed between the colors of foreground and background elements in an illustration. A background element may gradually be darkened and cooled (made more bluish) in hue as it moves toward its boundary with a foreground element, whose treatment is just the opposite: it is lightened and warmed (made more reddish) in hue as it approaches the same boundary. This is a useful way to make forms appear more distinct. These effects are easy to create and impart activity and sparkle to an illustration.

Fig. 1-3

Fig. 1-3 Gradations of color and tone occur on virtually every surface of this illustration as a result of illumination and reflected color. Gradations are particularly effective in making interior design illustrations appear vital and realistic.

Multiplicity of Color

You see your surroundings in a variety of colors. A green tree, a wall of red brick, a brown rock, and yellow field grass are common objects whose colors are familiar to you. But most of the colors you see are really visual averages or mixtures of a multitude of colors. The clump of winter field grasses that look yellow from a distance are, upon closer inspection, made up of such colors as magentas, ochres, grays, and greens—as well as a variety of different kinds of yellow.

As you observe your surroundings more closely, you may find these subtle variations of color in natural and exterior architectural surroundings difficult to describe or illustrate satisfactorily. This is in part due to these visual averages, called *medial mixtures* (1-4). It is also because many natural materials *refract* light as a result of their water, mineral, and cellulose content, splitting the light into its component colors on a microscopic scale. As indicated earlier, both exterior and interior man-made materials are also rarely of a single, consistent color, because of gradations, the reflection of color, and the impacts of such phenomena as simultaneous contrast.

Close observation of your surroundings will lead you to see that your world literally scintillates with color. Impressionist painters Seurat, Signac, van de Velde, and many others utilized these observations in their paintings. At a distance the colors of their forms appear soft and subtle, but closer inspection reveals that each area of color is made up of many different colors. These colors are not mixed, but placed side by side with tiny brushstrokes, which imparts an incredible richness to the painting and allows the viewer, rather than the artist, to create the final colors of the images. You will explore similar approaches to color illustration later, in Part II, by *mingling* a variety of color media to create your color images, including marker, pastel, and color pencil.

Fig. 1-4

Fig. 1-4 The colors in this illustration are composed of a mingling of many different colors applied with marker, pastel, and color pencil—all on pale green Canson paper. The color of the foreground grasses, for instance, was made with three markers, two pastel colors, and five color pencils.

Atmospheric Perspective

Forms that recede into the distance undergo a color change. Generally, they become lighter, cooler (more bluish), and more grayed. This is due in part to the layers of humidity, dust, and pollutants that accumulate in proportion to the distance between the form and the viewer (1-5). This phenomenon is known as *atmospheric perspective*.[1]

Your subconscious conditioning through lifelong experience with atmospheric perspective may lie behind a related phenomenon. Cool colors—blue greens, blues, and purple blues—appear to *recede* from the viewer. Conversely, colors opposite on the color wheel, warm colors—reds, yellow reds, and yellows—tend to *advance* toward the viewer, particularly when used in conjunction with cool colors. Another explanation for our apparent spatial positioning of color may lie in how the lenses of our eyes refract color. Reddish colors focus at a point behind the retina, whereas bluish colors focus at a point in front of the retina. The lens becomes convex to focus on a reddish image, "pulling it nearer," and flattens to focus on a bluish image. This flattening of the lens "pushes the [bluish] image back and makes it appear smaller and farther away" (Birren 1965, 130).

Reflections

Reflective surfaces present the colors they "see" back to you. In most cases, however, on such surfaces as glass, water, and polished furniture the reflected colors are less intense than those of the objects reflected. When a reflective surface is darker than its surroundings, such as a window in a sunlit wall, notice that the colors it reflects are less intense *and* darker than those of the objects reflected.

Mirrored surfaces such as chrome and polished stainless steel usually distort the *shapes* of the objects reflected, but reflect their colors exactly (1-6).

[1]The art world sometimes refers to this phenomenon as *aerial perspective*. The use of this term for our purposes would be confusing, since an aerial perspective in architecture and landscape architecture refers to a perspective view of a subject from above. Such views are also known as "birds-eye" views.

Fig. 1-5

Fig. 1-6

Fig. 1-5 In each successive layer of buildings and landforms, care was taken to lighten the colors, make them more bluish-to-pale purple, and make them weaker (more grayed). These color effects reinforce the diminution in size of the forms to create the illusion of distance. This effect was further enhanced by making the foreground elements warm (yellow reddish) in color.

Fig. 1-6 The colors reflected into the window and glass tabletop are weaker than those of the objects reflected, but those reflected into the polished stainless-steel column are not. As windows in a building become higher and more oblique to the viewer's sight line, they progressively reflect more sky.

Note the forced shadow on the patio surface and the gradation of the wall color.

Luminosity

Light colors and strong, vivid colors appear to be illuminated, or to glow, when they are surrounded by darker values or applied to or seen against toned backgrounds. The darker the background, the more *luminous* the color appears (1-7). This phenomenon can be used to create the effects of illumination, as many of the illustrations throughout this book demonstrate (1-8).

Fig. 1-7

Fig. 1-7 Notice how the color of the rectangle appears progressively more luminous as its background becomes darker.

Fig. 1-8 This study uses the luminous effect of light chromatic colors on dark backgrounds to illustrate a lighting design idea.

The image was made by first taking a Polaroid photograph of a model used to study the forms and spaces of the project. The photograph was simultaneously enlarged and photocopied onto clear photosensitized acetate on a standard black-and-white photocopier. The resultant acetate image was printed

onto blackline diazo paper, with the machine run at a faster-than-usual speed to create the very dark background. Color pencil and white gouache highlights were then applied to create the lighting effects. The notes were made with a *French Grey 50%* pencil, which minimizes their contrast with the background and prevents them from competing visually with the lighting effects.

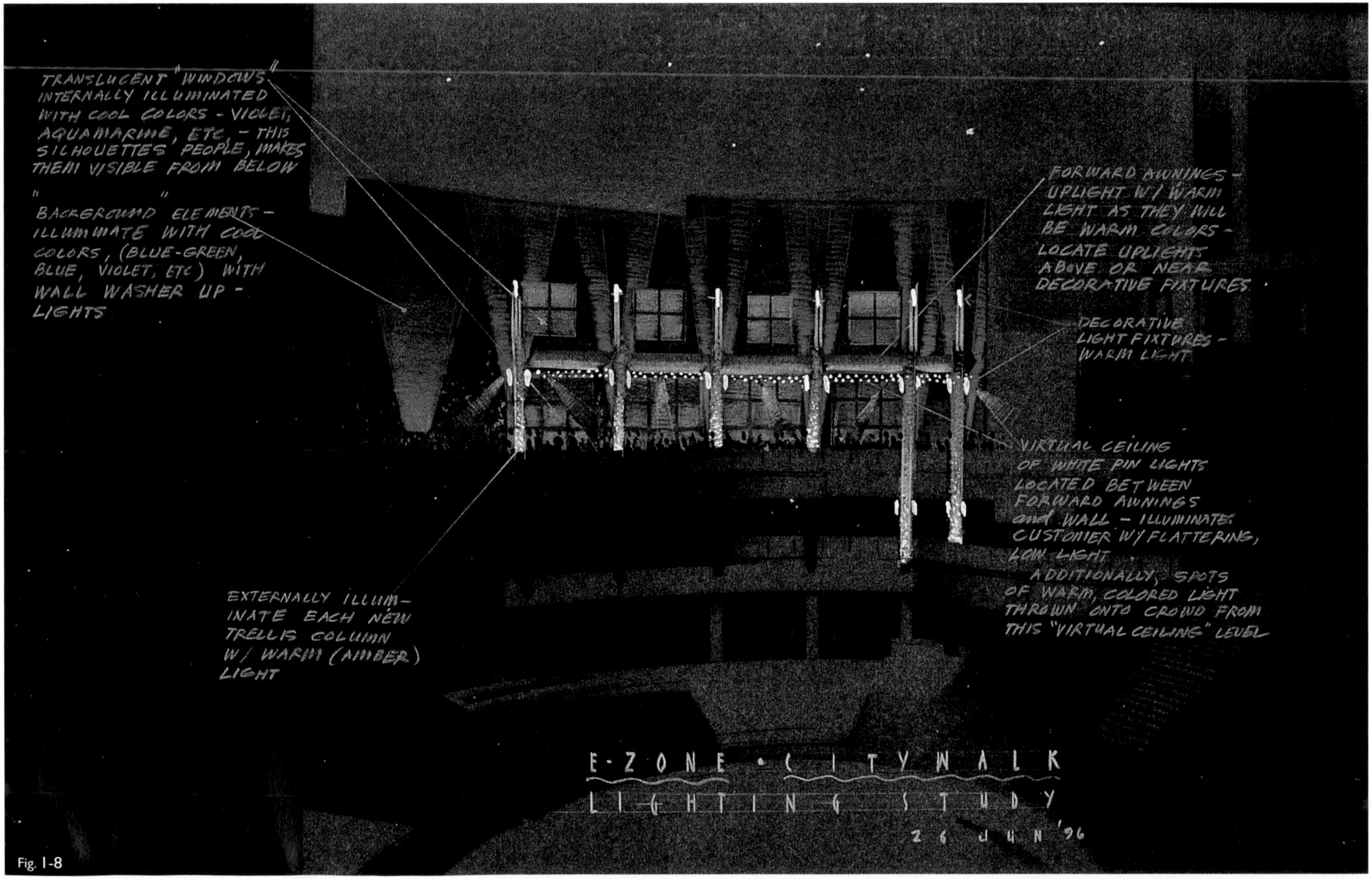

TRANSLUCENT "WINDOWS"
INTERNALLY ILLUMINATED
WITH COOL COLORS - VIOLET,
AQUAMARINE, ETC - THIS
SILHOUETTES PEOPLE, MAKES
THEM VISIBLE FROM BELOW

"BACKGROUND" ELEMENTS -
ILLUMINATE WITH COOL
COLORS, (BLUE-GREEN,
BLUE, VIOLET, ETC) WITH
WALL WASHER UP -
LIGHTS

EXTERNALLY ILLUM-
INATE EACH NEW
TRELLIS COLUMN
W/ WARM (AMBER)
LIGHT

FORWARD AWNINGS -
UPLIGHT W/ WARM
LIGHT AS THEY WILL
BE WARM COLORS -
LOCATE UPLIGHTS
ABOVE OR NEAR
DECORATIVE FIXTURES.

DECORATIVE
LIGHT FIXTURES -
WARM LIGHT

VIRTUAL CEILING
OF WHITE PIN LIGHTS
LOCATED BETWEEN
FORWARD AWNINGS
AND WALL - ILLUMINATE
CUSTOMER W/ FLATTERING,
LOW LIGHT

ADDITIONALLY, SPOTS
OF WARM, COLORED LIGHT
THROWN ONTO CROWD FROM
THIS "VIRTUAL CEILING" LEVEL

E·ZONE·CITYWALK
LIGHTING STUDY
26 JUN '96

Fig. 1-8

Color and Light Level

Your perception of color depends on a different kind of reflection from those discussed earlier. The various colored objects and forms that make up your surroundings absorb certain wavelengths of light—that is, they absorb certain colors—and reflect others. You see these forms and objects as certain colors because those are the colors reflected. A banana in a bowl of fruit absorbs most other wavelengths of light *except* yellow, which it reflects back to you.

As the light level diminishes, it follows that the amount of light available for objects to reflect also diminishes. The banana appears less yellow and more neutral, but yellow nonetheless when compared with the colors of other fruit in the bowl: "We judge colors by the company they keep. We compare them to one another and revise according to the time of day, light source, memory" (Ackerman 1991, 252).

However, in near darkness or on a moonlit night, color seems to disappear altogether. Our only sources of color come from those objects and surfaces sufficiently illuminated to reflect light (1-9). A nighttime walk will encounter color only in such places as windows that allow a view into an illuminated interior, or beneath streetlights and in illuminated signs. Most other forms and surfaces reflect only enough light for you to perceive them as low levels of light and dark.

Fig. 1-9

Fig. 1-9 The buildings have virtually no local color in this dusk illustration. The only areas of color are found in views into the buildings' interiors, the illuminated portions of the walking surface, and the illuminated signs. The flare of sunset color is caught by the chimney smoke and, partially, by the building to the right.

Arrangements of Light and Dark

There are a wide variety of tones in your surroundings, ranging from the brightest whites to the blackest of blacks. If you squint until your eyes are almost closed as you look around, you will notice fewer shadings of light to dark. In fact, every tonal group you see in the scene can fall into one of three categories: light, medium, or dark.

This way of viewing your surroundings is important because it provides a way to understand the underlying tonal arrangement of your surroundings and offers a way to approach strong tonal arrangements in your design communication illustrations as well. When the brilliant landscape illustrator Ted Kautzky prepared a scene, he first simplified it to three diagrammatic spatial planes of foreground, middle ground, and background. He assigned to each plane one of the three aforementioned tones—light, medium, or dark—which yielded six possible basic tonal arrangements (Kautzky 1947). This approach not only made his finished illustrations far more manageable to execute, but built into each one a surprising degree of impact. You will investigate tonal arrangements further in Chapters 6 and 7.

One of the most useful and powerful of these arrangements is frequently employed for illustrating evening and nighttime exterior views. Most of the background is illustrated as a medium tone, whereas the middle ground is the lightest—especially windows, as they are intended to be illuminated from within. When foreground elements, such as trees or figures, are made very dark, they appear to be in silhouette, further emphasizing the *brilliance* and luminosity of the middle ground (1-10).

Fig. 1-10

Fig. 1-10 This illustration uses medium background and building surface tones and very dark foreground tones so that the light, warm colors used for the building's interior make it appear illuminated. Notice how the layering of dark, medium, and light tones also helps create the illusion of depth.

THE DIMENSIONS OF COLOR

Certain groups and organizations, ranging from paint manufacturers to fashion designers, have descriptive names for colors that are commonly understood within a particular group. One may refer to a color as "Butterscotch," while another may refer to a similar color as "Goldenrod." Both names evoke an image of a yellow with perhaps a tinge of red, neither too light nor particularly vivid (1-11). Descriptive color names work well in instances where colors need only casual identification or when the user is attempting to summon particular associations or emotions in others, such as when these names are used for marketing purposes.

However, when asked to adjust a color or compare similar colors—like Butterscotch and Goldenrod—a designer must revert to a vocabulary capable of describing color in more accurate terms. He uses three dimensions to describe color, much the way he uses the dimensions of height, width, and depth to quantitatively describe form and space.

The term *hue* denotes the *name of a color,* such as "red," "yellow," or "blue green." When full-spectrum light, such as sunlight, is fractured into a rainbow by a cloud of water vapor or a prism, what you are seeing are the component colors that make up the light. You will see these colors blend or grade from one into another. Because the colors on either end of the rainbow are also related to each other, all the colors taken together form a circular relationship. This relationship is known as a *color wheel* or, more accurately, a *hue wheel,* inasmuch as most color wheels show only one representative color (usually vivid) for each hue (1-12). The terms *hue* and *color* are often confused. Hue is only one of the three dimensions required to make a color.

The degree of "darkness or lightness" of a color is known by the term *value.* The range of value of a color can extend from "very low" to "very high," that is, from very dark to very light. You may see other terms for value, such as *lightness* or *brightness,* used in other systems of describing color (1-13).

Fig. 1-11 "Butterscotch" *(left)* **and "Goldenrod"** **are casually descriptive names for these colors, but the names are almost meaningless when used to compare one color with the other.**

Fig. 1-11

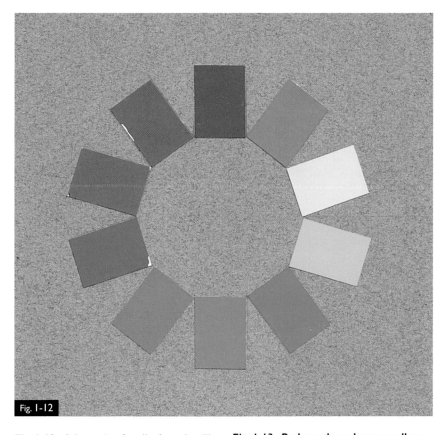

Fig. 1-12 A hue wheel or "color wheel" shows the relationships of hues to one another.

Fig. 1-13 Red-purple and green-yellow colors arranged vertically according to value. A corresponding neutral gray scale appears on the left. Note that although the colors change in value in each vertical row, the chroma of the colors is the same.

The terms *vividness* and *grayness* are observations that describe the strength of a color. This quality is known as the *chroma* of a color and can range from "very weak" (grayish) to "very strong" (vivid). Other commonly used terms for chroma are *purity* and *saturation* (1-14).

In theory, each of these three dimensions of a color can be altered *without affecting the other two*. For example, a color's value can be changed without affecting its hue or chroma, or a color's hue can be changed from green to blue while its value and chroma remain the same.[2] Notice that the qualities of hue and chroma cannot exist by themselves; you cannot create an image with *only* hue or *only* chroma. However, you *can* create an image exclusively with value,

as you often do when making a black-and-white drawing or photograph. Although the terms *hue, value,* and *chroma* will be used to describe the dimensions of color throughout this book, your choice of terms for these dimensions is important only insofar as those with whom you communicate are familiar with them.

---

[2] In reality, however, value and chroma are interrelated in strong-chroma colors. If you attempt to significantly change the value of a strong-chroma color, you find you must usually reduce its chroma to do so. This is because each hue reaches its strongest chroma at a particular value, called its *spectrum value*. For example, try to imagine a strong-chroma *dark* yellow. It is impossible to imagine, because the color does not exist. As a yellow becomes darker, its chroma grows weaker. Certain colors are simply not achievable.

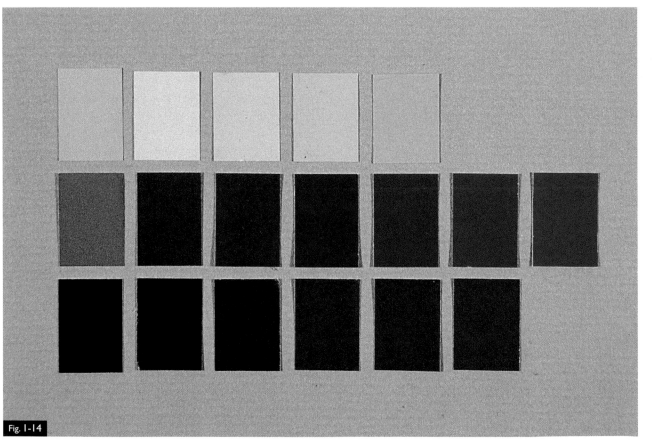

Fig. 1-14 In each horizontal row of colors, the hue and value of the colors remain constant. Only the chroma of the colors changes, progressing from gray on the left to stronger chroma on the right.

Fig. 1-14

Munsell Student Sets

A detailed knowledge of any particular organized system of color and the alphanumeric classifications of its colors is unimportant for the purposes of this book. What *is* important is that you have an understanding of the relationships between the dimensions of color and that you are able to identify and communicate the similarities and differences between colors that are intended to be seen together, as a composition.

You may find it worthwhile to purchase an inexpensive Munsell Student Set[3] to further explore the relationships between the dimensions of color. The set comes with a color wheel, value scale, chroma scale, 10 hue charts (one for each of the 10 hues of the color wheel), and packages of loose color chips. You must assemble the color wheel, scales, and hue charts by applying the color chips to their proper locations. During this process, each color chip must be evaluated according to its hue, value, and chroma, refining your ability to discriminate between the three color dimensions and to evaluate subtle differences within a particular dimension.

The student set can also be used to explore various combinations of color by arranging the loose color chips into small compositions, before they are adhered in their final locations on the scales and charts, similar to those in figures 6-4 and 6-11. Once you can visualize how a color's three dimensions can be manipulated, each independent of the others, it becomes easier to entertain the many possible relationships that can be established *between* colors. *Colors form relationships when their characteristics appear to affiliate or interact with one another.* Inasmuch as each and every color possesses the same three dimensions, it is the creative arrangement of the relationships between the dimensions of the colors in a composition that establishes the mood or expressive direction of the scheme. When these relationships are established, a perceptible order is introduced to the scheme. Color harmony is predicated on order, whether that color is arranged for a design idea for a place or for the *illustration* of an idea. For example, an exercise may explore the combination of five different hues with different chromas but all the same (or similar) values. You will notice that it is the similarity of the values of the colors that acts as the unifying agent of the composition. Such simple chip-arrangement exercises can help you build your skills in arranging colors in successful combinations, particularly with the guidance of Chapter 6.

Once a student set is assembled, it makes an excellent reference tool for evaluating and comparing the ranges of hues, values, and chromas of colors.

Simplified Color Descriptions

As you work with a Munsell Student Set, you will realize its value to the designer. However, its notation system, although simple, is of little value to the designer who wishes to describe a color to a client or colleague with more accuracy than the one-word names mentioned earlier. A typical *Munsell Student Chart* is shown with the numeric designations for value and chroma, accompanied by a verbal description of each (1-15). Thus, 5R 3/4 can be described verbally as a "low-value, weak-chroma red," whose relationship to all the other possibilities for red can be imagined from your mental picture of the chart. The verbal description lies between the very accurate description ("5R 3/4") and the casual description ("burgundy red"). Incidentally, you can see in figure 1-11 that Goldenrod is slightly more yellow red, lower in value, and of about the same medium-strong chroma as Butterscotch.

Computer Color Controls

You must understand and be able to manipulate the same three dimensions of color when creating illustrations and color studies on a computer. A typical computer color control is shown in figure 1-16. A hue is selected on the blended "color" (hue) wheel and adjusted with the *lightness* (value) and *saturation* (chroma) controls. Because a computer monitor creates each of its colors by an additive mixture of red, green, and blue light, the color of an object can also be adjusted by varying the amounts of those colors (1-17). Note that these two types of color control are linked together, so the color of an object can be created and adjusted using either control.

[3] Student sets can be ordered from:
Fairchild Books
7 West 34th Street
New York, NY 10001
Tel: (800) 247-6622 or (212) 630-3880, Fax: (212) 630-3868

Inquiries about the Munsell System of Color and products can be made to:
Macbeth
405 Little Britain Road
New Windsor, NY 12553-6148
Tel: (800) 622-2384 or (914) 565-7660

Initial Considerations

**Fig. 1-15 A Munsell Student Chart for
the hue red (5R) is accompanied by
descriptions of the numeric indications
for the increments of value and chroma.
The descriptions are by the author.**

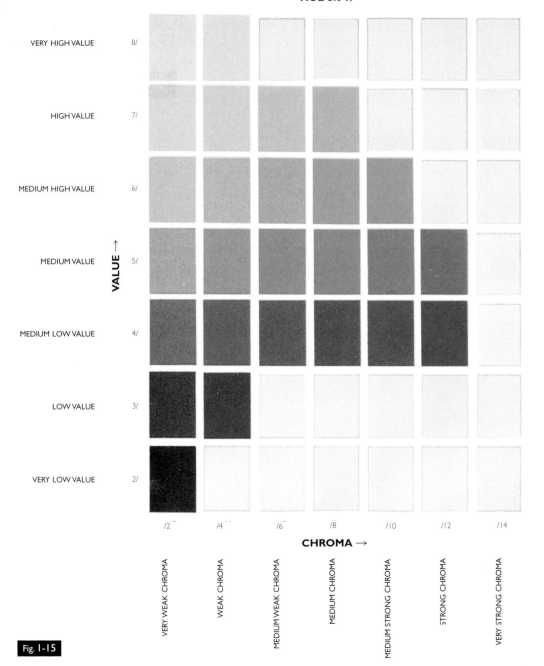

Fig. 1-15

The Pilot Razor Point is an excellent all-purpose felt-tipped pen to use with the color media displayed in this chapter. Its line is slightly wider than that of the Micron 01. Although it is not waterproof (it will smear if wetted), it is marker-proof and draws well over color pencil with a minimum of clogging. It is more difficult to eradicate with an electric eraser than the Micron pens, but its line can be partly eradicated with the use of a pink erasing strip. Line remnants can be hidden with color pencil during the coloring stage.

The "pointed nib" tip of the black Eberhard Faber Design Art Marker 229-LF makes it a good felt-tipped marker for making wider lines, adding small areas of black to a drawing, and creating rough conceptual diagrams. It should not be used over color pencil, because its solvent will dissolve and consequently smear the pencil. Like all markers, it should be capped immediately after each use because it can dry out very quickly.

One of the most versatile of the line media shown in figure 2-1 is the *Black Prismacolor pencil*. Its line is very dark and can, of course, vary in width. It is often used with a straightedge if its lines must be kept very thin. It reproduces well on a photocopier, especially as compared with graphite pencil lines made with pencils harder than an "H." It erases fairly well, though not entirely, when an electric eraser is used. It can make very even tones because of its slight waxiness and is particularly good for applying shade and shadow.

Color Media

Markers

Markers can apply a transparent color to paper that appears similar to watercolor. Most markers use a concentrated colorant, usually *aniline dye,* mixed with a carrier, typically a volatile solvent of xylene or alcohol. Their tips, once made from felt, are now made from proprietary plastics. However, most designers still refer to them as "felt-tipped" markers. Marker does not buckle paper the way water-based color media do, because the carrier evaporates quickly. This quality makes it an excellent color medium for designers, because it is compatible with the kinds of paper they most frequently use (2-2).

In our design work, we often use markers to create the "base," or underlying colors, for drawings that are subsequently modified by applying colored pencil, pastel, and sometimes line media to achieve the illusion of materials, patterns, and light. Many interesting effects can be created quickly and easily, as you will see throughout this book. You should note that some kinds of markers

Fig. 2-2

Fig. 2-2 There are a variety of marker brands and types on the market. The Design 2 Art Marker, AD Marker Spectrum, and Prismacolor markers are all alcohol-based. The AD Marker and Design Art Marker are xylene-based.

are incompatible with certain line media. Marker should not be used over color pencil. Not only will the pencil smear because of its dissolution by the marker's solvent, but the dissolved pencil color will adhere to the marker's tip, waiting to surprise you with a revised marker color, usually when you least want it. Moreover, *only alcohol-based markers should be used on black-and-white photocopies.* Xylene-based markers will dissolve and smear the black toner that creates the photocopy image. Alcohol-based markers can cause certain kinds of felt-tipped pen line and the lines of diazo prints to smear slightly *if applied with excessive hand pressure.* However, as a general rule of thumb, both alcohol- and xylene-based markers can be safely used over most felt-tipped pens, on diazo prints, on all papers, and even over each other with no ill effects, provided they are used with restraint.

Because marker colorant is aniline dye, it tends to fade with continuous exposure to ultraviolet light, even the small amounts found indoors. If you intend to display a color design drawing that uses marker, make a more lightfast color photocopy or bubble-jet copy of the illustration for display purposes. Store the original in the dark. Contemporary color reproduction methods, such as that of the *bubble-jet photocopier,* can provide an excellent rendition of your original.

Always use markers in a place that has adequate ventilation. The prolonged inhalation of marker solvents, particularly *xylene* (which has the stronger, more pungent odor of the two marker types), can cause headaches and nausea. This can also happen if you work with your face too close to the page, especially when your markers are new.

The largest-selling marker brands together have hundreds of colors from which to choose, but you can create most of your color design illustrations with a limited number. There are two basic *palettes* of markers recommended in this book:

a palette of grays and a general color palette. Each palette is described in both alcohol-base and xylene-base in figures 2-3 and 2-4. They are recommended as minimum starting palettes for general color design drawing for architects, interior designers, and landscape architects. These palettes have evolved from the repeated marker choices made by designers at CommArts during our work in these areas. In your pursuit of design solutions for your particular design specialty, you may choose to substitute others or augment the number of colors shown here.

The most important is the palette of grays, because these markers are used most frequently (2-3). Gray can set the value of a color, whose hue and chroma can be determined later with subsequent applications of color pencil or pastel. *French grays* are slightly yellow reddish, *warm grays* slightly reddish, and *cool grays* a touch bluish in hue. The same observations apply to gray color pencils.

The markers shown in the general color palette (2-4) are derived from those we consistently select to illustrate frequently used natural and ubiquitous materials (wood, stone, metals, glass), those found on building exteriors, and landscape materials. Special marker colors, particularly for interiors, can be chosen in addition to the general palette for specific projects.

Xylene-based markers appear capable of delivering slightly richer, smoother color, particularly on diazo prints. They also usually last longer than alcohol markers. However, if you must choose one marker system, the best all-around system is the alcohol-based, inasmuch as it can be used on both diazo prints *and* photocopies. If you have a limited budget for drawing materials, purchase a palette of gray markers first, because the grays can set the values of colors and other less expensive color media can be used to bring up their hue and chroma, as you will see in Chapters 3 and 7.

Fig. 2-3 A recommended palette of gray markers. You can choose either the AD marker (xylene-based) or Prismacolor marker (alcohol-based) grays—or a range of each. It is not necessary to buy both kinds.

AD MARKER

PRISMACOLOR MARKER

WARM GREY #1

COOL GREY #1

FRENCH GREY 10%

COOL GREY 10%

WARM GREY #3

COOL GREY #3

FRENCH GREY 30%

COOL GREY 30%

WARM GREY #5

COOL GREY #5

FRENCH GREY 50%

COOL GREY 50%

WARM GREY #7

COOL GREY #7

FRENCH GREY 70%

COOL GREY 70%

WARM GREY #9

COOL GREY #9

FRENCH GREY 90%

COOL GREY 90%

Fig. 2-3

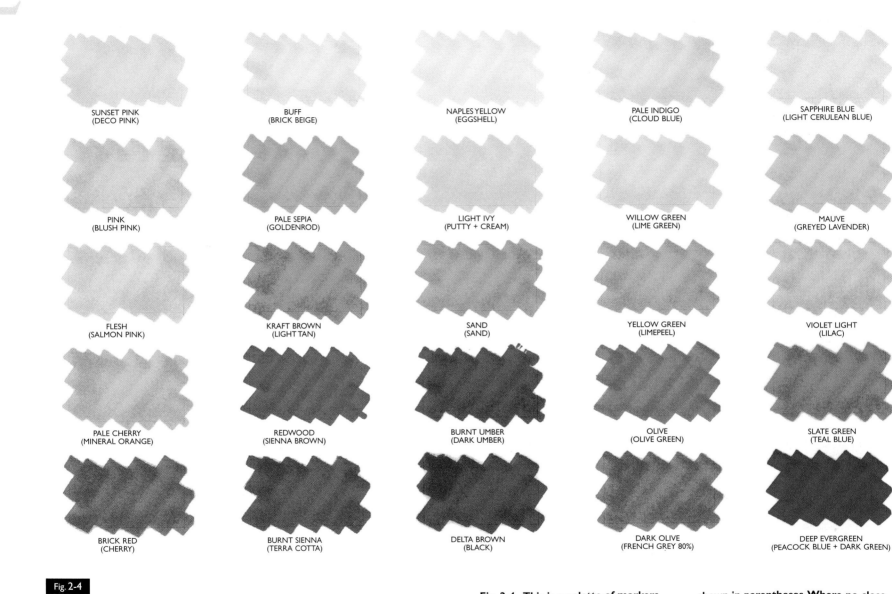

SUNSET PINK
(DECO PINK)

BUFF
(BRICK BEIGE)

NAPLES YELLOW
(EGGSHELL)

PALE INDIGO
(CLOUD BLUE)

SAPPHIRE BLUE
(LIGHT CERULEAN BLUE)

PINK
(BLUSH PINK)

PALE SEPIA
(GOLDENROD)

LIGHT IVY
(PUTTY + CREAM)

WILLOW GREEN
(LIME GREEN)

MAUVE
(GREYED LAVENDER)

FLESH
(SALMON PINK)

KRAFT BROWN
(LIGHT TAN)

SAND
(SAND)

YELLOW GREEN
(LIMEPEEL)

VIOLET LIGHT
(LILAC)

PALE CHERRY
(MINERAL ORANGE)

REDWOOD
(SIENNA BROWN)

BURNT UMBER
(DARK UMBER)

OLIVE
(OLIVE GREEN)

SLATE GREEN
(TEAL BLUE)

BRICK RED
(CHERRY)

BURNT SIENNA
(TERRA COTTA)

DELTA BROWN
(BLACK)

DARK OLIVE
(FRENCH GREY 80%)

DEEP EVERGREEN
(PEACOCK BLUE + DARK GREEN)

Fig. 2-4

Fig. 2-4 This is a palette of markers useful for general color tasks. The colors of the AD markers are reproduced here. The names of the closest corresponding matches in the Prismacolor markers are shown in parentheses. Where no close Prismacolor marker match was found for an AD marker, a mixture of two Prismacolor markers is indicated with a plus (+) sign between the two.

Color Pencils

Color pencils are the mainstay of the color drawings shown in this book. They are the most frequently used of the color media, the most flexible (they can be applied very lightly or quite heavily), and the most precise. On small drawings, marker is frequently less necessary as a color base, because small drawings require only a color medium that can be applied precisely to a given area but still be removed if the designer makes a mistake or changes her mind. In fact, color pencil is often the only color medium necessary to complete small drawings, particularly those that are highly detailed.

Sanford Prismacolor and Design Spectracolor pencils are two of the best brands of color pencil to use for the kind of color drawing discussed in this book. Both brands come in a wide variety of colors, are soft enough to apply easily and smoothly, and are able to impart a solid, brilliant color when necessary. The Bruynzeel design Fullcolor color pencils (Holland) and the Derwent Studio color pencils by the British company Rexel Cumberland are slightly harder than the Prismacolor and Spectracolor pencils, making it somewhat more difficult to create brilliant colors without indenting the paper surface. However, the Bruynzeel and Derwent pencils both offer colors that are unavailable in the American brands (2-5).

In this book, Prismacolor pencils are used for the drawings. Recommended palettes of grays and general colors are shown in figures 2-6 and 2-7. As with the recommended palette of markers, these pencils are not the only ones we use at CommArts. Rather, they are the pencils selected most frequently for a wide variety of illustration tasks.

Fig. 2-5

WHITE

FRENCH GREY 20%   COOL GREY 20%

FRENCH GREY 30%   COOL GREY 30%

FRENCH GREY 50%   COOL GREY 50%

FRENCH GREY 70%   COOL GREY 70%

Fig. 2-6

Fig. 2-5 These brands of high-quality color pencil are widely available, and each brand has many different colors.

Fig. 2-6 This palette of gray pencils is adequate for most every drawing task that requires their use.

Fig. 2-7 A general palette of Prismacolor pencils (and one Derwent pencil), useful for illustrating a wide variety of materials.

BLUSH PINK   LIGHT PEACH   CREAM   DECO AQUA   CLOUD BLUE

ROSY BEIGE   DECO ORANGE   CANARY YELLOW   CELADON GREEN   GREYED LAVENDER

PINK   PEACH   YELLOW CHARTREUSE   LIMEPEEL   BLUE SLATE

CARMINE RED   MINERAL ORANGE   JASMINE   APPLE GREEN   LIGHT CERULEAN BLUE

POPPY RED   BURNT OCHRE   YELLOW OCHRE   OLIVE GREEN   DERWENT BLUE VIOLET LAKE 27

TUSCAN RED   TERRA COTTA   BRONZE   PEACOCK GREEN   COPENHAGEN BLUE

DARK UMBER   DARK GREEN   INDIGO BLUE

Fig. 2-7

Pastels

Pastels are the fastest and most directly manipulated (worked with the fingers) of the color media featured in this book. They are also the least controllable at the edges of shapes; that is, they tend to "go outside the lines" more than the other color media. They are meant to be used loosely, in order to apply very quick color to a *sketch* or study illustration. They blend extremely well and are most effective in "high key" schemes of color—those in the lighter ranges of value. They are especially well suited for creating very light, subtle colors.

A designer can produce very successful color illustrations without using pastels. However, larger areas of mixed media color illustrations (those using marker and colored pencil) can be colored quickly and easily with this medium. Skies and clouds in particular lend themselves to illustration in pastel.

Pastels are made by combining dry pigment with a methylcellulose binder. Because of their dry, powdery composition, they erase very easily and cleanly from most kinds of paper. Use a soft, high-quality stick pastel for large areas of color (2-8). These pastels are in the more expensive range, but are worth the cost inasmuch as cheap pastels tend to leave streaky deposits of color and do not blend well. The Rembrandt stick pastels can be found in most art supply stores and have been used for the illustrations that required pastel shown in this book.

If you want to use pastels on small drawings, use them in pencil form. These pastels are somewhat harder and more pointed than stick pastels, which enables the designer to color small areas of a drawing more easily and accurately. Streakiness is not usually a problem, owing to the small areas of color. Just as with stick pastels, use a high-quality pastel pencil. The Schwan Stabilo pastel pencils are widely available and are shown in various illustrations in this book.

If you wish to limit your initial exploration of pastel to a few colors, a useful palette to select from is shown in figure 2-9. If you are an architect or landscape architect, purchase at least the blue stick pastels for creating skies in your illustrations. These skies can take on the more dramatic qualities of a sunset with the help of subsequent additions of pastels in the pink and orange range. If you are an interior designer, you may first wish to test various pastel colors in the store to find a few colors you will tend to use in your work.

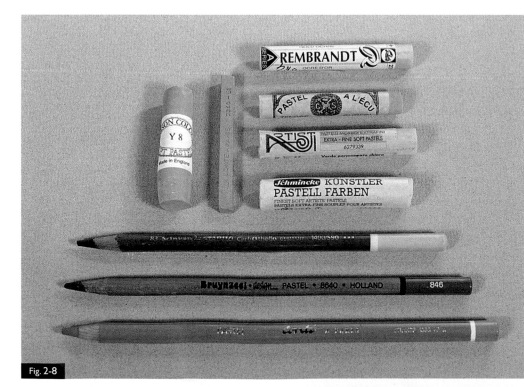

Fig. 2-8

Fig. 2-8 A variety of high-quality pastels. The stick pastels arranged horizontally are, from top to bottom: Rembrandt by Royal Talens (Holland), Pastel a l'Écu by Sennelier (France), Artisti by Maimeri (Italy), and Künstler Pastell Farben by H. Schmincke & Co. (Germany). The two stick pastels arranged vertically are the Conté stick by Conté a Paris (right) and Unison Colour, made in England (left). The pencil pastels are, from top to bottom, Schwan Stabilo (Germany), Bruynzeel design pastel (Holland), and the Conté a Paris pastel (France). Note that the Conté a Paris pastel has a wider shaft diameter than most pencils and will not fit into many electric pencil sharpeners. It must be sharpened with a knife.

Fig. 2-9 A useful palette of both stick and pencil pastels. You may wish to revise or supplement these palettes, depending on your specific color design needs.

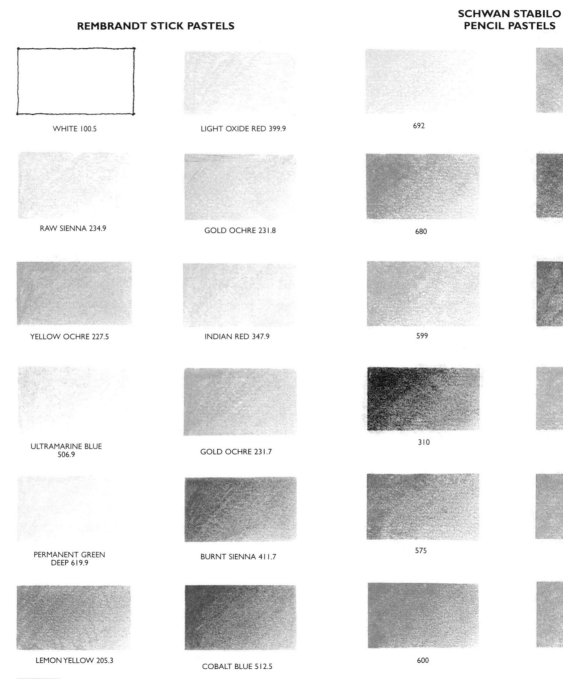

REMBRANDT STICK PASTELS

WHITE 100.5

LIGHT OXIDE RED 399.9

RAW SIENNA 234.9

GOLD OCHRE 231.8

YELLOW OCHRE 227.5

INDIAN RED 347.9

ULTRAMARINE BLUE 506.9

GOLD OCHRE 231.7

PERMANENT GREEN DEEP 619.9

BURNT SIENNA 411.7

LEMON YELLOW 205.3

COBALT BLUE 512.5

SCHWAN STABILO PENCIL PASTELS

692

690

680

620

599

675

310

435

575

500

600

430

Fig. 2-9

Pastel works well over marker and gives the marker a smoother appearance as it modulates its color. Color pencils also work well over pastels. However, avoid using felt-tipped media—pens and markers—over pastel, because the pastel will eventually clog them and tend to dry them out.

Once you have used pastels on part of a drawing, avoid touching that part. Pastel can lift, smear, and show fingerprints. If you must rest your hand on a part of a drawing where you have used pastel, place a piece of bond paper under your hand while you draw. When you are finished with your drawing, you may wish to apply a light coating of spray *fixative* to preserve the pastel, but this can somewhat deaden its luminous quality. If possible, avoid using fixative. Instead, make a good color copy of your drawing to use for presentation purposes and safely store the original between two sheets of clean paper.

Accents

You may frequently find yourself in a drawing situation where you need those "final touches" or accents that bring a design drawing to life (2-10). Touches of white *gouache* are good for effecting *highlights* or "sparkle" on chrome, water, polished stainless steel, and the edges of glass objects—anywhere a specular reflection may occur. A touch of gouache is also good for creating the illusion of an illuminated lamp in drawing light fixtures.

Touches of metallic gold or silver may also occasionally be necessary for a drawing. These can be easily added with pointed liquid marker pens; the highlights glisten convincingly when they catch the light. However, metallic pen accents work best as small touches or dots and should not be substituted for the designer's illustration of polished metals (see figures 4-60 through 4-63). Metallic pen accents will not copy effectively on a color photocopier or bubble-jet copier, so, when necessary, they must be added to each copy.

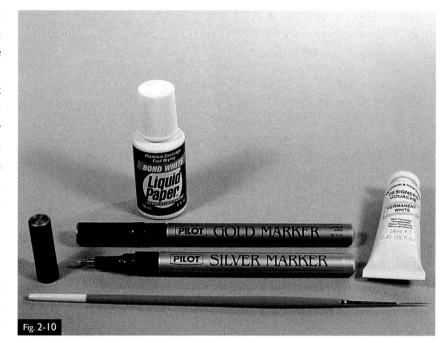

Fig. 2-10

Fig. 2-10 Media for creating accents in drawings. You will find a small tube of Windsor & Newton *Permanent White* gouache and a long, thin "lining brush" useful for applying both dots and lines of white accent. Dots can be applied full-strength, but lines require that the gouache be diluted slightly with water in a mixing tray. Liquid Paper correction fluid is a good "emergency" white accent medium when gouache is unavailable, but it can absorb and turn into a tint of the color of certain kinds of marker.

Pilot's Gold Marker and Silver Marker come in an extra-fine point, good for applying spots of metallic accent.

PAPER

The variety of paper types commonly used in the design professions can be successfully used for color design drawings. Each of these papers—even roll tracing paper—can be used to receive images from a black-and-white photocopier. This allows the easy transfer of line drawings from, say, tracing paper to Canson paper for a more finished color drawing. This capability also enables the designer to make more than one copy of a line drawing in case an illustration must be repaired or redone.

Tracing Paper

White roll tracing paper is the most frequently used paper in professional design offices for the illustration and development of ideas early in the design process (2-11). It can be used for drawings of many types, ranging from pre-conceptual doodles to finished color illustrations.

Tracing paper is an excellent surface for color design drawings. It takes all pencil, dry media, and felt-tipped line media well and erases cleanly. Markers bleed only slightly and appear muted—usually an advantage. Its translucency is less refined than that of mylar or vellum. This, too, is an advantage, because when color pencil is applied on the back of a line drawing on white trace, it appears softened, more even, and less mottled or streaky when viewed from the front. When toned paper is slipped behind a color illustration that is drawn on white trace, its lighter pencil colors appear more luminous. This quality, which is also imparted to color photocopies of this arrangement, is advantageous in creating lighting effects in both exterior and interior illustrations.

We usually use Bienfang brand, No. 106, white tracing paper in 12" or 18" rolls. One of the few disadvantages of white trace is that its thinness makes it somewhat fragile. It is susceptible to holes from electric erasure, particularly if the harder erasing strips are used. Because oils and perspiration from your hand can cause it to curl, use a piece of paper under your hand if you find you must rest it for any length of time on the tracing paper as you draw.

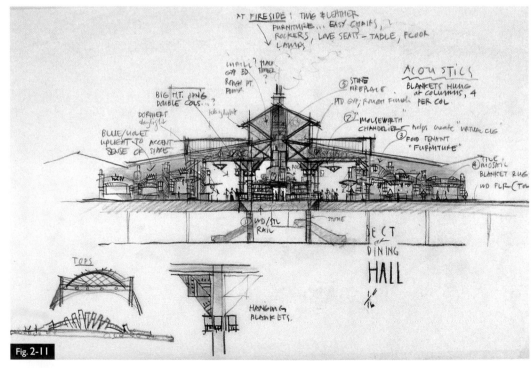

Fig. 2-11 A typical exploration of a design concept on white tracing paper. The linework was drawn with *Black Prismacolor* on the front of the sheet, and color pencil was applied to the back. Note the white accents applied to the front with *Liquid Paper* correction fluid.

Toned Papers

One of the greatest advantages of *toned paper* is that it allows the designer to complete a color design drawing very quickly, as only the center of interest need be colored for the illustration to have a visual impact. This is because the greatest contrasts will most likely occur within the colored area. If the same is attempted on white paper, the strongest contrasts are often inadvertently created at the *edges* of the colored area, where, frequently, the marker stops and the white paper begins. This area competes with the center of interest. This is not to say that partially colored drawings on white paper are impossible, but the designer must take more care to fade from the colored area into the uncolored part of the drawing.

Toned papers also allow the designer to create dramatic effects very easily and efficiently. Highlights become vivid, and the colors of pastels and color pencils can be made to appear luminous with little effort. Darks can be added where necessary, and middle tones need only be lightly colored or even left uncolored. Far less effort is spent trying to adequately cover the white of the paper when illustrating medium- or low-key color schemes.

There are two common types of toned paper that work especially well with the color media discussed in this book: diazo print paper and Canson paper.

Diazo Print Paper

The diazo reproduction process is widely used throughout the design professions. Diazo reproductions or *prints* of drawings originally created on such translucent drawing surfaces as vellum, mylar, and tracing paper are easily obtained in most design offices, design schools, and copy shops (2-12). Reproductions of working drawings are often made on "blueline" paper, which has blue lines and a blue background, but blackline and brownline papers are also available. Blackline paper is preferable for color drawings, because its lines and background color, a cool gray, are relatively neutral in hue.

Diazo print paper has excellent *tooth* (ability to extract smooth, rich deposits of color or tone from dry color media, such as pencil or pastel) but a smooth texture. It takes marker well, although new markers tend to bleed owing to the paper's lack of density.

Fig. 2-12 A study of the stern for a proposed riverboat. Marker, color pencil, and white gouache on blueline diazo paper. (Drawing: Bryan Gough)

Fig. 2-12

In addition to carrying a reproduced image of your original drawing, a major advantage of the *diazo print* is that the value of its background can be varied, ranging from no background (hence, white) to nearly jet black. The faster the speed of the machine is set, the darker the resultant print. Backgrounds in the medium to medium-light range will give applied pencil and pastel colors a degree of luminosity, whereas medium-dark to very dark backgrounds are excellent for creating night scenes. If the speed control is varied *as the print is being made,* the background will correspondingly gradate from lighter to darker. A graded background can create a dynamic effect and can be used to set up various lighting effects for the drawing (2-13).

Fig. 2-13 In this streetscape study, a pencil drawing on vellum was printed on blackline diazo paper. The vellum was fed bottom-first into the diazo machine, and the speed was gradually increased to its fastest as it reached the top, or sky, portion of the drawing. The bottom of the resultant print appears to be illuminated by the streetlights. Note how little color—marker, pencil, and white gouache—is necessary to illustrate the idea.

Fig. 2-13

Canson Paper

The Mi-Tienes line of paper manufactured by Canson-Talens is called *Canson paper* in this book. It is a high-quality textured, toned art paper that comes in a wide variety of subtle colors as well as a number of different colors of gray. It provides an excellent background for color design drawings and accepts marker, color pencil, and pastel quite well (2-14). Canson paper has a more pronounced texture than the other papers described in this chapter, and this quality helps to mask errors and streakiness inherent in pencil application. In fact, the textural quality of the finished drawing is a unifying factor that helps tie the elements of the illustration together. You can see that the texture of the paper is slightly more pronounced on one side than on the other. Either side can be used.

Line drawings can be transferred to the lighter colors of Canson paper with the use of a light table, which is helpful particularly if you want to keep the lines very light. If line value is not an issue, a faster and easier way to make the transfer is by using a black-and-white photocopier. Once a line drawing is photocopied onto the Canson, it should be lightly sprayed with Krylon Crystal Clear, because the photocopier toner often does not fuse completely to the rough paper. This clear acrylic coating, which dries in a few minutes, will help prevent the lines from smearing with normal use. Remember to use only alcohol-based markers on photocopies.

Fig. 2-14

Fig. 2-14 This is a study of suggested modifications to an existing building. A line drawing was photocopied onto Canson paper, and color pencil was subsequently used to highlight the modifications.

White Paper

Bond Paper

During the design process you will frequently want to make an ordinary black-and-white copy of a line drawing and then add some quick color for an impromptu review or meeting. Photocopiers are usually stocked with ordinary *bond paper* ranging from letter size (8½" x 11") to ledger size (11" x 17"). Large-format black-and-white photocopiers, such as the Xerox 2080 or the OCÉ Bruning 9400, can produce enlargements on sheet sizes up to 36" wide and of any length.

The bond paper used in large-format photocopiers is somewhat thicker than that used in office copiers, but the quality of the paper is similar. It is relatively smooth, yet has sufficient *grain* (tooth) to allow the use of color pencils and pastels (2-15). Markers can also be used successfully on bond paper, but they will bleed more than on the other papers described in this chapter, due to its greater absorbency (see figures 3-9(a) and 3-9(b)). If possible, use a high-quality, heavyweight (24 lb.) type when using bond paper for color drawing.

Fig. 2-15 A photocopy of a line drawing on ordinary 8½" x 11" bond paper was colored with alcohol markers, color pencil, and touches of white gouache.

Fig. 2-15 ...UE · LINEAR OASIS STUDY

Bristol Paper

Bristol paper is a dense, high-quality paper that yields excellent results when used with the color media described in this book. It has the right amount of tooth to take pencil and pastel beautifully. Because of its density and makeup, markers bleed very little when applied to Bristol paper (2-16).

This versatile white paper can be run through many black-and-white photocopiers, and the toner usually fuses well to its surface. Because it is very translucent on a light table, drawings can be traced onto it quite easily. If you prefer the lines to be subtle, trace the original drawing onto the Bristol with .5 mm mechanical pencil using a 6H lead.

A number of high-quality Bristol papers are available in most art supply stores. Some of the best for color design illustration include the Strathmore Bristol, 100 lb., and Canson Bristol. Both are two-ply and have a *vellum finish*. The 11" x 14" pad size is adequate for most illustration tasks. Bristol paper, like toned Canson paper, has one side with a very slightly rougher texture than the other. Although either side can be used, the texture is so subtle that the rougher side is usually preferable.

Fig. 2-16

Fig. 2-16 This design study of a combination sign and light fixture is drawn on Bristol paper with marker and color pencil. The shade of the light fixture is subtly colored with two colors of pastel that grade from warm to cool. Note also the subtle highlights of white gouache. (Drawing: Henry Beer)

TECHNIQUE

Designers usually work within time constraints. The reasons vary, ranging from tight fees to looming construction starts. This time pressure trickles down, of course, to all parts of the design process, including the illustration of design ideas.

The techniques discussed and illustrated in this chapter form the basis for the approach to color design drawing presented in this book. They have evolved because they help make the process of illustrating ideas during the evolution of a design—from conception to design development—efficient and effective.

If you are unfamiliar with the media and paper introduced in Chapter 2, experiment with them. As you become more familiar with them, you will discover that there are few firm rules that govern their use. This chapter offers some guidelines for getting the most from these media and papers. Feel free to modify them in a way that works best with your specific approach to the illustration of your design ideas.

WAYS TO APPLY COLOR MEDIA

The techniques that follow show ways to apply a variety of color media. Once you familiarize yourself with them, you may wish to create variations that more closely meet your own approach to design drawing.

Color Washes

A *wash,* a term originally used in watercolor art, describes a deposit of color on paper. There are two kinds of color washes you will use continually in color design illustration—the *even* wash and the *graded* wash.

The Even Wash

An *even wash* is often used as the base color for many parts of a design illustration, such as a wall or sky. Certain media described in Chapter 2 lend themselves to even washes more than others. Markers, for example, usually leave a faint striped effect. Although this is not a problem in most illustrations, there are ways to minimize the effect when necessary (3-1). The faster you work with marker, the smoother the results, because the carrier (alcohol or xylene) remains fresher, allowing each successive swipe of color to blend more thoroughly with its neighbors.

Washes of pencil or pastel are easier to create, as these media do not "bleed" and are thereby more controllable (3-2 through 3-5). Although they alter a marker's color, they tend to smooth its appearance, as figure 3-10 shows.

Applying a very faint wash of color, often with pastel or pencil over marker, is referred to in this book as *flavoring* a color.

Fig. 3-2

Fig. 3-3

Fig. 3-1

Fig. 3-1 When you apply marker, first outline the shape of the area you intend to color using the marker's tip (*left*). When you subsequently fill in the shape with color, there is less chance that the color will stray beyond the lines.

If the marker color must appear smoother than usual, apply a second marker coat by stroking the marker in a direction perpendicular to the first (*right*).

Fig. 3-2 Use the side of the pencil point when applying a pencil wash to get a more even application. Stray pencil color can be easily removed with an electric eraser.

Fig. 3-3 Use the side of a piece of stick pastel (*top*) or the side of a pastel pencil (*right*) to apply these media to paper. Maintain light hand pressure to avoid streakiness. You can also scrape the side of a stick pastel with a knife (*left*) to deposit the color onto a drawing.

Fig. 3-4a

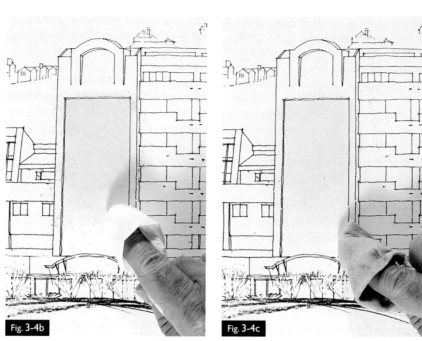

Fig. 3-4b

Fig. 3-4c

Fig. 3-4 Once the pastel is deposited onto the drawing surface, there are a number of ways to distribute it. You can use your finger (a), which will give you the least smooth, though darkest, deposit of color. By wrapping a tissue over your finger, you can make your pastel color more even and somewhat lighter (b). The use of a piece of soft leather chamois (the kind used to polish cars) will make the pastel application even smoother and lighter (c). Chamois can be obtained at an auto supply store.

Fig. 3-5

Fig. 3-5 An electric eraser with a soft white erasing strip can be used to easily clean up the edges of an overextended pastel application.

3

The Graded Wash

A wash of color that progressively changes in color dimension over a surface is called a *graded wash*. A graded wash may change in hue, such as from red to yellow, in value from lighter to darker, or in chroma—for example, from grayed to saturated. In your surroundings, a surface often changes in more than one dimension at a time, as when a sky grades from a tint of violet at the horizon to a more saturated blue at its zenith.

Very few surfaces in your world appear evenly colored, owing usually to the play of direct and reflected light. You will see gradations of color everywhere, from the surfaces of the room that surrounds you to the way light influences the colors of a tree. Gradations of color make an illustration appear more realistic and far more dramatic. They can be used to build necessary contrasts subtly, almost unnoticeably. These washes can be made with marker, color pencil, and pastel (3-6).

Fig. 3-6a

Fig. 3-6b

Fig. 3-6c

Fig. 3-6 Graded washes of marker are usually made with the grays, inasmuch as their progressive value designations lend themselves to this kind of application (a). Dark-to-light applications are easiest.

It is important to work quickly. If, for example, you begin with a *Warm Grey #5* marker, briefly scrub the leading edge of the marker deposit you make with the next lightest marker to blend the edge between the two. Most likely, this will be

Warm Grey #3. Continue with *Warm Grey #3* until you begin with *Warm Grey #1*, and repeat the process at the edge. If you want to grade back into the paper color, repeat the edge treatment at the edge of *Warm Grey #1* with a colorless blender marker. After you experiment with this kind of gradation, it becomes quite easy.

A graded wash with pencil (b) is best accomplished with the side of the pencil point. Here, Derwent *Blue Violet Lake #27, Mineral Orange,* and *Jasmine* pencils

were progressively blended one into the other. Each color was extended far enough into the next to ensure a smooth gradation.

The pastel graded wash (c) was easily created by scraping the Rembrandt stick pastels *Permanent Green Deep 619.9* on the ceiling on the left, *Ultramarine Deep 506.9* in the center, and *Raw Sienna 234.9* on the right side. The three colors were distributed by finger, then evened and blended with a chamois.

Ways to Modify Colors

Design ideation is an iterative process. In most cases, you will find that once an idea initially bursts forth onto paper, you instantly begin a dialogue with yourself: Move this here, shift that to there, add this, delete that. All those thoughts and feelings happen at lightning speed, without words and almost beneath notice.

Color is one of the elements in early design illustrations you will most certainly want to adjust easily. You will want to "massage" it, shift its dimensions, sometimes only slightly and at other times more significantly as your design effort progresses.

Any combination of color media, whether similar—such as pencil over pencil—or differing—such as pastel over marker, is legitimate for the purposes of color mixing and adjustment as long as the media are compatible. When you attempt to modify a color, you will achieve the best results when you use another color to do so. Extensive use of a *neutral color* (gray, black, or white) applied over chromatic colors to modify them can make your drawing dull or muddy.

Fig. 3-7 A *Deco Blue* pencil (a Munsell blue, *top left*) is applied over a *Pale Cherry* marker (a Munsell yellow red, *bottom left*). Because the colors are complements, the result is the gray shown on the right.

Fig. 3-7

Keep in mind that, in general, when two colors are mixed, the resulting color will be somewhere between the two. An exception to this precept applies to markers. Because marker applications are transparent, the darker markers will predominate and overwhelm lighter markers. But with most media, including markers of similar value, the rule of thumb holds. If, for example, a light red pencil is applied over a dark blue marker, the resulting color will be a medium-value purple. If a color pencil with a blue-green hue, such as *Deco Aqua,* is applied as a wash over a pencil color (of similar value) that is green-yellowish in hue, such as *Yellow Chartreuse,* the resultant color will be somewhere between the two, in the green hue range.

The further away the two colors are from each other on the color wheel, the more grayish the resultant hue. Refer to the color wheel in figure 1-12. If a *Deco Blue* pencil (a blue hue) is used to draw over its visual complement, a yellow-red hue made with a *Pale Cherry* marker, the result will yield a gray. This gray is a livelier, more interesting gray than a perfectly neutral gray, however, and much better suited for the purposes of color design drawing (3-7).

Although pencils and pastels can and should be blended with themselves to create more interesting colors, some less common combinations of color drawing media can also yield rich, though subtle, colors. Such combinations are discussed and illustrated in the following paragraphs.

Marker over Marker

The best way to begin a color illustration that requires marker is to apply a *marker base* color that most closely approaches the color you intend. If you want to modify it—adjust its hue, value, or chroma—you can do so by applying other marker colors, pastel, and/or color pencil over the original marker color (3-8 through 3-11). If your marker colors tend to "bleed" past their intended boundary, see figure 3-9 for ways to control them. Markers tend to bleed more on less dense papers, such as bond and diazo prints. This happens particularly when the markers are new, owing to an excess of the alcohol or xylene carrier. This problem will self-correct as you use your markers.

Fig. 3-8a

Fig. 3-8b

Fig. 3-8 Markers can be applied over other markers to create new colors. One of the most common uses of marker blends is to reduce the chroma of the underlying color. This can be done by using complementary marker colors. In example (a), a *Willow Green* marker is applied over a *Burnt Sienna* marker. Another way to achieve similar results is simply to apply a gray marker over the first color. In example (b), a *Warm Grey #3* marker is applied over the *Burnt Sienna*.

Fig. 3-9a

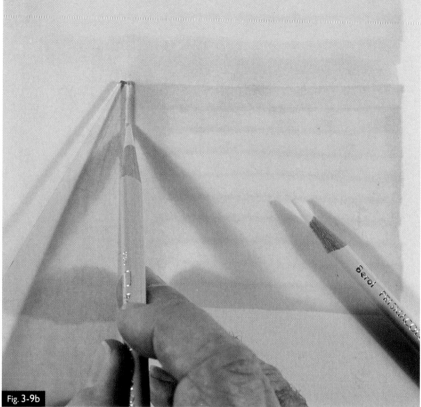

Fig. 3-9b

Fig. 3-9 Marker that "bleeds" past an edge can be controlled by gently blowing on the marker tip as you apply it near the edge (a). This accelerates the evaporation of the carrier solvent and reduces the spread of the dye.

If bleeding has already occurred, the edges of the marker colors can be "trimmed" with color pencils that are similar in color to the markers (b). The semiopaque pencils will cover the bleeding fairly well. In the example here, *Cloud Blue* pencil is applied with a straightedge where the *Sapphire Blue* marker meets the *Flesh* marker, and *Light Peach* pencil is used to cover areas where the *Sapphire Blue* has bled into the *Flesh*.

Pastel over Marker

Pastel can be applied over marker quite effectively. The resultant color is a visual mixture of the underlying marker color and the coating of pastel. The more pastel you apply, of course, the more the resultant color will shift toward that of the pastel (3-10).

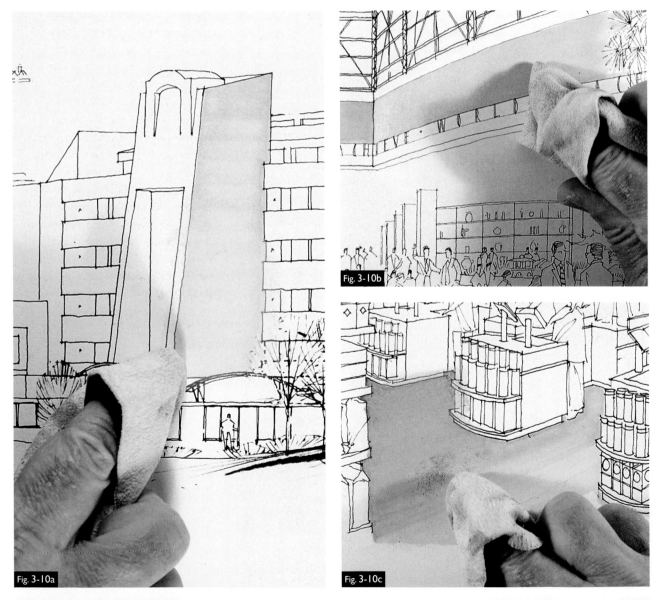

Fig. 3-10a

Fig. 3-10b

Fig. 3-10c

Fig. 3-10 Pastel smooths the streaked appearance of the marker base as it also shifts the dimensions of its color. In (a), a near-complementary *Permanent Green Deep 619.9* is applied over *Flesh* marker, resulting in a grayish green. As more pastel is wiped from atop the marker, the more the marker will show through.

Marker colors can be tinted with pastel. In (b), *White* pastel has been applied over the *Light Ivy* marker on the curved fascia to the right.

Pastel can be used to "bring up" color from gray, as in (c), where *Raw Sienna 234.9* pastel is applied over the graded wash of *Warm Grey* markers shown in figure 3-6a.

Pencil over Marker and Pastel

Color pencil works well over marker and pastel. It not only can shift the dimensions of the marker color, it can add texture while doing so (3-11). This is a benefit particularly in illustrating materials, as you will see in Chapter 4.

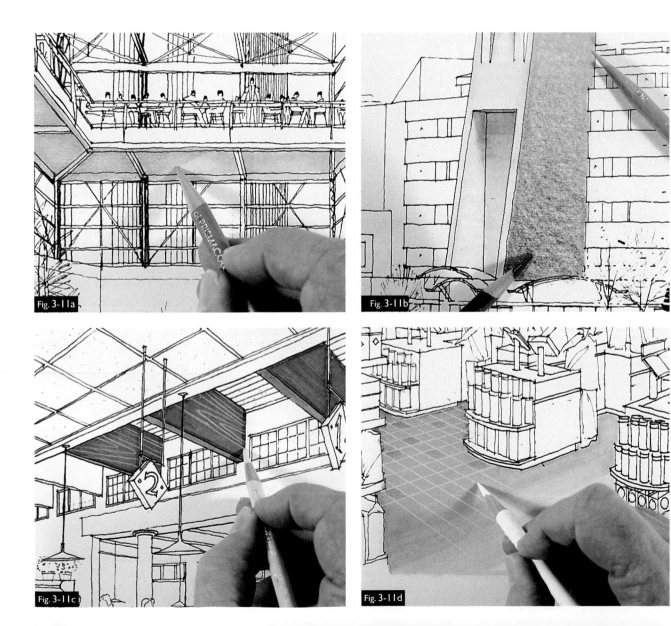

Fig. 3-11a

Fig. 3-11b

Fig. 3-11c

Fig. 3-11d

Fig. 3-11 Color pencil over marker can simultaneously shift the color of the marker as it creates texture and pattern. Figure 3-11 (a) shows *Celadon Green* pencil applied over *Mauve* marker. These near complements result in a lively gray. In (b) a graded wash of color pencil, from *Light Peach* to *Terra Cotta,* is applied over *French Grey 30%* Prismacolor marker. Although the grain of the paper causes the pencil to produce a texture, the underlying gray marker diminishes the impact of this texture. In (c) *Light Peach* pencil is used to apply the grain pattern to a beam initially colored with a *Kraft Brown* marker. *White* pencil is used over the pastel and *Warm Grey* marker in (d) to draw the grout joints of the tile floor.

IMPRESSIONS OF MATERIALS

Many newcomers to color design drawing often feel overwhelmed when they attempt to create an illustration that shows a variety of different materials. This happens because they assume that each material must be illustrated in time-consuming detail to adequately communicate its character. But this is to confuse design illustration with photography.

Most of us have gained much of our impressions of the world through the photographic image—imagery whose every part is usually in sharp focus. It should come as no surprise, then, that beginning designers assume they must replicate a similar level of detail to communicate their ideas. However, this is not how we see.

Look up from this page and focus on something in your field of vision—near or far. Without moving your eyes from this object, notice that you perceive everything surrounding it *in much less detail*. In fact, as you fix your eyes forward, the very edges of your field of view are so indistinct that they are simply colorless blobs of light and dark. The average content of your field of view is far more impressionistic than a photograph.

One of your jobs in the early stages of the design process is to utilize the language of illustration to quickly assemble the many decisions about the form, space, proportion, scale, and *character* of a project into pictures—usually called studies or *sketches*—for feedback to yourself and review by others. Some of these pictures can be adequately communicated through line drawings. However, it is the visual communication of the additional information about the character of the space—color, light, materials, pattern, texture, and furnishings—that transforms a *space* into a *place*.

Because much of the way you see is impressionistic, your illustrations of previews of your ideas about places can be likewise impressionistic without seeming inappropriate. These impressions of materials can also be created far more quickly than detailed illustrations (3-12). Attempt to create impressions of materials that are easily understood by an untrained viewer.

Chapter 4 offers time-efficient approaches to illustrating a wide variety of materials commonly used by architects, landscape architects, and interior designers. Experiment with these approaches until you find those that work best for you.

Fig. 3-12a

Fig. 3-12b

Fig. 3-12c

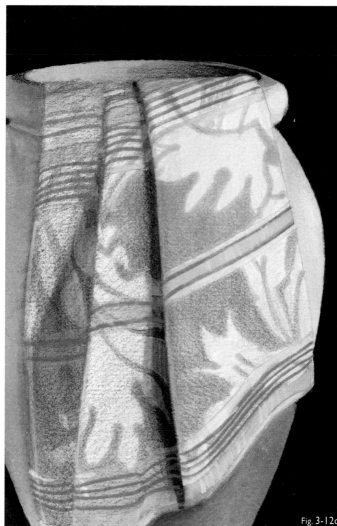

Fig. 3-12d

Fig. 3-12 Impressions of materials almost always begin with a line drawing to guide the color application. These line drawings can be quick and loose, because the color will more clearly define the images.

An impression of the stone in (a) has been drawn in (b) by rapidly mixing *Sand, Kraft Brown, Willow Green, Flesh,* and *French Grey 30%* markers. *Light Peach, Yellow Ocher, Celadon Green,* and *French Grey 30%* pencils were loosely washed over the marker. The shadow between the stones was applied last, with *Black* marker, to complete the illustration.

The fabric in (c) has been approximated in (d) by first drawing the diffuse shadows with *Cool Grey #1, #3,* and *#5* markers. The entire fabric surface was then washed with the lighter *Sapphire Blue* marker and the design approximated by delineating the negative spaces with a darker *Ice Blue* marker. *Celadon Green* and *Jasmine* pencils were used to add the colored stripes, and *Cool Grey 70%* pencil delineated the thin stripes. The shadows were softened further with *Indigo Blue* pencil, and the darker parts were washed lightly with the side of the *Cool Grey 70%* pencil.

CREATING THE EFFECTS OF LIGHT

In addition to creating successful impressions of materials, a designer can further communicate the character of proposed places by cultivating skills in the illustration of the effects of light. This is also the most convincing means of revealing the intended forms and spaces to the viewer of an illustration.

It is assumed in this book that you understand the basics of how to illustrate and "cast" typical exterior and interior *shade* and *shadow*. This is a critical (but easily learned) skill for all designers of places, because a thorough understanding of how light works on forms and in spaces will, ultimately, influence your design decisions. As mentioned in Chapter 1, much can be learned about the behavior of light on forms and in spaces by careful observation of the world around you.

There are two important qualities you should understand about shade and shadow before you attempt to illustrate them in color. First, the shade and shadow should appear *transparent* (as opposed to "applied"), and, second, the *distinctness of the edges* of the shadows should be appropriate to the lighting conditions.

In drawings of exterior views, shadows usually have *distinct* edges, inasmuch as a sunlit condition is typically illustrated. In fact, the contrast at these edges can be intensified through the use of gradations of value. This is known as "forcing the shadow." Shadows in interior settings are often caused by diffused or indirect sources of light and have *indistinct* edges. Indistinct shadows can also be caused by reflected light from "secondary" light sources, such as sunlight reflected from a wall. *Interior shadows are generally more subtle* and have less contrast with their neighboring illuminated surfaces than exterior shadows. Interior objects often have multiple shadows, as interiors usually have multiple sources of light. Notice, too, that interior shadows appear to gradate in value more than exterior shadows, appearing darker at the base of the casting object and becoming lighter as they progress away from the object. Make studies of interior shadows, using the color media described in this book, to build your skills in illustrating interior shadows. Do not be discouraged at their apparent complexity. In your interior design illustrations, placing interior shadows, not too dark, in approximately the right locations, will in most cases be sufficient to "anchor" the shadowed objects to the page and help communicate your design ideas (3-13).

Surfaces in shade and shadow will appear transparent if they are of a value appropriate to the sunlit portion of the same surface. That is, shades and shadows on light-value surfaces will be lighter than those on dark surfaces (see also figure 1-1). In addition, the textures and patterns that appear on the sunlit parts of a surface should be continued into the shaded and shadowed portions of the surface If the patterns and textures are not continued, these portions of the surface appear obscure and muddy, as if painted with black or gray paint (3-14).

Interior shadows often grade in value, becoming darker toward their point of origin.

Interior shades and shadows have edges that are diffuse rather than distinct.

You will usually see shadows within shadows in interiors as well as multiple shadows cast by the same object.

Fig. 3-13

These shadows were made with warm grays #3 and #1: their colors were developed and their edges softened with color pencil. The gray markers are good for illustrating diffuse shadows because they can be made into any color and have predictable values.

Fig. 3-13 A typical interior shadow.

Fig. 3-14 The basics of exterior illumination and color are explained in terms of typical errors (a) and corresponding recommendations (b).

SKY
Single marker color (*Sapphire Blue*) for sky is time-consuming, and gives cartoonlike appearance.

MODELING
No light-to-dark modeling on trees leads to flat appearance.

GRADATION
Lack of gradation of color leads to flat, "dead" illustrations.

MINGLING
Colors not "mingled" results in colors that are too bright, and to a lack of cohesiveness in the illustration.

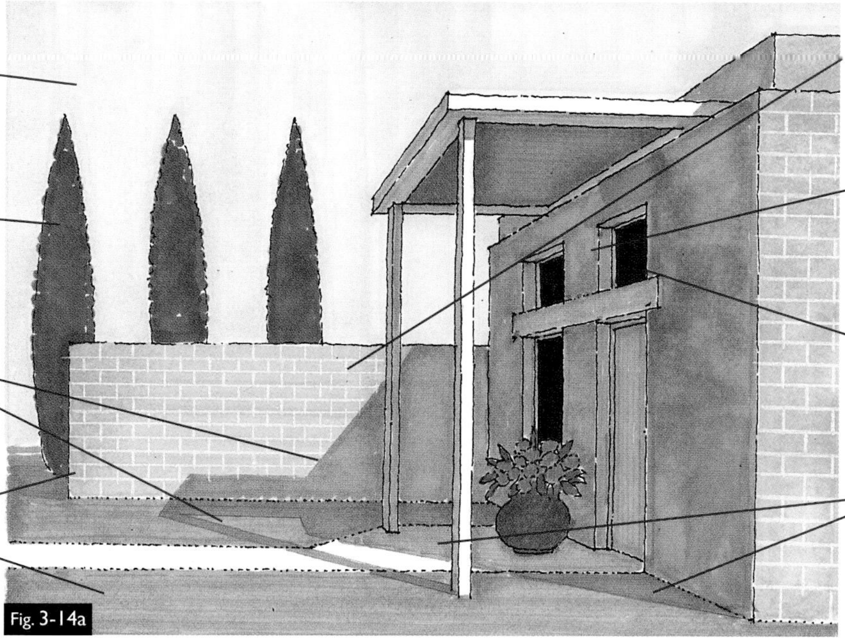

MATERIALS
Material indication too detailed, time-consuming.

SHADOW TRANSPARENCY
Cool Grey #3 marker was simply applied over sunlit marker color, resulting in a hue mismatch. Lack of material indication gives shadow a "painted on" appearance.

REFLECTIONS
Windows with no indication of reflectivity appear "dead."

SHADOW VALUE
Same marker (*Cool Grey #3*) used for shadows, regardless of value of material, creating a mismatch between the sunlit and shadow values of each material.

Fig. 3-14a

SKY
Sky indicated as gradation of hue with pencil (*Light Peach* to *Light Cerulean Blue*).

MODELING
Trees modeled with light and dark gives them a substantial look.

GRADATION
Values of color from light to dark; helps to "force" the shadows.

MINGLING
Colors mingled extensively help tie the illustration together while reducing chromas of the colors. For example, *Limepeel* and *Light Cerulean Blue* pencils were used over the brick; *Terra Cotta* pencil was used on the grass.

MATERIALS
Materials indicated as impressions instead of literally.

SHADOW TRANSPARENCY
Shadow color is a lower value, but same hue and chroma as sunlit colors. (Note the exception on the trees—used to create appearance of sunset light.) Material indications, grass and tree textures occur in shade and shadow as well as on sunlit surfaces. Note how mortar joint value is light in shadow to maintain visibility.

REFLECTIONS
Simple reflections in windows allow them to appear more alive.

SHADOW VALUE
The values of various materials correspond to one another in sunlight and shadow. Dark materials have dark shadows; light materials have lighter shadows.

Fig. 3-14b

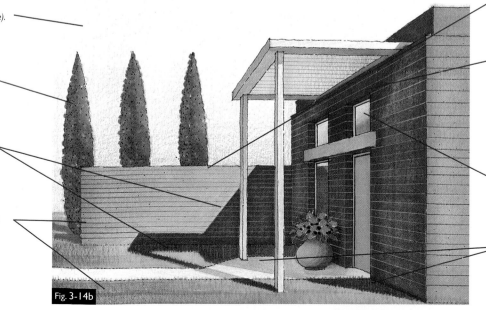

Lighting Situations

There are a variety of lighting situations that can be created easily with the media and papers shown in this book, including exterior daylight (3-15), interior light (3-16), dusk—or dawn—light (3-17), and nighttime light (3-18). The approaches to illustrating these kinds of lighting situation are explained in detail in Chapters 4 and 7.

Fig. 3-15

Fig. 3-15 This entry study for a retail project shows a typical exterior daylight lighting condition. Note how the shadow on the building is "forced." *White* pencil is used to grade the sunlit portion of the wall to a lighter value, and the shadow is darkened toward the same edge.

Bubble-jet copy of felt-tipped pen, marker, color pencil, and white gouache on white tracing paper. 8" x 12". **(Drawing: Bryan Gough)**

REMOVE WOOD from columns to reduce their size; treat columns in a more contemporary way...

TENANT CRITERIA would allow fresher, more interesting tenant presentations

ADD SKYLIGHTS for natural light, brightness

STREET LANTERN add scale, sparkle

NEW FLOOR FINISH could lighten food court, reduce floor maintenance

LIGHTER AND FRESHER

Skylighting would enhance the feeling of freshness in the food court. A lighter, more easily maintained floor could be accomplished with terrazzo.

4.5

Fig. 3-16

Fig. 3-16 The shadows in this interior study have *diffuse edges* and grade in value. Color was added only to the center of interest, then graded back into the line drawing and white paper to save illustration time. The figures are darkened somewhat to help the food-service tenants appear more luminous.

Alcohol-based marker and color pencil over black-and-white photocopy on bond paper. 11" x 17".

Fig. 3-17

Fig. 3-17 This dusk rendition of a building study was drawn with a **Micron 005** felt-tipped pen on white tracing paper. *Black Prismacolor* pencil was used to darken the roof, parts of the building front, trees, and the lower portion of the drawing in order to accentuate the building's internal glow by way of value contrast. Color was added to the back of the drawing with color pencil, and white accents were added as a final touch to the front of the drawing with white gouache.

Color photocopy with gray Canson paper behind original. 11" x 17".

Fig. 3-18 This night scene began as a line drawing on vellum, fed diagonally through a diazo machine. The lower right of the drawing was fed first into the machine, and the speed gradually increased to maximum as the drawing progressed to the upper right. Color was added to the print with color pencil. Pastel was used on the wedge-shaped banners on the building facade to make them especially luminous. A wash of white pastel was added to the ground at the entry and graded with a chamois. In this special case, the figures were added with black marker *over* the pastel—far easier than attempting to work *around* each figure. A large black marker was also used to make the sky darker, so that the searchlight effect (applied with white pastel on a chamois, using a cut-paper template) would be more visible. White gouache was added when the illustration was complete, to create stars, lighting, and to brighten the interior. 18" x 24". (Drawing: Henry Beer)

Fig. 3-18

THE RETROCOLOR TECHNIQUE

The *retrocolor* technique is a fast and highly effective color illustration technique we use frequently at CommArts, because it works best on common white roll tracing paper. It permits color design illustrations to be created quickly, lends itself to a wide variety of lighting situations, allows easy alteration, and reproduces (and enlarges) beautifully.

These illustrations are easy to make. The linework is drawn (or photocopied—see figures 7-5 through 7-9) on the tracing paper as usual (3-19). Shade and shadow are applied to the same side of the paper as the linework (3-20). However, the color is applied to the *other* side of the paper, where it cannot dim, obliterate, or smear the linework and shade and shadow application (3-21). This technique opens new opportunities in combinations of media. For example, *Black* Prismacolor—easily erasable and capable of beautifully producing smooth shade and shadow—can be used with marker. Photocopies can be colored with xylene-based markers. Felt-tipped lines stay crisp and dark, no longer dimmed by color pencil. Color media of all types can be applied much more quickly and loosely, inasmuch as when the drawing is turned right-side-over, the unobliterated linework continues to organize the image into a coherent illustration (3-22). The color also appears smoother and more even. In addition, both the color and the linework can be easily altered, each without interfering with the other. Finally, design drawings done in the retrocolor technique lend themselves to a variety of dramatic lighting effects with little or no additional effort, as explained in the following discussion.

Fig. 3-19 Line drawing on white tracing paper made with *Black* Prismacolor pencil and straightedge. A straightedge can help a designer "aim" her lines more easily toward the vanishing points, keep the lines thin, and apply them more quickly.

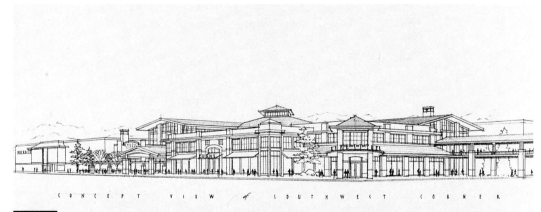

Fig. 3-19

Fig. 3-20 Shade and shadow have been applied, also with *Black* Prismacolor pencil, to the same side of the paper as the linework.

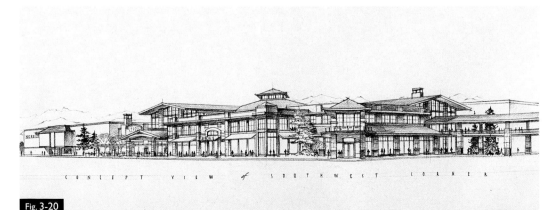

Fig. 3-20

Fig. 3-21

Fig. 3-21 Color is applied to the *back* of the drawing with color pencil. This step should be done while working on a toned surface, such as kraft paper, because the drawing is repeatedly turned over to evaluate progress. The color for this illustration took about an hour to apply.

Fig. 3-22 The finished drawing. Notice how the linework, unaffected by the color application, neatly organizes the rapidly applied color. Lighter colors have been used in the windows, as the drawing is transformed into an evening scene in subsequent steps. 4" x 17".

Fig. 3-22

TONED BACKGROUNDS

Illustrations with toned backgrounds have three distinct advantages over those created on opaque white paper. First, they can be made more quickly, as less time and effort must be spent "fighting the white" that often shows through the application of color media. The reason is that, unless you are intentionally creating a very light illustration, the average value of a typical illustration is lower than that of white paper. Second, you can "apply"—and thereby more carefully manipulate—the *illumination* as well as the shade and shadow in the illustration. Finally, toned papers provide a wider range of opportunities for easily creating drama and impact in your design illustrations. In many kinds of toned-background illustrations, markers are applied first, creating the values that are darker than the paper. Color pencils and pastels are then applied to create the effects of light and colors that are lighter than the paper. *All toned backgrounds lend themselves most readily to illustrations in which the viewer is looking from larger, darker surroundings into areas of smaller, lighter conditions.*

Diazo prints, mentioned in Chapter 2, can easily be made with either even or graded *background* tones. The designer need only provide the *highlights* and *lowlights* at the center of interest to bring the illustration to life (3-23).

Fig. 3-23 This restaurant study uses a blackline diazo print, run at a faster-than-usual speed, to illustrate the impacts of a proposed exterior view. Marker was used to apply the dark values, color pencil the lighter ones. 18" x 24".

Fig. 3-23

Canson paper can be used in a similar way to diazo prints, but offers a greater choice of background colors that you can use to complement the scheme of colors used in your illustration (3-24).

Design illustrations that use the retrocolor technique can be turned into toned-background illustrations simply by slipping colored paper (kraft paper, Canson, or Pantone paper, for example) behind the illustration to enhance its lighter values (3-25 and 3-26). Color is often applied on the back of these illustrations while the designer is working on a toned surface, such as kraft paper, in order to judge where and how much color pencil and pastel should be applied.

Once a portion of the back of the drawing is colored, it can be turned right-side-up and rested on the kraft paper for evaluation. These illustrations in particular lend themselves to dramatic dawn, dusk, and early evening lighting effects, because it is at those times of the day that the exterior surfaces, lighting, and interior illumination are simultaneously evident (3-27 and 3-28).

Black backgrounds are also used to create impact in design illustrations other than night scenes, such as in the illustration of illuminated signing (3-29) and high-finish objects (3-30).

Fig. 3-24 The shade and shadow were applied to this felt-tipped pen line drawing with the use of horizontal lines to create their tones, because even tones often do not copy well on a black-and-white photocopier. The drawing was then photocopied onto Canson paper (#343, "Pearl"), sprayed lightly with Krylon Crystal Clear, and finished with color pencil. The light value is *White Prismacolor pencil*; the shadow color is *Blue Violet Lake #27*, a Derwent pencil. 10" x 12".

Fig. 3-24

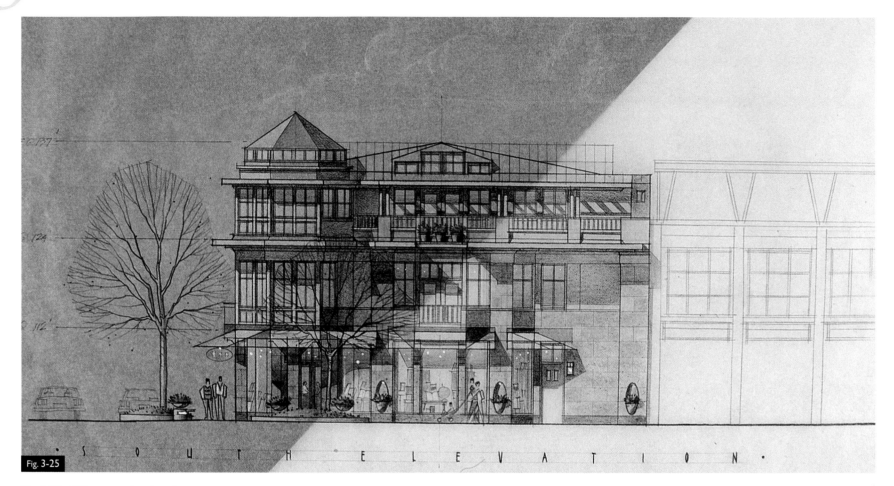

Fig. 3-25

**Fig. 3-25 This retrocolor drawing on
white trace uses *Black* Prismacolor
pencil on the front for line and shadow;
color has been applied to the back. The
blue Pantone paper (# 18-4051, "Strong
Blue") placed behind the upper left half
enhances the drawing's lighter values,
giving it a moonlit quality. 12" x 18".**

Fig. 3-26

Fig. 3-26 This test print is a bubble-jet copy of a retrocolor drawing with strips of "Pearl" Canson paper *(left)*, darkened blueline diazo paper *(middle)*, and kraft paper *(right)* placed behind the original. It was used to decide on the best backing paper color for a "dusk" effect. The blue was chosen for the enlarged final copy. 11" x 17".

Fig. 3-27 The illustration shown in figure 3-22 with kraft paper placed behind it. Note how the windows now appear illuminated.

Fig. 3-27

Fig. 3-28 The illustration shown in figure 3-27 with Pantone paper (# 18-4051, "Strong Blue") placed behind it to the ground line of the building. This darker paper intensifies the lighter pencil colors even more than the kraft paper, instantly creating an evening scene. By adding a graded value to the lower part of the remaining kraft paper with *Black* Prismacolor pencil, a slight "glow" from the building was easily effected. The bubble-jet copy process, shown here, strengthened the effect.

Fig. 3-28

Fig. 3-29

Fig. 3-29 This black-background illustration was made by running an acetate "reversal" (black background, clear lines) of a felt-tipped pen line drawing through a diazo machine. The copy, a blackline print, has a black background with white lines. The neon is created by applying white gouache over color pencil (see also figures 4-76 through 4-78). 12" x 14". (Drawing: Henry Beer)

3

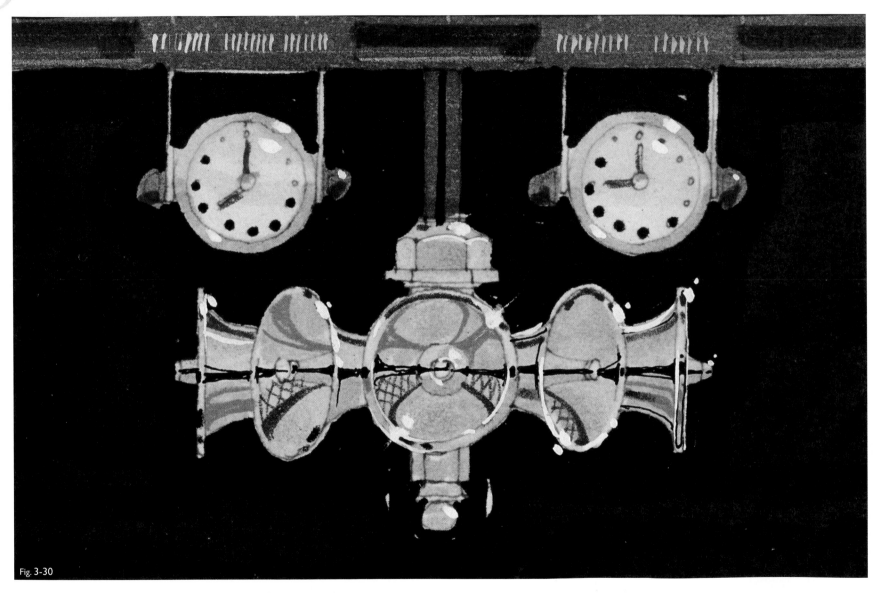

Fig. 3-30

Fig. 3-30 The creation of a medium-value blackline print of a line drawing was the first step in making this chromed public address/time station. The background was then quickly covered in black marker. Highlights and lowlights were added with gray marker, felt-tipped pen, color pencil, and white gouache. 12" x 14". (Drawing: Henry Beer)

ELEMENTS, MATERIALS, AND FINISHES

This chapter presents an encyclopedia of techniques you can use to illustrate a wide variety of typical elements, materials, and finishes used to create places for people. These techniques illustrate the most difficult—and most widely used—middle-ground views of these elements, materials, and finishes; distant views of design ideas have little or no detail, and close-up views are rarely drawn or, if they are, are frequently shown in silhouette.

The approaches to these techniques follow a similar pattern. First, the paper type is selected that will create the most effective background for the illustration. White paper is used for many of the techniques where ordinary lighting effects are required. Bristol paper is used in this chapter for the white paper, as it presents the techniques most clearly. However, these techniques can be effectively employed on the bond, trace, and diazo papers you typically use in practice. You will notice that toned papers, such as Canson and diazo print paper that has been run through the machine at a faster-than-usual speed, are used for techniques that depict various effects of light.

Second, once the linework is on the paper, the shade and shadow are added. In the examples shown, shade and shadow are often applied with gray marker, because the values can be chosen readily. An exception is the retrocolor technique, where—owing to the paper type (white trace) and small size of the illustration—the shade and shadow are more effectively applied with *Black* Prismacolor pencil.

Once the shadows are drawn, the marker base is applied, over which the pastel and/or color pencil follows. Fine-line felt-tipped pen (often Pilot Razor Point) is used to add the final delineation and augment the patterns and textures. Accents of white gouache are usually the last touches. Gold or silver marker accents, if necessary, are added to the final *copy* of the illustration, because they will not photocopy.

This chapter illustrates only one material, finish, or element at a time. When you approach an entire drawing, however, all these parts will evolve *together,* as Chapters 6 and 7 will show. Your drawings may often not look like much after the first few steps, but don't be discouraged; a drawing usually does not "come alive" until the latter steps or even until you apply the accents.

You will find it very useful to have a wide variety of visual references at your fingertips while creating design illustrations. This *source file,* whether books with photographs, whole magazines, clippings, or snapshots, allows you to complete your illustrations much more quickly. Your source file may include such referents as people (sitting, standing, walking, leaning), architectural materials, landscape elements (trees, shrubs, ground covers, distant landscapes, and cityscapes), vehicles (including bicycles), lighting conditions of all kinds (both indoors and out), reflective materials (moving and still water, glass, windows, and metals), interior materials and finishes, furnishings, and a miscellany of whatever you may need if your project is specialized, such as animals, boats, or airplanes.

This chapter is organized around the space-defining planes for both interiors and exteriors as well as the elements that typically accompany each. An approach to illustrating people and automobiles is discussed separately in Chapter 5.

Your design illustrations need not be photographic, but instead should convey a coherent impression of the myriad ideas you have in response to the programs that guide the development of your projects. The detail in the illustrations that follow need not be included in your own color design drawings if it is not necessary. Remember, the point of design drawing, from conceptual through schematic, is to focus on overall ideas. Add only as much detail as necessary to communicate the character of those ideas. Let photographs of specific elements, such as furniture, and the sample boards that accompany your drawings provide the detail during these early stages of the design process.

The marker colors listed in this book name the xylene-based AD markers first, followed by the corresponding alcohol-based Prismacolor markers in parentheses. Where only an AD marker or only a Prismacolor marker is recommended, the marker is listed by itself. The color pencils listed are Prismacolor.

INTERIOR MATERIALS

Space-Defining Planes

Each of the three planes that make up all interior spaces—floor plane, wall plane, and ceiling plane—have typical elements, materials, finishes, textures, and ways of carrying light that give these planes, and thereby the interior itself, their character.

In one sense, the step-by-step techniques that follow are intended to provide you with a ready reference for at least one approach to illustrating the various elements that constitute these planes. In another sense, however, this approach is intended to facilitate the development of your own approach to design illustration. You can easily extrapolate from these techniques when you undertake to illustrate the myriad other elements you will encounter in your interior design work.

FLOOR FINISHES

The general issues you will confront when illustrating floor finishes are layout of the pattern, color, play of light (shadows and gradations), texture (smoothness, nappiness, etc.), reflections, and clarification of the pattern—in approximately that order. Most floor finishes can be illustrated by using the general approach shown here.

Wood  (4-1, 4-2)

1 **Apply marker base.** *Sand (Sand), Kraft Brown (Light Tan),* and occasional strokes of *Redwood (Sienna Brown)* markers are used as the base colors, following the penciled help lines.

Fig. 4-1

Fig. 4-2

2 Develop wood colors with pencil. *Jasmine* and *Cream* pencils were applied randomly in horizontal streaks, following the help lines. A light *Peach* pencil wash was then evenly applied over the entire wood floor surface.

3 Add diffuse shadows and reflections. A *Dark Umber* pencil was used to add the diffuse shadows under the table and chairs. The window reflections were added with *White* pencil; the reflections were made most obvious nearest their source.

Rugs and Carpets (4-3, 4-4)

Impressions of patterns can easily be created to effectively illustrate those rugs and carpets intended for a room. Their textures should remain subtle.

1 Draw the outline of the rug pattern with pencil.

2 Apply base color with marker. Approximate the rug pattern *(left)* using the marker tip. *Sapphire Blue (Light Cerulean Blue)* and *Deep Salmon (Carmine Red)* markers were used for the pattern. *Buff (Brick Beige)* marker was applied to the interior, stroking toward the vanishing point.

Mid tone the carpet *(right)* was also colored with *Buff (Brick Beige)* marker, and its border was colored with *Light Ivy (Putty + Cream)* marker. Shadows were added to both with *French Grey 30%* and *French Grey 50%* markers.

Fig. 4-3

3 **Refine color with pencil.** Yellow accents were added to the rug with *Yellow Ochre* pencil. This pencil was also used to add a wash of color to the interior of the rug with the side of its point. This helped to bring up the texture of the paper, thus giving nap to the rug. The graded wash was continued on the rug toward the right with *Terra Cotta* and *Olive Green* pencils. The red and blue borders and patterns were washed with *Terra Cotta* pencil. The red only was muted with *Olive Green* pencil.

The carpet *(right)* was washed with *Bronze, Peach,* and *Burnt Umber* pencils. The subtle border pattern was added with *White* pencil, then flavored with *Bronze* pencil.

Fig. 4-4

Terrazzo (4-5, 4-6)

Terrazzo has a number of distinguishing characteristics. It can be made in just about any color, its patterns can be large and complex, and many—although not all—of the colors have a unique grainy texture owing to the combinations of stone chips and matrix used to create the material. It is usually somewhat reflective, because it is polished during the final stages of installation.

1 **Draw the outline of the pattern** in pencil, so that the lines remain subtle. A .5 mm mechanical pencil with a 6H lead was used here.

2 **Apply marker colors** to the terrazzo pattern. *Cool Grey #1 (Cool Grey 10%), Cool Grey #3 (Cool Grey 30%), Brick Red (Cherry), Pale Cherry (Mineral Orange), Flesh (Salmon Pink), Buff (Brick Beige),* and *Warm Grey #1 (French Grey 10%)* markers were used for these particular colors.

3 **Apply graded washes with pencil.** The right side was washed with a mix of *Light Peach* and *Jasmine* pencils, and the left side was washed with *French Grey 90%* pencil. The two sides were graded into each other. Note how the wash on the left brings up the grain of the paper and imparts a texture similar to terrazzo.

4 **Stipple** the areas of terrazzo that have a highly visible stone chip content (this happens when the color of the stone chips differs significantly from that of the matrix). The central and outermost gray areas were stippled with *White* pencil that had a sharp point. The pencil was quickly rotated as its tip was lightly touched to the surface so that it would make an adequate mark. The pinkish areas were stippled in the same way with a *Terra Cotta* pencil.

5 **Add reflections** using white gouache, very slightly diluted, with the side of a long-tipped brush (see figure 2-10).

6 **Clarify the pattern.** The part of the pattern closest to the viewer was "enhanced" (re-outlined) with a Micron 005 felt-tipped pen.

Fig. 4-5

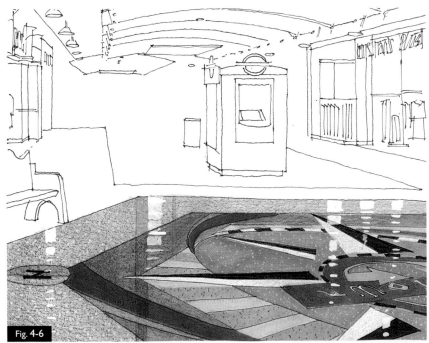
Fig. 4-6

Stone, Honed, and Polished (4-7, 4-8)

It is usually a good idea to illustrate floor surfaces last in an illustration, particularly those that have reflective qualities. By doing so, you will know which colors you will have to reflect in these surfaces.

1 **Apply color to stone.** *Cool Grey #1 (Cool Grey 10%)* marker was used to color the banding, and *Raw Sienna 234.9* pastel was applied to the remaining floor areas. The pastel that crept beyond the yellow portions of the floor area was removed with an electric eraser.

2 **Add reflections and shadows.** Reflections in the honed stone floor *(left)* are softer and less distinct than those for a polished floor. Nor do they go as far "into" the floor. The light-value reflections were added with *White* pastel, and the dark reflections and indistinct shadows were applied with pencil. *Cool Grey 50%* pencil was used to add reflections and shadows to the cool-colored stone banding; *French Grey 30%* pencil was used to apply the reflections and shadows to the warm-colored stone.

The reflections in the polished floor *(right)* have more distinct edges, *but should not have a visible outline.* They were delineated extremely lightly with a hard pencil. Colors are also reflected in polished surfaces but are more muted than the objects themselves. Here, the same color pencils were used for both the objects and their reflections, although the reflections were colored using a *much* lighter touch with the pencils. The white reflections were created simply by using an electric eraser, with an erasing template, to remove the yellow pastel.

Fig. 4-7

3 **Add stone texture, coloration, and joints.** Subtle coloration and veining were added to the stone with *Burnt Ochre* and *French Grey 30%* pencils. Some foreground stippling was added with a Micron 005 felt-tipped pen. A final and very important step was the addition of the stone joints, which were added with a .5 mm mechanical pencil with a 6H lead. These joints were drawn over everything—reflections, shadows, and highlights.

Fig. 4-8

Tile (4-9, 4-10)

Tile can be found in a wide variety of materials, colors, and finishes—from vinyl to ceramic, from matte to polished. Apply the techniques shown for the various floor materials to the tile type you happen to be illustrating. For example, if you are illustrating a ceramic tile with a high sheen (but not polished), you can add highlights similar to those shown in the illustration of the terrazzo.

The tile shown here is intended to be a simple vinyl tile with matte finish. However, most hard floor finishes will have *some* degree of reflectivity, as they are often buffed during maintenance.

1 **Lay out tile** lightly with pencil. The tile layout should be in correct perspective, because an error in its perspective can make the floor appear warped or tilted. Tile layouts, particularly those with a pattern that uses vanishing points that differ from those used for the rest of the picture, as shown here, can most easily and quickly be accomplished using a computer.

2 **Apply marker color.** Wash the entire floor with the *lighter* marker first. *Naples Yellow (Eggshell)* marker was used here for the wash, then *Light Ivy (Putty + Cream)* marker was used to touch color to the alternating tiles. The shadows were added beneath the tables with *French Grey 10%* and *French Grey 30%* markers.

3 **Apply pencil washes** to the floor. A *Light Peach* pencil wash was graded into a *Burnt Ochre* pencil wash on the right.

4 **Add highlights.** Because the tile has a matte finish, diffuse highlights were added with *White* pencil.

5 **Trim edges** of foreground tile. In this example, a .5 mm pencil was used to delineate or "trim" the foreground tiles. These rough edges can be trimmed with color pencil, which appears as a grout joint, in illustrating ceramic tile. In that situation, light-colored pencils should be used on dark ceramic tile and vice versa.

Fig. 4-9

Fig. 4-10

Interior Floor Plans (4-11, 4-12, 4-13)

A plan view is an abstract device used for organizing circulation, architectural, and interior elements in a place. When color is added to a plan—even diagrammatic color—the viewer can understand its information much more quickly and easily.

When the color and pattern of a plan are coordinated to the perspective views of the project, the viewer is yet more easily oriented. Impressions of floor materials and patterns not only make the plan seem more real and more attainable, but also pull the viewer's eye all the way to the floor plane. Quickly applied diffuse shadows help to visually "anchor" the various plan elements. Select only quick and easy techniques for applying plan color, inasmuch as you are only creating an impression in an attempt to clarify your plan view.

1 **Draw the plan;** *poché* **the wall cuts.** The plan was drawn with a Micron 005 felt-tipped pen. The walls were pochéd with a *French Grey 70%* marker (4-11).

2 **Add marker color.** Marker colors were added to the materials on the floor plane (4-12). The rug patterns were dotted in with the tips of the markers. Remember that the rug patterns need only be approximate; a color photocopy or a strike-off (sample) of the real rug can be included on your accompanying materials board to provide the details. Diffuse shadows were added with *French Grey 10%, 30%,* and *50%* markers. Note how they contribute to the three-dimensional quality of the plan and help anchor the elements to the floor.

3 **Add color pencil detailing.** The marker colors of the outdoor patio pavers and the living room rug were both muted with a wash of *French Grey 30%* pencil, and the *Buff (Brick Beige)* marker on the bleached oak floor was simultaneously textured and muted by lines applied with a *Blue Slate* pencil and a straightedge. Other subtle washes of pencil color were added to adjust the colors of the furniture and tiles on the kitchen floor. *Deco Aqua* pencil was added to the glass line to help emphasize the location of the glazing.

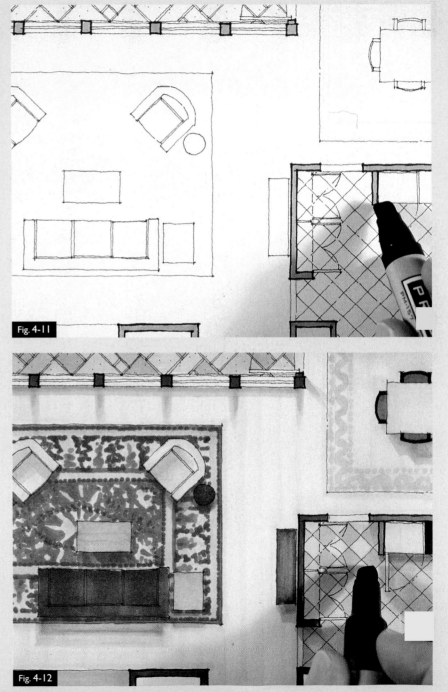

Fig. 4-11

Fig. 4-12

Fig. 4-13

WALL PLANE ELEMENTS

Wall Finishes

Consider two important issues. First, keep your rendition of these surfaces subtle and muted, because wall surfaces are the *backdrops* to the room. As in reality, wall surfaces that appear too intense and contrasting tend to overpower both the room and its occupants. It is much easier to make a wall surface more intense (if it appears too muted) than to mute one that is too intense.

Second, because wall surfaces are often smooth, take care to avoid graininess in your pencil washes. Graininess can occur when the pencil reveals the grain of the paper and the pencil's value contrasts too greatly with the value you have chosen for the wall surface. If you are applying graded pencil washes to a light wall, stick to light-colored pencils; on a dark wall, use darker pencils.

Painted Wall (4-14, 4-15)

1 **Apply pastel base.** In this example (4-14), the darker-colored end wall was first lowered in value with a *French Grey 10%* marker. However, unless you are faced with a special condition like this, use pastels to create a smooth wall color base. *Raw Sienna 234.9* stick pastel was scraped with a knife onto the wall area of the drawing, rubbed in with a facial tissue, then smoothed with a chamois. On the darker end wall, *Gold Ochre 231.7* stick pastel was applied in the same way.

2 **Trim; apply gradations.** The overapplication of pastel on areas where it doesn't belong was cleaned off or "trimmed" with an electric eraser using a soft, white erasing strip.

Graded washes were applied (4-15) to bring up the subtle, diffuse shadows and gradations of light with a *French Grey 20%* pencil. These gradations were then flavored with *Jasmine* and *Mineral Orange* pencils.

The darker end wall was treated in a similar way with *French Grey 30%* and *Mineral Orange* pencils. Some touches of even darker value were applied with *Terra Cotta* pencil.

Fig. 4-14

Fig. 4-15

Decorative Paint Finish (4-16, 4-17)

There are many kinds of decorative paint finish that can add interest and richness to wall surfaces, such as sponging, cloth distressing, stippling, color washing, and dragging. The example shown in these drawings simulates a color wash finish called "brush wash" in multiple colors.

An excellent reference to follow when attempting to illustrate decorative paint finishes is *Recipes for Surfaces* by Drucker and Finkelstein (New York: Fireside, 1990). Experiment first with combinations of pastel and color pencil to find appropriate color combinations before you attempt an illustration.

1 **Apply pastel; distress with electric eraser.** A knife was used to scrape a *Cobalt Blue 512.5* stick pastel onto the drawing. It was spread with a facial tissue and smoothed with a chamois. Note that less pastel was applied to the more illuminated parts of the surfaces. An electric eraser with a soft white erasing strip was used (4-16) to "distress" the even blue finish. Slightly more pastel was removed from the illuminated areas. An erasing template was used to edge the shadows.

2 **Apply additional pastel colors; trim; apply gradations.** *Permanent Green Deep 619.9* stick pastel was scraped with a knife onto the wall surface, dabbed into the blue with a facial tissue, and wiped lightly with a chamois. *Light Oxide Red 339.9* stick pastel followed in the same way. These colors not only shift and mute the blue, but also soften the eraser marks.

The gradations were emphasized by lightly applying a *Cool Grey 30%* pencil with the side of its tip, then flavored with a *Blue Slate* pencil. Some touches of *Peach* and *Light Peach* pencils were added, using the sides of the pencils' tips, to bring up the warm color slightly (4-17).

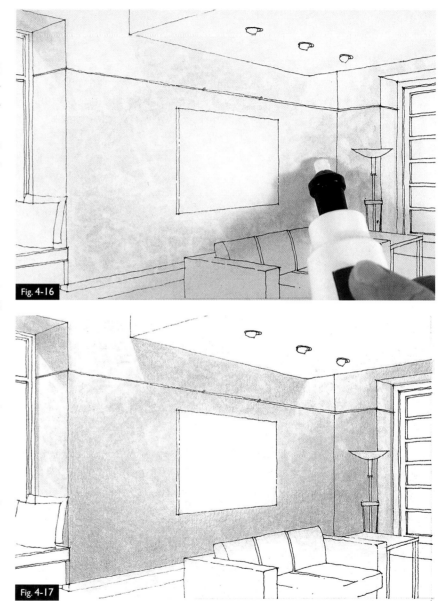

Fig. 4-16

Fig. 4-17

Patterned Finishes (4-18, 4-19)

A patterned wall finish is usually created by the use of wallpaper or stencils. The techniques shown here can suffice for either.

The patterns illustrated follow those produced by Bradbury and Bradbury Art Wallpapers for their Arts & Crafts collection. "Springfield Stripe" is used for the body of the wall, with a "Vienna Check Border" top and bottom. A "Thornberry Border" is used at the top of the wall as a frieze.

1 **Draw patterns in pencil; apply light markers for base.** First, the patterns were drawn lightly using a .5 mm pencil with a 6H lead. Light-colored markers were applied to the pattern so that the pattern would stay sufficiently in the background (4-18). *Naples Yellow (Eggshell)* marker was used for every other stripe as well as the sinuous stem in the frieze at the top. *Light Ivy (Putty + Cream)* marker was used for the leaves in the frieze and the tiny squares on the checkerboard borders. *French Grey 10%* marker was used for the edges of both the borders and the frieze.

Note that felt-tipped pens were *not* used to draw the patterns, so the edges would remain soft and unassertive.

2 **Apply pastel wash.** After the marker was applied, *Raw Sienna 234.9* stick pastel was scraped with a knife onto the wallpaper, rubbed in with a bare finger, then smoothed with a chamois. This both provided a background wall color and muted, softened, and unified the marker colors.

The pastel was erased from the berry locations on the frieze, and *Pale Indigo (Cloud Blue)* marker was applied as a final touch (4-19).

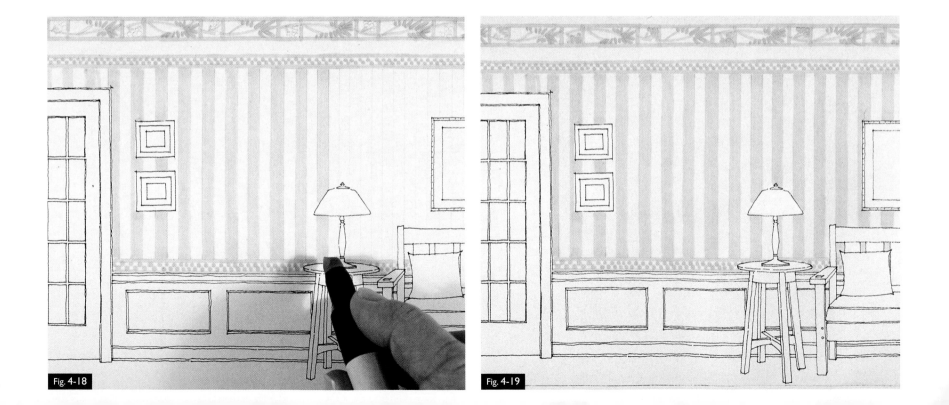

Fig. 4-18

Fig. 4-19

Wood Wainscot   (4-20, 4-21)

The oak wainscot shown here is typical of the kind used with the wallpapers shown in figure 4-19. Wood wainscot can have more or less detail and, often, less apparent grain than that shown here.

1 **Apply marker base.** *Kraft Brown (Light Tan)* and *Pale Cherry (Mineral Orange)* markers were applied to the wainscot and door (4-20).

2 **Add pencil grain.** Swipes of *Terra Cotta, Mineral Orange,* and *Jasmine* pencils were applied, stroking along the direction of the wood grain, using the *sides* of the pencils' tips. Thin graphite pencil lines were applied for additional wood grain, using a .5 mm pencil with a 2H lead.

3 **Apply highlights and lowlights.** Highlights were added to those edges that roll toward a probable light source, with a *White* pencil. White gouache was applied to the same locations. Note that the gouache highlights are long, smooth, and lens-shaped. They were dimmed slightly by coloring them with a *Jasmine* pencil. Lowlights and shadow were added with a *Dark Umber* pencil and a straightedge (4-21).

Fig. 4-20

Fig. 4-21

Windows

Because windows are important elements in the design of an interior, they should neither remain blank nor attract too much attention. Detailed views through windows, unless presented for the purpose of illustrating specific relationships between indoors and outdoors, should be avoided. Instead, just enough visual information should be given to allude to something beyond, so that the viewer's attention remains in the room.

When you look at a professional photograph of an interior, the lighting of the space appears normal, but the view through the window is often indistinct and overexposed. The illustrated image works much the same way. The window wall should be darker—even if only slightly—than the exterior. If your interior view includes windows and you want to illustrate a very light interior view, you may want to consider a nighttime view through the windows.

Daytime View, White Paper (4-22, 4-23)

1 **Color window wall.** Light-value—even white—walls will appear darker than the windows. In this illustration, *Warm Grey #1 (French Grey 10%)* marker was applied vertically, followed by *Sunset Pink (Deco Pink)* marker, stroked horizontally to diminish streakiness. *Raw Sienna 234.9* stick pastel was applied by finger, smoothed with a chamois, and trimmed with an electric eraser (4-22).

2 **Add color to exterior view.** Because the wall now has a value, you will know how much color you can add to the exterior view without making it too dark. An effective combination of pencils starts with *Cool Grey 20%* applied first and lightly, with the side of the point, in abstract and rather random motions. This is followed by *Yellow Chartreuse* pencil, also applied with the side of the point and very lightly. *Cloud Blue* pencil is then applied over the gray pencil and in any remaining white spaces in the same manner. You may wish to blend the colors with a *White* pencil, if necessary. All three colors here were applied very quickly and right over the windows' muntins. Remember that the result should remain lighter than the interior wall.

3 **Add color to window muntins, frames, and trim.** In this illustration, the window trim, frames, and muntins were colored with *Cool Grey #1 (Cool Grey 10%)* and *Pale Indigo (Cloud Blue)* markers, one over the other. Because the trim was intended to be lighter than the walls, it was further colored with *Cool Grey 20%* pencil and flavored with a *Blue Slate* pencil. The frames and muntins were made darker, because they were silhouetted by the bright exterior, by using a *Cool Grey 50%* pencil and flavored with the same *Blue Slate* pencil.

At this point, the exterior appeared too dark in value, so an electric eraser was used to quickly lift off some of the exterior color without touching the muntins (4-23).

Fig. 4-22

Fig. 4-23

Daytime View, Toned Paper (4-24, 4-25)

1 **Apply color to exterior "view."** When using toned paper (Canson "Pearl" is used here), both the light and dark colors can be applied, giving the designer more control. *Yellow Chartreuse* and *Cloud Blue* pencils were applied first with fairly light hand pressure. *French Grey 10%* marker was used for the tree trunks. *White* pencil was then applied overall, with firm hand pressure, to create the sense of the illuminated exterior (the tree trunks received less pressure) as shown in the window on the right (4-24).

2 **Apply color to window frames and muntins.** *Pale Indigo (Cloud Blue)* marker was applied to window frames and muntins. *Blue Slate* pencil was then used to flavor the marker color. A *White* pencil was applied with a straightedge to add a highlight just inside the line of the window trim.

3 **Apply color to wall.** You now know how light you can make the wall color without diminishing the effect of the brighter exterior (that is, if you make the wall *too* light, the exterior will no longer appear illuminated). In this illustration, the wall was partially washed with *Peach* and *Mineral Orange* pencils (4-25).

    Note: Pastel was not used on the wall in this illustration, because photocopy toner does not fuse particularly well to heavily grained and textured papers. When the overapplication of pastel is erased from paper of this type, the lines are erased as well.

Fig. 4-24

Fig. 4-25

Nighttime View (4-26, 4-27)

1 **Apply very dark marker.** A *Black* or very dark blue (such as a *Prussian Blue* AD marker or a *Navy Blue* Prismacolor marker) can be applied over the windows, including the muntins, to begin a simple night view. In figure 4-26, a *Black* marker was used to begin a slightly more complex night view, drawing in the foreground trees and shrubs. *Cool Grey #7* and *#9 (Cool Grey 70%* and *90%)* markers were used to add distant landforms. *Mauve (Greyed Lavender)* marker was used to color the sky.

2 **Draw window muntins with very light pencil.** The window muntins were drawn back in with a *White* pencil and a straightedge. These muntins can be flavored with other light pencil colors if necessary.

3 **Add highlights if desired.** Distant city lights were added with white gouache (4-27). The interior can be completed in the usual manner.

Fig. 4-26

Fig. 4-27

Drapes (4-28, 4-29)

1 **Draw folds, shadows, and major pattern elements with marker.** The recesses of the folds were drawn with a *French Grey 30%* marker, as shown in the drapes on the right (4-28). The major pattern elements were dotted in an even distribution with a *Pale Cherry (Mineral Orange)* marker. The shadows were added to the wall with a *Cool Grey #1 (Cool Grey 10%)* marker.

2 **Apply color wash.** The drapes were washed with *Lemon Yellow 205.3* and *Yellow Ochre 227.5* stick pastels and smoothed with a chamois. This wash could also have been applied with color pencil, creating a slightly more textured effect. After the color wash, the drapes will appear like those on the upper right (4-29). The pastel overcolor was trimmed with an electric eraser, removing some color from the inside of the drape next to the window. This easily creates the effect of the edges of the drapes being illuminated by the daylight.

3 **Apply secondary pattern.** A secondary "squiggly" pattern suggests finer print detail or embroidery. It was applied with a *Bronze* pencil, as shown in the lower right of figure 4-29.

4 **Accentuate recesses in folds.** The recesses in the folds, originally drawn with marker, were emphasized with *Bronze* pencil followed by a thin line of *Dark Umber* pencil, as the completed drapes illustrate. *Dark Umber* pencil was also used to create the pinch pleats at the top.

Fig. 4-28

Fig. 4-29

Sheer Curtains (4-30, 4-31)

The illustration of sheer (translucent) curtains can be somewhat tricky, in that they can quickly become too heavy looking. The following steps can reduce the risk of that happening.

1 **Draw curtains' surroundings.** The wall, window trim, and exterior view are all drawn first (4-30). Note that the curtains are outlined only in very light pencil, instead of felt-tipped pen, so they maintain a light appearance.

2 **Draw folds with marker.** The curtains on the left show the folds being drawn with a *Cool Grey #1 (Cool Grey 10%)* marker. Avoid drawing too many folds, especially over the glazing, so the curtain does not become too dark. This marker was also used to dot in the window frame and muntins behind the curtains. The pencil guidelines were erased after the marker was applied.

If your folds appear too dark or severe, they can be softened by an application of *White* pencil or pastel.

3 **Lightly tone window frame and muntins with pencil.** In figure 4-31, on the left, a *French Grey 20%* pencil was used to very lightly tone the frame behind the curtain, so that the glazed areas would appear brighter by contrast.

4 **Add subtle coloration.** You may wish to subtly flavor the color of the curtain. In the finished curtain on the left, *Cloud Blue* pencil was used to flavor the recesses of the folds and *Light Peach* and *White* pencils were used on the ridges.

Fig. 4-30

Fig. 4-31

Shades (4-32, 4-33)

1 **Draw the shades' surroundings first.** The shades should be drawn last so they can remain appropriately light.

2 **Add base color to shades.** A wash of *Ultramarine Deep 506.9* stick pastel was applied here (4-32), but any light pastel can be used.

3 **Create silhouette of window frame and muntins.** *Cloud Blue* pencil was applied over the pastel base with a straightedge, then darkened slightly with a *Cool Grey 30%* pencil.

4 **Add horizontal pleats.** A straightedge was used with a *Blue Slate* pencil to lightly apply the horizontal pleat lines (4-33).

Fig. 4-32

Fig. 4-33

Shutters (4-34, 4-35)

1   **Draw shutter elements with marker.** The shutters were drawn with a *Willow Green (Lime Green)* marker over light pencil layout lines. Felt-tipped pen lines can make the shutters appear too busy and diminish their softness. Note that the horizontal lines were drawn all the way across the shutter pair (4-34), with the frame elements added afterward. Use a marker sufficiently dark so the spaces between the louvers appear adequately bright.

2   **Trim edges of louvers** and darken if necessary. The top and bottom of each line of louvers were trimmed with a sharp *Blue Slate* pencil drawn along a straightedge. These trim lines were drawn right across the middle frame line and later erased.

     The *Blue Slate* pencil was then used to slightly darken the louvers—a step you can skip if your louvers are sufficiently dark.

3   **Lighten and edge.** If you accidentally draw your horizontal marker lines for the louvers too close together, use white gouache and a thin brush to reintroduce the white spaces.

     The frames of the shutters, as well as the center adjustment bar, were delineated using a .5 mm pencil with a 2H lead (4-35).

Fig. 4-34

Fig. 4-35

CEILINGS

Ceilings often exhibit subtle gradations of value as a result of their being illuminated from below by direct and reflected light. These gradations are often easiest to accomplish with pastel, combined with marker when necessary. Use photographs in books and magazines to help guide you when illustrating specific ceiling types.

Lay-In Ceiling, Tegular (4-36, 4-37)

1 **Lay out ceiling in pencil.** A .5 mm pencil with a 6H lead was used to lay out the ceiling illustrated here.

2 **Add graded color with pastel.** This ceiling was washed with *Raw Sienna 234.9* stick pastel, with *Gold Ochre 231.7* stick pastel used in the corners. Both colors were blended and smoothed with a chamois. Care was taken to allow the areas illuminated with reflected ground light to remain the white of the paper. *Ultramarine Deep 506.9* stick pastel was then used to lightly tint the back part of the white ground light reflection. It too was smoothed with a chamois (4-36).

3 **Erase layout lines.** When the layout lines are erased with an electric eraser and erasing template, a white T-bar grid is created. Because the ceiling is tegular, the shadow side of the recess is drawn in with the .5 mm, 6H pencil. This technique creates a grid pattern that is appropriately subtle (4-37).

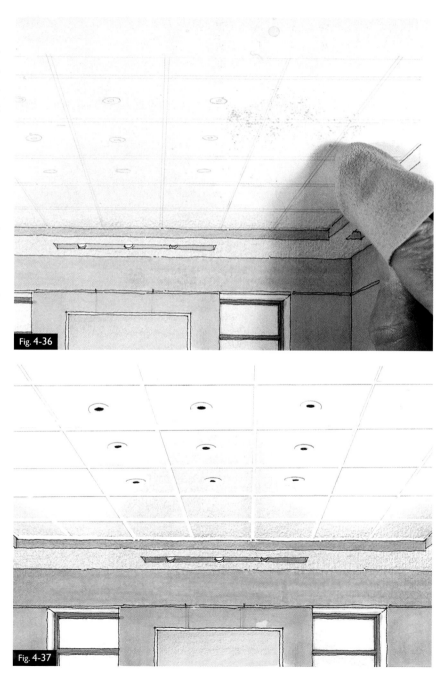

Fig. 4-36

Fig. 4-37

Beam Ceiling (4-38, 4-39)

1 **Apply shade and shadow with marker.** *French Grey 10%, French Grey 30%,* and *Clear Blender* markers were used to create shade and shadow that respond to uplight from the windows (4-30). Use a photograph of a similar condition for guidance if necessary.

2 **Apply ceiling colors.** *Indian Red 347.9* and *Raw Sienna 234.9* stick pastels were applied to the beams/joists and decking, respectively, including shade and shadow. Highlights were erased out with an electric eraser.

3 **Add detail.** The decking joints were added with a .5 mm pencil with a 6H lead and a straightedge (4-39). Shadows were touched up using a *Yellow Ochre* pencil on the decking and a mix of *French Grey 30%* and *Rosy Beige* pencils for the beams and joists.

Fig. 4-38

Fig. 4-39

Furnishings and Fixtures

Each kind of furnishing and fixture displays its own particular combination of telltale characteristics. These characteristics provide the visual clues that tell the viewer what he is looking at in a design illustration. Wicker, for example, is quite different from stainless steel in appearance. Why? Because wicker furniture is a combination of shapes, colors, textures, patterns, and kinds and degrees of reflectivity that differ sharply from the characteristics of stainless-steel furnishings and fixtures. The more often you attempt to draw those elements relevant to your profession, the more you will understand how to identify the clues necessary to communicate their most visually relevant qualities. This section will help you begin that understanding.

Those new (and many not so new) to the design profession often ask how to locate and draw furnishings in perspective design studies, both individual pieces and groupings. The gray "sidebar" pages that follow offer some suggestions.

Delineation and Location of Furniture (4-40 through 4-43)

You will frequently have to delineate and locate furnishings in design illustrations of places you are designing. Because your job is to create the places where the furniture belongs rather than the design of the furniture itself, it is best to delineate existing furniture designs appropriate to the place rather than attempt to invent furniture or draw it from memory. Unless you are an excellent furniture designer, invented furnishings can often look clumsy and seriously detract from an otherwise good design.

Figure 4-40 shows a "cut sheet" of a club chair and ottoman intended for the space in figures 4-41 through 4-43. (Courtesy Donghia Furniture and Textiles, 485 Broadway, New York, NY 10013)

Fig. 4-40

© Jeff Goldberg/Esto

Fig. 4-41

Fig. 4-42

Fig. 4-43

1   **Draw a standing figure in the desired location of the piece; rough-in the piece.** Figure 4-41 shows a roughly drawn standing scale figure, its head on the horizon line of the room perspective and its feet located at a corner of the furniture piece. This gives you a familiar reference with which to estimate the scale and proportions of the piece.

The pieces were roughed in, using the cut sheet as a reference, focusing on position and approximate shape. Accuracy of perspective is not important at this step.

2   **Refine perspective, scale, and proportions.** Once you have something on paper, you have something to manipulate. In figure 4-42, a new piece of trace was placed over the rough drawing. The most obvious straight lines of the piece, those that are perpendicular to one another, were extended to the *same* horizon line used for the room's perspective.

Vanishing points were established where these lines intersect the horizon. Of course, these points are different from those used to draw the elements of the room itself, although the horizon line is the same. From these new vanishing points, the chair and ottoman can be drawn so that, although rotated, they appear to be resting on the floor rather than awkwardly tilted.

The chair and ottoman were lightly redrawn using these vanishing points. Heights, widths, and depths of the parts were more accurately established, using both the standing figure for scale and a comparative visual estimation of proportion of one part to another. In other words, they were "eyeballed" as accurately as possible.

When the chair and ottoman were lightly blocked out, a *Black Prismacolor* pencil was used to refine the shapes in accordance with the cut sheet.

3   **Make final tracing.** The refined version of the chair and ottoman, shown in figure 4-42, was traced onto the final sheet using a Micron 005 felt-tipped pen. This step afforded yet one more opportunity to subtly refine the line illustration. Figure 4-43 shows the finished line drawing, ready for color.

Note that in the process of illustrating a selected piece of furniture, you become far more intimate with its nuances and subtleties. This is an invaluable dividend paid to those designers who create illustrations by hand.

Grouping of Tables and Chairs, with People (4-44, 4-45, 4-46)

You have probably had to draw a room or restaurant filled with tables, chairs, and people. These situations need not require the detailed, time-consuming effort you may imagine.

1 **Draw a foreground scale figure and table.** Begin by drawing the horizon line of the illustration's perspective, as shown in figure 4-44. Draw a rough figure in the foreground, where you intend to draw your first table, making sure its head is on the horizon. You will be able to estimate the sizes of furniture far more easily in the proximity of something as familiar in size as the human figure.

Draw in the approximate size of the tabletop (relative to your figure) at about midthigh. If the table is square or rectilinear, make sure its edges vanish to points on the horizon so it appears flat and not tilted. If the table is circular, draw an appropriately flat ellipse (freehand), or draw what appears to be a horizontal square in perspective, as shown here, and inscribe the ellipse within. Draw a vertical line from the center of the table shape down to align with the feet of your figure. This is where the base or legs of the table will be located.

Draw additional figures in the area where you intend to locate tables, always placing their heads on the horizon. This will help you estimate the size of additional tables within your seating area. Although the first ellipse was carefully drawn, enough of its shape is known so that the subsequent ellipses in the distance can be eyeballed, taking care only to relate their size to the nearest figure and make them progressively flatter as they near the horizon.

In this illustration, the surroundings for the tables and chairs were previously drawn on an underlying sheet. The layout step you see here was drawn with *Black* Prismacolor pencil, the perspective layout lines with a .5 mm pencil.

Fig. 4-44

2 **Rough-in figures and chairs.** In figure 4-45, seated figures were added to the tables, again using a *Black* Prismacolor pencil. The scattered standing figures were used as scale referents. This stage is often the most difficult to those new to design illustration. However, it becomes easier the more you do it. Collect and use photographs of similar situations to help you with the gestures and postures of the seated figures. Note that the detail should diminish as you progress into the background until you are drawing little more than heads and shoulders.

3 **Create final tracing.** A fresh piece of tracing paper was laid over the rough to make the final tracing in figure 4-46. The people, the furnishings, and the surroundings were drawn simultaneously. This ties everything together and gives the line drawing a unified look. A Micron 005 felt-tipped pen was used, so the linework remains thin and the final color drawing does not take on a "cartoonish" look.

With your rough as your guide, you can focus on editing and refining the drawing during this step. Note how the detail has been simplified as this part of the drawing progresses into the distance. This part of the information is kept fairly *simple,* because creating highly detailed people occupies too much time relative to their purpose in the illustration. Further detail can be added to the furnishings through the application of the color.

Fig. 4-46

Fig. 4-45

Leather (4-47, 4-48)

Leather and leatherlike materials can be found in most any color. Here, two classic colors are represented on a matching sofa and club chair.

1 **Apply marker base; consider direction of light.** In figure 4-47, *Delta Brown (Black)* marker was applied to the darker surfaces of the sofa, and *Burnt Umber (Dark Umber)* marker was used on the lighter, upward-facing surfaces. Note that although *Delta Brown (Black)* marker was used on the lower front of the sofa, the slightly lighter *Burnt Umber (Dark Umber)* marker was used behind the glass table. This is because colors appear slightly lighter behind glass as a result of veiling reflections.

    Redwood (Sienna Brown) marker was applied to the shaded parts of the club chair, and *Pale Cherry (Mineral Orange)* marker was used on the more brightly illuminated faces. In both cases the lighter markers were used as blenders.

    Note that wrinkles in the leather are indicated in this step with the darker markers.

2 **Add highlights.** The highlights on leather are often quite bright but most always have diffuse edges. In figure 4-48, a *White* pencil was used to add graded highlights on those surfaces that bend toward the light source, in this case the large window. Once the highlights were created with pencil, white gouache lines were added to the middle of the highlights to enhance their effect.

    Note that *Mineral Orange* pencil was used on the brown sofa to indicate reflected light from the club chair, and *Blue Slate* was used on the other end to simulate a cooler light—such as daylight—from an "off-picture" light source.

Fig. 4-47

Fig. 4-48

Fabric, with Pattern (4-49, 4-50)

1 **Apply marker base.** In figure 4-49, darker-value markers were applied to the shaded surfaces, and lighter markers were applied to the illuminated surfaces. *Cool Grey #1 (Cool Grey 10%)* marker was applied to the upward-facing surfaces of the sofa; *Cool Grey #3 (Cool Grey 30%)* marker was applied to the surfaces that face away from the window. The stripes were added to those surfaces with *French Grey 10%* and *French Grey 30%* markers, respectively.

The pillow on the left has a *Naples Yellow (Eggshell)* marker base with *Light Ivy (Putty + Cream)* marker stripes and *Pale Cherry (Mineral Orange)* marker spots. The shadows were added with *French Grey 30%* marker. The plain pillow on the right has a *Buff (Brick Beige)* marker base with *French Grey 10%* and *30%* marker shadows.

The club chair has a *Naples Yellow (Eggshell)* marker base. The shaded faces were darkened with *French Grey 30%* marker.

Fig. 4-49

2 **Apply highlights, shading, and detail.** The sofa's illuminated surfaces were washed with *White* pencil, and the shaded faces were lightly washed with Derwent *Blue Violet Lake #27* pencil (4-50). The stripes and surfaces near the pillows were lightly washed with *Deco Orange* pencil.

Highlights were added to the pillows with *White* pencil, and *Deco Orange* pencil was applied to the shadowed parts of the folds. A *Bronze* pencil was used to add horizontal stripes to the left pillow, and detail was added to the pillow's orange spots with dilute white gouache.

The club chair's shaded faces were washed lightly with *Deco Orange* pencil, and graded washes of *White* pencil were applied to its illuminated surfaces. The pattern was added with a *Rosy Beige* pencil on the illuminated surfaces and lightly touched with *Henna* pencil on the shaded surfaces.

The glass table received a light wash of *Deco Aqua* pencil. Its foremost edge was lined with *Celadon Green*.

Fig. 4-50

Wicker, Rattan, and Cane (4-51, 4-52)

1 **Begin by applying the marker base.** The illuminated surfaces of the natural wicker and rattan chair and side table, as well as the wicker basket, were colored with a *Sand (Sand)* marker, and a *Kraft Brown (Light Tan)* marker was used on the shaded surfaces (4-51).

The same marker colors were used on the cane seat and back of the foreground chair. The white-painted wicker rocker required its immediate surroundings and background to be colored so that the white wicker would be visible in forthcoming steps.

2 **Apply pencil detail.** In figure 4-52, the natural wicker chair and side table were washed lightly with a *Yellow Ochre* pencil, after which vertical lines were added with a *Burnt Ochre* pencil. Horizontal lines were applied with a *Dark Umber* pencil. This quickly imparted a wickerlike texture. The shaded areas were darkened with a *Dark Umber* pencil.

The basket required the addition of a *French Grey 30%* marker, stroked horizontally along its contour, before a *Dark Umber* pencil was used to apply evenly spaced dashed lines in the same direction. Evenly spaced vertical lines were added along the basket's contour with a *Burnt Ochre* pencil.

The cane seat and back of the foreground chair received a wash of *Yellow Ochre* pencil, after which rows of black dots (to simulate openings) were applied with a Pilot Razor Point. Fine lines of diagonal cross-hatching were added with a *Dark Umber* pencil.

The fine strips of wicker were added to the white wicker rocker with a *White* pencil. To *one side* of the white pencil lines, *Cool Grey 70%* pencil lines were added so that certain portions of the wicker strips would be visible against insufficiently dark parts of the background. The sunlit surfaces of the white rocker were lightly washed with *Cream* pencil, and *Blue Slate* pencil was used to flavor the shaded surfaces.

Fig. 4-51

Fig. 4-52

Wood (4-53, 4-54)

The marker colors you choose as a base will largely depend on the kind of wood you intend to communicate in your design illustrations. In the illustration sequence shown here, the kitchen cabinets are intended to be a clear-grained wood, such as maple or fir, with a light stain and a matte finish. The table is a dark wood with reddish highlights, such as rosewood or Brazilian walnut, with a high finish. The freestanding pantry is intended to be an antique pine piece.

1   **Apply marker base.** *Sand (Sand)* and *Sunset Pink (Deco Pink)* were applied in sequence on the upper cabinets in figure 4-53, and *Kraft Brown (Light Tan)* and *Sunset Pink (Deco Pink)* markers were used on the lower cabinets. The lower cabinets were made slightly darker because they receive slightly less ambient light.

     Burnt Umber (Dark Umber) and *Burnt Sienna (Terra Cotta)* markers were applied to the table. *Sand (Sand)* marker was added over the *Burnt Sienna (Terra Cotta)* marker to mute it slightly.

     Pale Sepia (Goldenrod) was applied to the lighter face of the pantry, followed by *Sunset Pink (Deco Pink)* marker. The shaded and shadowed parts of the pantry were colored with *Kraft Brown (Light Tan)* marker, followed by *Sunset Pink (Deco Pink)* marker.

2   **Add detail.** Figure 4-54 shows both upper and lower cabinets subtly streaked with *Jasmine, Peach, Mineral Orange,* and *Cream* pencils.

     Reflections were added to the table with a *White* pencil. In a typical full-color design illustration, the reflections in a horizontal surface are aligned with the lightest values and brightest sources of light that are located above and beyond that surface. In this case the window is the source of the strongest reflection. Because the objects and surfaces beyond are not all colored, a few light reflections have been "dropped into" the table surface to show how reflections work on a polished wood surface. Note that the reflections are strongest at the far edge, then fade away as they drop into the table.

Fig. 4-53

Fig. 4-54

Local reflections, such as the pitcher of flowers, are created by making a reverse image in the table with the same pencils used to color the actual image. No pen outlines are used to delineate reflections, and less hand pressure is used with the pencils so that the reflection appears dimmer than the actual object. The lines formed by the table leaves were redelineated with a Pilot Razor Point.

French Grey 50% marker was used to add knots to the pine pantry. Streaks of *Mineral Orange, Cream, Jasmine,* and *Burnt Ochre* pencils were applied with the sides of the points. A straightedge was used with *Cream* and *Burnt Ochre* pencils to apply highlights and shadows to the moldings. Hints of wood grain and cracking were added with a .5 mm pencil with a 2H lead.

Stone (4-55, 4-56)

The colors of the markers you choose as a base are largely determined by the type of stone you wish to indicate. In the illustration here, a rose granite is indicated for the counter, and the backsplash is intended to be Chinese slate.

1 **Apply marker base.** In figure 4-55, *French Grey 10%* marker was applied to the granite counter, and *Cool Grey #2 (Cool Grey 20%), Cool Grey #3 (Cool Grey 30%),* and *Buff (Brick Beige)* markers were scribbled on the backsplash area.

Fig. 4-55

2 Add detailing. Shadows were added beneath the bowls and vase on the counter with a *French Grey 30%* marker in figure 4-56. The countertop was washed lightly with a *Light Peach* pencil, and a *White* pencil was used to add reflections of the uncolored objects. The counter was then stippled with *White, Black,* and *Peach* pencils. You will find that a sharp point and a slight twist to the pencil as it strikes the surface will make the stippling more delicate and effective.

Mineral Orange, Terra Cotta, and Burnt Ochre pencils were very lightly applied, using the sides of the points, to individual stones of the backsplash. A *French Grey 50%* pencil was used to darken the backsplash where it meets the counter, grading lighter as it moved up. A *White* pencil was likewise used to wash the wall beneath the cabinets, fading away as it moved downward. This creates the effect of under-cabinet lighting.

Fig. 4-56

Glass (4-57, 4-58, 4-59)

1 Draw table's surroundings first. Figure 4-57 shows the glass table saved until last in the illustration, so that the designer will know what colors are reflected.

2 Color objects on the table and the surfaces beneath. In figure 4-58, color was added to the objects on the table in the usual fashion. However, only marker was used to color those surfaces seen through the tabletop.

Fig. 4-57

When the reflections are drawn in the tabletop, they will remain crisp instead of becoming muddied by mixing with other pencil colors. *Willow Green* marker was applied to the tabletop after marker was applied to those surfaces seen beneath.

3 **Draw reflections with pencil; add finishing touches.** Figure 4-59 shows the reflections, drawn with the same color pencils used to draw the objects reflected. Note that no outlines are used on the reflections. To avoid confusion, the reflections of the objects resting on the table were drawn first, as they will partially block reflections of objects in the room beyond. The reflections of objects beyond, such as the brick of the fireplace and the window, were then added with pencil.

White gouache, thinned somewhat with water, was applied to the two far edges of the table with the use of a ruling pen. Ruling pens can be hard to find, so use *White* pencil and a straightedge as a substitute in this step. *Celadon Green* pencil and a straightedge were used to color the two closer edges, with a thin *White* pencil line added above. Highlights of white gouache were added to the corners of the table and to the two wineglasses.

Fig. 4-58

Fig. 4-59

Metals (4-60 through 4-63)

The following series of steps illustrates types of metal typically encountered by interior designers: brushed stainless steel, polished stainless steel, chrome, and polished copper.

Metals usually reflect the colors that surround them. The more polished a metal, the more distinct from one another are its darks, lights, and reflections; the less polished and more brushed the finish, the less distinct and more diffuse the reflections.

The shape of the metal determines the shape of the reflections. Flat pieces reflect like a mirror; if a flat surface is slightly warped, the reflection is likewise distorted. Cylindrical and tubular surfaces elongate reflections, stretching them into lines. Half-round objects curve reflections, and a truly spherical reflective object (particularly a polished sphere) gathers curving reflections into an intensely contrasting horizon along its middle.

1 **Illustrate everything that surrounds the metals.** In order to know what colors to reflect into the metals, they should be drawn last in an illustration (4-60).

2 **Add marker base.** The value of stainless steel can range from very dark to very light, depending on how it reflects the light. You can therefore successfully illustrate stainless steel at any value, depending on the lightness or darkness of the markers you choose to begin the illustration.

In figure 4-61, a *Cool Grey #2 (Cool Grey 20%)* marker was applied to the left side of the brushed stainless-steel cabinets, and *Warm Grey #3 (Warm Grey 30%)* marker was applied to the right side. *Warm Grey #1 (Warm Grey 10%)* marker was used as a blender between the warm and cool grays. The use of subtly different colors of gray indicates subtle differences in the hues of the light reflected from the cabinets. *French Grey 20%* marker was applied to the part of the stainless-steel countertop that reflects the red tile backsplash.

Note the wavy white spaces left in the cabinet faces. These will be turned into diffuse reflections in later steps. These reflections are wavy

because the stainless steel used in applications of this kind is rarely perfectly flat, but instead has some degree of "oil canning." The vertical orientation of the reflections indicates that the reflected light sources are vertical.

The espresso machine and teapot were touched with *Redwood (Sienna Brown)*, *Cool Grey #4 (Cool Grey 40%)*, *Warm Grey #3 (Warm Grey 30%)*, and *Warm Grey #1 (Warm Grey 10%)* markers.

The copper pot was colored with *Burnt Sienna (Terra Cotta)* and *Pale Sepia (Goldenrod)* markers.

3 **Add diffuse highlights and color washes to brushed metal; add sharp-edged lowlights to polished metals.** The edges of the white spaces left by the marker on the brushed stainless steel were softened and "diffused" by applying *White* pencil to their edges—exerting most hand pressure at the

Fig. 4-60

edge, then grading outward by using increasingly lighter hand pressure on the pencil (4-62).

Slate Blue and *Cloud Blue* pencils were used to wash the left side of the cabinets; *Peach, Light Peach, Jasmine,* and *Cream* pencils were used to wash the right side and the cabinet faces near the floor. These colors were applied because stainless steel reflects the colors of its surroundings, even though these reflections are quite diffuse rather than crisp-edged.

Burnt Ochre and *White* pencils were used to reflect the color and grout lines from the backsplash into the countertop. *French Grey 50%* pencil was then applied to mute these colors somewhat.

You will notice that the closer an object is to a brushed stainless-steel surface, the more clearly it reflects in that surface. Hence, the bottom of the blue bowl, the espresso maker, and the vertical tile grout lines of the backsplash are the most distinct reflections, whereas parts (such as the fruit) and elements farther away are more diffuse or (like the stool) do not reflect at all.

Very dark reflections with sharp edges have been added to the stool legs, the espresso maker, the teapot, and the copper pot. Because these objects are highly polished, they have very distinct-edged reflections. These dark reflections were added with a Pilot Razor Point.

4 **Add final touches.** In figure 4-63, small touches of reflected colors were added to the espresso maker, teapot, copper pot, and stool legs, using *Peach, Slate Blue, Orange, Poppy Red, Yellow Chartreuse,* and *Jasmine* pencils.

Highlights were added with white gouache to these elements and to the nosing of the stainless-steel countertop.

Fig. 4-61

Fig. 4-62

Fig. 4-63

Bathroom Fixtures (4-64, 4-65, 4-66)

These illustrations were colored on a blackline diazo print that was run through the machine at a faster-than-usual speed.

1 **Apply color to the fixtures' surroundings.** This makes it easier to determine how dark or light to make the fixtures and fittings.

In figure 4-64, the mirrors' images were drawn in pencil and colored with pencil. Then a wash of *Deco Aqua* pencil was applied to the mirrors to give them the slightly greenish characteristic tinge of mirrors and glass.

The marble counter, tub surround, and shower wall were easily created by first applying shading to their darker edges and surfaces with a *Cool Grey #5 (Cool Grey 50%)* marker and then washing all the marble surfaces with *White* pencil. Firm pencil pressure was applied to the upward-facing surfaces to make them the brightest. The surfaces in shade or illuminated by daylight were flavored with *Blue Slate*, and those surfaces illuminated by incandescent light were flavored with *Light Peach.* The shower wall grades from *Light Peach* at the upper left to *Blue Slate* on the lower right. The marbling was then applied with both the side of the tip and the point of the tip of a *Cool Grey 70%* pencil.

Fig. 4-64

2 **Apply darks and lights.** In figure 4-65, *Cool Grey #5 (Cool Grey 50%)* marker was applied to the chromed waste pipes beneath the lavatories, the deepest visible part of the tub, and the shaded sides of the water closet and bidet. *Cool Grey #3 (Cool Grey 30%)* marker was used to diffuse the edges of the darker marker.

Micron 01 and Pilot Razor Point pens were used to apply blacks to the chromed fittings, including the waste pipes, faucets, towel bars, and shower head. A straightedge was used to keep the lines straight and crisp. *White* pencil was then applied to those parts of the fittings that appear to bend in such a way that they may reflect light toward the viewer of the illustration.

Deco Aqua pencil was used to color the glass lavatory bowls, including the glowing translucent bottoms that are visible beneath the counter. *Celadon Green* pencil was applied to their rims.

White pencil was applied to the tub, water closet, and bidet, with more hand pressure on the pencil where the surfaces face probable sources of light.

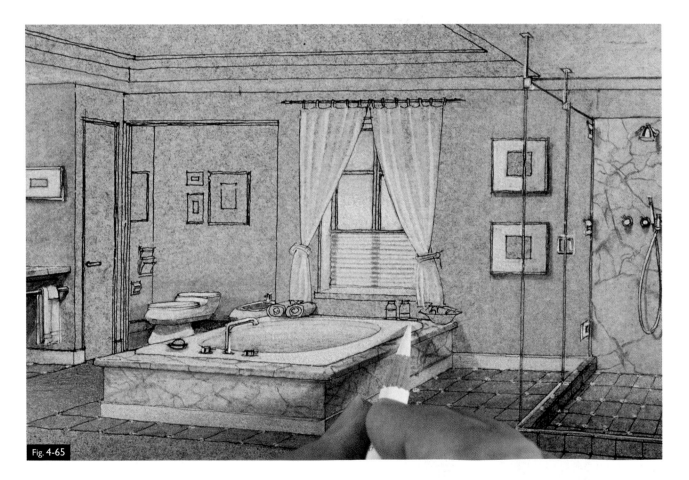

Fig. 4-65

3 **Apply flavorings and highlights.** Figure 4-66 shows the result of the addition of the final touches to the illustration. *Blue Slate* pencil was used to flavor the side of the tub that "sees" the bluish daylight from the window. The same pencil, along with *Celadon Green* pencil, was used to shade the side of the white water closet. *Light Peach* pencil was used to flavor the illuminated sides of the tub, water closet, and bidet. This is an important step, inasmuch as white bathroom fixtures reflect the colors—and colors of the light—in their surroundings.

Celadon Green pencil was applied, using a straightedge, to the edges of the glass walls of the shower, and *Deco Aqua* pencil was used to flavor the face of the glass.

White gouache highlights were applied, as the final touch, to the chrome, porcelain, glass lavatory bowls, and light fixtures.

Fig. 4-66

Lighting

Nothing so completes the effort spent in the creation of the mood or feel of a place as masterful lighting. Lighting effects are easy and fun to create. You will encounter basic lighting illustration techniques in this section, and you can see them deployed throughout this book.

In illustration, the successful creation of lighting effects depends fundamentally on making light sources and illuminated surfaces adequately *luminous.* As you have seen in Chapter 1, this means that the stronger the contrast between two adjacent values, the brighter and more luminous the lighter portion appears. The following illustrations will show that, on white paper, luminosity is created by surrounding light surfaces with values that are sufficiently dark. However, if you are creating design illustrations that are intended to show extensive lighting effects—whether sunlight or artificial light—

you may find it easier to work on toned papers or white roll tracing paper. The reason is that on these papers, both dark *and* light value pencil colors are easily visible.

You will find lighting effects easier to create after you have mastered the easily attainable skill of making graded washes, in both marker and pencil, because you will discover that color, light, and shading must be constantly graded one into the others. Your chances of successfully creating the effects of lighting, particularly indoor lighting, will also be greatly increased if you first make a quick, rough value study of a proposed illustration. Once your study is complete, you can use it as a strategic reference for value arrangement, allowing you to concentrate on the tactics of technique as you create your illustration. You can find such a study in figure 4-70.

Ceiling-Mounted Lighting (4-67, 4-68, 4-69)

If ceiling-mounted light sources are to appear illuminated, the ceiling must be sufficiently darker than those sources. In most cases this is not a problem, because unless a ceiling is directly illuminated by uplighting, it usually appears slightly darker than the lower parts of a room.

Ceiling-mounted recessed "cans," adjustable "eyeball" spotlights, and track lighting often create parabola-shaped patterns on walls or artwork. When necessary, use an ellipse template to help create these shapes.

This illustration is shown on "Pearl" Canson paper.

1 **Create a quick lighting study.** See figure 4-70 as an example.

2 **Create the appropriate graded values on the ceiling; outline illumination patterns on walls.** *Cool Grey #5 (Cool Grey 50%)*, *Cool Grey #3 (Cool Grey 30%)*, and *Cool Grey #1 (Cool Grey 10%)* markers were used in figure 4-67 to create the ceiling gradations. Note that although the pendant light fixture is surrounded by some of the darkest marker values to make it appear sufficiently bright, the part of the ceiling it uplights is quite light. This inverted pool of light becomes progressively darker at its edges.

French Grey 30%, 10%, and *Clear Blender* markers were used on the suspended portion of the ceiling. Note that the marker was applied directly over the recessed can lights so that the gradation of values could be made more easily.

A *White* pencil was used with an ellipse template to make the parabolic shapes of light on the wall.

3 **Develop light effects with pencil.** *Deco Orange* and *White* pencils were used with firm hand pressure to color the pendant fixture in figure 4-68. Derwent *Blue Violet Lake #27, Blue Slate, Cloud Blue,* and *White* pencils were used to color the cool-colored portion of the ceiling, the pencil values corresponding to the ceiling values already in place.

White, Light Peach, Deco Orange, Mineral Orange, and *Burnt Ochre* pencils (named here in order of descending value) were used to create gradations on the ceiling shapes, walls, and floor. Note that the parabolic washes of light on the wall are most intense at the upper crown of the shape. It is in the same location that the wall value is graded to its darkest. The wall value is also graded darker against the merchandise, beginning a higher-contrast relationship that will help the merchandise to appear illuminated in the next step. Subtle shadows were added beneath the merchandise and the wall-mounted letters with a *French Grey 30%* marker, subsequently flavored with a Derwent *Blue Violet Lake #27* pencil. Avoid creating value contrasts between light and shadow that are *too* strong in interior design illustrations, because such value relationships will make the lighting appear too harsh.

Fig. 4-67

The track lights on the pendant stems were darkened with *Black* marker and Pilot Razor Point in order to silhouette them against the wall. This helps the wall to appear more brightly illuminated by contrast.

Upward-facing surfaces—countertops, floor, and so forth—are more brightly illuminated as a result of the recessed ceiling-mounted downlights.

4   **Add final touches and highlights.** In figure 4-69, a variety of color pencils were used to add color to the items displayed, with *White* pencil added to the tops of the items and graded into their local colors farther away from the light sources.

The viewer's attention is kept on the illuminated wall and ceiling by the foreground elements being darkened with *French Grey 90%, 70%, 50%, 30%,* and *10%* markers. Color pencil was then lightly added to give them some hue. Silhouetting is a useful technique for both creating the sense of illumination and guiding the viewer's attention *if it works with your design intent.* Do not darken elements of your illustration if they play a critical part in the overall design idea you are trying to communicate. Silhouetting works here, because the purpose of the illustration is to feature the wall and ceiling.

White gouache was added as a final touch to the lights and the wall-mounted letters.

Fig. 4-68

Fig. 4-69

Lighting at the Wall Plane

Wall sconce, table lamp, and floor lamp (4-70 through 4-75)

1 **Create a quick lighting study.** A *Black* Prismacolor pencil and an electric eraser were used to make a quick lighting study (4-70) on a black-and-white photocopy of the line drawing. This 20-minute exploration will be used, during the creation of the more finished version of the illustration, as a guide in making its value arrangements and gradations of colors.

When creating lighting effects on white paper, such as Bristol (4-71, 4-72), use the following steps:

2 **Apply marker base.** In figure 4-71, marker base colors have been applied to the furniture, pictures, and floor. The walls have been left white, as they will be high in value. The shapes of the light patterns have been drawn and partially colored with *Cream* pencil.

Fig. 4-70

Fig. 4-71

3 **Add pencil.** Figure 4-72 shows graded washes applied to the walls with *French Grey 90%, 70%, 50%, 30%, 20%,* and *10%* pencils. The upper left wall, for example, was graded from gray to white with *French Grey 30%, 20%, 10%,* and *Cream* pencils. The *Cream* pencil grades into the white of the paper just above the lamp shade of the floor lamp. *Cool Grey 70%, 50%, 30%, 20%, 10%, Blue Slate,* and *Cloud Blue* pencils were used to create the gradations on the right side to suggest an off-picture incursion of daylight.

Note how the *French Grey* pencil series, with the addition of some *Black* pencil, was used to surround the table lamp shade with values dark enough to make it appear illuminated. The shade itself was colored with a light wash of *Deco Orange* pencil, followed by a heavy application of *Cream* pencil.

A combination of *Dark Umber* and *Burnt Ochre* pencils was used to grade the rug and soften its shadows. *Olive Green* pencil was used to darken the patterns in the shadow.

The white mats around the pictures were lightly flavored, grading from *Cream* to *Blue Slate* pencil, indicating reflection of both incandescent light and daylight.

Touches of white gouache were applied to the wall sconce, the table lamp base, and the ashtray.

Fig. 4-72

When creating lighting effects on **white roll tracing paper** (4-73, 4-74) with the retrocolor technique, use the following steps:

2 **Apply shade and shadow with** *Black* **Prismacolor pencil.** Graded washes of *Black* Prismacolor pencil are lightly applied to the line drawing to create the shade and shadow. One advantage of this technique is that the illustration is usable, if necessary, as soon as the shade and shadow are applied. A portion of the drawing is shown in figure 4-73.

3 **Apply color pencil to the** *back* **of the drawing.** In figure 4-74, *White, Cream,* and *Light Peach* pencils were applied most heavily, in the order named, to the crown of the parabolic shapes of light on the wall, then graded into the natural color of the paper. This was done on the back of the tracing paper, with a piece of brown kraft paper beneath as a work surface. The shadow area behind the lamp shade was washed with *Light Peach* pencil, again with color applied to the back of the drawing.

The creation of this illustration was significantly faster than that done on white paper, inasmuch as the light could be applied as well as the shadow. The color could also be applied more quickly and less carefully, because the translucent quality of the paper tends to smooth the look of the result when turned right-side-over. If color went past the lines, it could be quickly erased without harming the linework.

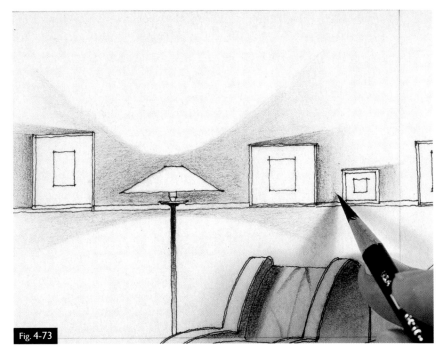

Fig. 4-73

Fig. 4-74

4 **Make a color reproduction.** Color design drawings using the retrocolor technique are more effective as color reproductions, because reproduction tends to slightly intensify their effects. While being reproduced, your drawings can be enlarged up to 400% to accommodate any presentation format. The reproduction shown in figure 4-75 was made on a large-format bubble-jet copier.

Fig. 4-75

Specialty Lighting

Neon and pin lights (4-76, 4-77, 4-78)

Common specialty lighting is grouped in two categories: linear display and point display. Linear display lighting, such as neon, "light pipe," and linear fiber-optic lighting, are best illustrated in surroundings shown as very dark—at least those in the vicinity of the lights themselves. Point display lighting, including the many varieties of tiny incandescent "pin" lights or fiber-optic ends, are also best illustrated against dark surroundings. Both kinds are easy to draw.

The drawing series that follows is created on a diazo print of a *reversal* and shows a neon sign, including clear incandescent lamps, and pin lights on the surrounding plant materials.

1 **Mute white lines on all except neon tubes.** All the black felt-tipped pen and pencil lines become white on a reverse-image print. To allow the lighting to have the strongest value contrast with its surroundings, the remaining white lines are muted with marker. Any dark gray—even black—marker will do, as long as the line images can still be seen. In figure 4-76, a *Cool Grey #9 (Cool Grey 90%)* marker is used to mute the structure supporting the sign and the plant materials, and a warmer *French Grey 70%* marker is used to mute all sign elements except the neon tubes themselves.

2 **Add strong-chroma pencil colors to neon tubes and their backgrounds.** White neon tubes can be colored with a variety of strong-chroma, light-value pencils. The "neon" pencil series by Prismacolor—*Neon Red, Neon Orange,* and so on—is especially good for this purpose. Color pencil should also be applied to the letters and miscellaneous metals on the sign during this step. Of course, these metals will not be as bright as the neon, because only the neon has a white background.

In figure 4-77, the neon letters in the word "Eat" were colored with *Deco Orange* pencil, and the surrounding pan channel letters were colored with *Carmine Red* and *Poppy Red* pencils. *Tuscan Red* pencil was used on the sides, or "returns," of the letters.

Fig. 4-76

Fig. 4-77

Fig. 4-78

The neon lettuce in the hamburger and the pointing fingers are *Yellow Chartreuse* pencil, and *Jasmine* pencil was applied to the large arrow behind the word "Eat." Note how much dimmer the pencil colors are when applied to the black part of the print.

Olive Green and *Jasmine* pencils were applied quickly and roughly to the plant materials, using the sides of the points, to give them both color and texture.

3 **Apply light "haloes" and washes; add pin lights.** Neon light is usually intense enough to cast a glow of light in its immediate vicinity. In figure 4-78, graded washes of *Yellow Chartreuse, Deco Orange,* and *White* pencils were added to the vicinity of similarly colored neon. These pencils, with the addition of *Pink* pencil, were also lightly applied to the pavement and figure beneath the sign.

White gouache was used to create the impression of clear incandescent lamps on both the large arrow behind the word "Eat" and the pin lights in the plant materials.

Accessories

Accessories have a surprising effect on interior places, as well as on the design illustrations of such places. Artwork, books, flowers, pottery and vases, bowls of fruit, plants, sculpture and candles, even lamps and fireplaces, all provide an opportunity for focal points and accents of color. They contribute a finer level of scale to a room and can make a place seem rich and interesting.

Paintings, Prints, and Photographs (4-79, 4-80)

Graphic art in real places provides points of interest. Part of what gives a picture its ability to focus attention within a place is often its wealth of detail. However, its purpose in a design illustration is somewhat different. Because it is usually the designer's job to orchestrate the development of a place in its entirety, graphic images in design illustrations are simplified so that they take their place as part of the larger idea.

1 **Apply marker base** to frames and picture images. These images can be imitated or invented and are drawn using the marker tip only (no lines). As figure 4-79 shows, this also allows the designer to create the images quickly and keep them appropriately indistinct. *Pale Sepia (Goldenrod)* marker was applied as a base for the gilded frame.

Fig. 4-79

2 Add details. In figure 4-80, a *White* pencil line was applied with an ellipse template to the painting over the fireplace. A graded wash of *White* pencil was then applied below to create a parabolic wash of light from the ceiling-mounted eyeball spotlight. The colors in the picture were then enhanced slightly with color pencil to prevent them from appearing too washed out by the white, with care taken to keep the colors within the parabolic shape *lighter* in value than those outside its shape.

The mat surrounding the picture was colored with a *Sand (Sand)* marker, then darkened at the top with a *French Grey 70%* marker. *Jasmine* and *Yellow Ochre* pencils were used to add color to the gold frame, which was then highlighted with white gouache.

The white mats around the pictures to the right were flavored with *Cream* and *Cloud Blue* pencils.

French Grey 30% and *10%* markers were used to create the diffuse shadows behind and beneath the pictures.

Fig. 4-80

General Accessories (4-81, 4-82, 4-83)

Books, flowers, plants, bowls of fruit, and various kinds of pottery are common accessories in interiors. They take additional time to illustrate, but are important to include in design illustrations to impart a degree of animation and realism to your ideas that help them appear probable.

1 **Make accessories legible by darkening backgrounds as necessary.** In most cases, diffuse shadows will add presence to your accessories. In figure 4-81, *French Grey 90%, 50%, 30%,* and *10%* markers were used to create the diffuse shadows. Other marker colors can, of course, be used for this step, depending on the local colors of the surfaces on which the shadows occur.

Sometimes the backgrounds of accessories must be darkened to give the accessories emphasis. Note, for example, how the cabinet doors behind the tulips on the coffee table are progressively darkened. This was done so that the tulips would be a bit more vivid in the finished illustration.

2 **Apply base colors with marker.** Marker base colors are applied in figure 4-82. *Sand (Sand), Naples Yellow (Eggshell), Sunset Pink (Deco Pink), Kraft Brown (Light Tan),* and *Burnt Sienna (Terra Cotta)* markers were used on the stone fireplace, and *Willow Green (Lime Green)* marker was applied to the bookshelves and cabinets. The blue marker used in the illustration is *Pale Indigo (Cloud Blue)*. The large foreground vase has a *Pale Sepia (Goldenrod)* marker base, and the smaller vase is a combination of *Willow Green (Lime Green)* and *Pale Indigo (Cloud Blue)* markers. These colors were used randomly for the base colors of the books as well.

3 **Add pencil detailing; apply highlights.** At this stage, color pencil can be applied to add smaller touches of color, more brilliant color, and to shift base colors. In figure 4-83, *Cool Grey 50%* and *30%* pencils were used to mute the green of the bookcases. *Black* pencil was added to the darkest recesses between and behind the books. *Carmine Red* and *Jasmine* pencils were applied to the flowers; *Yellow Chartreuse* and *Limepeel* pencils were added to the leaves of the tulips. Touches of *Celadon Green* and *Blue Slate*

Fig. 4-81

Fig. 4-82

pencils were used to flavor some of the stones in the fireplace. *Olive Green* and *Limepeel* pencils were used to color the plant on the right; *Poppy Red*, *Jasmine,* and *Black* pencils were added to the books. The apples were colored with *Poppy Red* and *Tuscan Red,* and *Limepeel* and *Jasmine* pencils were used for the pears. *White* and *Jasmine* pencils were applied to both

large vases in the foreground. *Deco Aqua* was added to the tulip vase on the coffee table and to the bottles on the counter.

White gouache was used to add highlights to the fruit, vases, and small lamp to the left of the fireplace, as well as to the flowers on the mantle and the plant on the right.

Fig. 4-83

Fire in a Fireplace (4-84, 4-85)

1 Outline flames; blacken surroundings. In figure 4-84, the flames were lightly outlined in pencil. Black marker and Pilot Razor Point were used to darken the soot-blackened surroundings—the back of the firebox, foreground logs, and andirons. *French Grey 50%* marker was used to darken the sides of the firebox.

These very dark surroundings will, of course, help make the fire appear more luminous. Note the bits of flame separated from the main body of the fire.

2 Apply color pencil to flames, firebox, and hearth. *Neon Orange* pencil was applied to the outside edges of the flames in figure 4-85. A light wash of the same color was added to the side of the firebox and the hearth. *Canary Yellow* pencil was graded from the *Neon Orange* to the centers of the flames, which were allowed to remain white. *Yellowed Orange* pencil was used to lightly wash the boundary between the edge of the flames and their black background, giving the fire a subtle glow.

Fig. 4-84

Fig. 4-85

E X T E R I O R   M A T E R I A L S

You will notice that the discussion and illustration of materials for exterior views is not separated into those for "architecture" and those for "landscape architecture." Rather, they are integrated into groups similar to those used for interior materials: ground plane materials, wall plane materials (and windows), and roofs/skies.

There are two reasons for this grouping. First, architectural and landscape materials exist together. That is, landscape materials are just as important as architectural surfaces in composing effective exterior spaces and forms. The best design teams are facile in utilizing both to create exemplary exterior surroundings. Second, because the fields of architecture and landscape architecture are typically categorized as separate disciplines, teachers, practitioners, and, particularly, the print media sometimes tend to emphasize one at the expense of the other. One is exalted while the other is ignored. In fact, this separation is unfounded. Both fields are mere categories in the larger and more important endeavor facing the designer in making good places for people. The approach to the organization of the material that follows is but a small attempt to acknowledge this fact.

Ground Plane Materials

Ground plane materials, like those of wall and roof planes, need be distinguished only close at hand. Detail should be applied to these materials only in the foreground of the view, allowing them to simplify as they proceed into the distance.

PAVING

Brick (4-86, 4-87)

This illustration shows brick paving in a typical herringbone pattern. Note how the pattern becomes simplified as it recedes into the distance.

1 **Apply marker base.** *Redwood (Sienna Brown)* marker was applied, stroked toward the 45° vanishing points on the horizon.

To find the 45° vanishing points, draw a simple square shape on the walkway surface, estimating a square as best you can. This square should be drawn using the vanishing point(s) for the picture. In this picture, the vanishing point is in the center and the "H" denotes the horizon line. Draw diagonals through opposite corners of your square and extend them until they come to the horizon line. In this illustration, you will notice arrows to either side of the walkway, inasmuch as the 45° vanishing points are outside the edges of the picture.

Stroking the marker toward these vanishing points (first one, then the other) has established a subtle diagonal gridded texture on the walkway surface. Touches of *Willow Green (Lime Green)* and *Pale Indigo (Cloud Blue)* markers were also added, in the same way, to weaken the chroma of the base marker (4-86). Note how the marker application begins to appear like brick.

2 **Add shadow with marker.** *Burnt Umber (Dark Umber)* marker was used to add the shadow.

3 **Apply joint pattern.** Figure 4-87 shows the finished material. The actual herringbone pattern was drawn in the foreground with a .5 mm pencil using a 2H lead. This pattern is time consuming, so if you do not have to communicate the pattern in detail, it is best to avoid its exact replication. Instead, use the diagonal dashed-line pattern shown just behind, drawing the dashed lines toward the same 45° vanishing points mentioned earlier. Note that in the shadow a *French Grey 30%* pencil was used to continue the pattern.

Berms and Banks (4-94, 4-95, 4-96)

1 **Make line drawing.** As figure 4-94 shows, the ridge lines should be drawn first, using a gradually sloping contoured line. These lines should be drawn light enough that they do not show in the final drawing.

2 **Add help lines and apply marker base.** Thin help lines run approximately perpendicular to the axes of the berms, curving smoothly and gently. Because the forms are grass covered, *Light Olive (Leaf Green)* and *Sand (Sand)* markers were applied, following the help lines as indicated in figure 4-95. *Dark Olive (French Grey 80%)* marker is used to indicate tree shadows, which originate to the right of the drawing. Note how the shadows conform to the terrain.

3 **Add highlights, shading, and texture.** In figure 4-96, the same techniques were used to finish the drawing as those used for lawn grass in figure 4-93. *Olive Green* pencil was used to darken the hollow in the distance, and *Cream* pencil was used on the hillside. The resulting graded value gives a sense of volume to the landforms and distinguishes between them.

Fig. 4-95

Fig. 4-94

Fig. 4-96

Ground Covers (4-97, 4-98)

1 **Apply marker base.** In figure 4-97, *Olive (Olive Green)* marker was applied to the foreground ground cover, with a horizontal, curving stroke used to approximate pachysandra. The white spaces between the *Olive (Olive Green)* marker strokes were colored with *Yellow Green (Limepeel)* marker. To the right of the pachysandra, iris leaves were created with *Yellow Green (Limepeel)* marker, followed by *Pale Indigo (Cloud Blue)* marker. Just beyond, among the rocks (as well as among the more distant rocks by the gazebo), a *Willow Green (Lime Green)* marker was applied to the low, mounded grasses.

The water grasses were colored with a quick upward stroke of *Yellow Green (Limepeel)* marker, and *Olive (Olive Green)* marker was used to add darker color to their base.

Beyond the water grasses on the left, the tip of an *Olive (Olive Green)* marker was used to dot in a ground cover that recalls vinca. Note the white areas that remain between the dots of green.

The lawn in both foreground and background is intended to approximate a bluegrass, illustrating a quicker grass technique than those illustrated in figures 4-92 through 4-96. *Yellow Green (Limepeel)* was applied in long horizontal strokes, followed by *Pale Indigo (Cloud Blue)* marker applied similarly. The shadows on the grass were made with *Olive (Olive Green)* marker.

Fig. 4-97

The short vertical strokes in the distance are stems of a flower mass. These were made with an *Olive (Olive Green)* marker followed by a *Pale Indigo (Cloud Blue)* marker.

2 **Add details.** In figure 4-98, *Black* marker was added to the foreground pachysandra-like ground cover to give it depth. *French Grey 50%* and *Black* markers were applied between the iris leaves to the right.

French Grey 50%, 30%, and *10%* markers were used to create the rocks. *Black* marker was used to emphasize the horizontal fissures.

Yellow Ochre and *Jasmine* pencils were used to bring out the colors of the yellow flowers in the center and to the left of the rock mass, respectively. *Pink* pencil filled in the white spaces as flowers on the shrub just above.

Black marker was added to the water grasses with a quick upward stroke of the marker tip. This stroke was used to create the grasses in shadow and silhouette.

Blue Slate pencil "flowers" were added to the white spaces between the vinca leaves, beyond the water grasses on the left.

Poppy Red pencil was applied to the top of the distant flower mass to approximate tulips.

Fig. 4-98

SHRUBS

Deciduous Shrubs (4-99, 4-100)

The shrubs shown here are generalized indications and not intended to represent specific plant types. Specific shrubs can be drawn with these techniques, however, by approximating their habit, size, and coloration.

1 **Apply marker base.** Shrubs of various colors are shown in figure 4-99, each with a marker base applied using the point of the marker tip, stipple fashion:

(1) *Light Olive (Leaf Green)* and *Olive (Olive Green)* markers
(2) *Slate Green (Teal Blue)* and *Cool Grey #7 (Cool Grey 70%)* markers
(3) *Yellow Green (Limepeel)* and *Olive (Olive Green)* markers
Cool Grey #9 (Cool Grey 90%) was stippled on all the shrubs to create the darkest areas. *Dark Olive (French Grey 80%)* marker was used to indicate shadows on the grass.

Fig. 4-99

2 Create highlights, shadows, and contrasts. Figure 4-100 shows the finished illustration. *Apple Green* pencil was added to the sunlit parts of shrub (1), with *Cream* pencil applied over it. *Pink* pencil was used to make the flowers. A graded pencil wash was applied to the fence behind, allowing the shrub to stand out by contrast.

The sunlit leaves on shrub (2) were washed with *Olive Green* pencil and again lightened with *Cream* pencil. *Indigo Blue* pencil was applied to the shaded parts. *French Grey 20%* pencil was used to draw the branching beneath.

Shrub (3) was colored with a *Jasmine* pencil on its lightest foliage, then lightened with *Cream* pencil. *White* pencil was used for the blossoms. A Pilot Razor Point was used to add vertical strokes to texture the shrub shadows on the grass.

3 Stipple for texture. A Pilot Razor Point was used to stipple the shrubs for additional texture.

Fig. 4-100

Evergreen Shrubs (4-101, 4-102)

Juniper and pine shrubs, two typical evergreen shrub types, are illustrated in the following steps.

1 **Apply marker base.** *Slate Green (Teal Blue)* marker was applied to the junipers with the point of the marker tip flicked in a series of fanlike patterns, as shown in figure 4-101. The pines on the right were drawn with the broad side of the tip of an *Olive (Olive Green)* marker. Again, the tip was flicked upward from the center of the shrub.

2 **Add highlights, texture, and shading.** In figure 4-102, the junipers to the side and rear of the fountain are shown in their summer foliage color. *Cream* pencil with *White* pencil over it, was applied to the sunlit sides of each shrub, with the pencil flicked upward to maintain the spiky habit of

Fig. 4-101

the foliage masses. On the shaded sides *Terra Cotta* pencil was added to dull the somewhat intense marker color (and to repeat the brick color). Pilot Razor Point was used to create dark areas in each shrub, again flicked upward with the stroke, and to stipple the shrubs for additional texture. The junipers in front of the fountain at the bottom middle of the drawing are shown in their winter foliage color, similar to that of an andorra juniper *(Juniperus horizontalis plumosa).* They were drawn by washing each shrub

with *Terra Cotta* and *Greyed Lavender* pencils, with *White* pencil flicked upward on the sunlit sides. Pilot Razor Point was used to create the darkest texture and for stippling. The pine shrubs on the right are similar to the mugo pine *(Pinus mugo mughis).* The sunlit needles were highlighted by flicking *Jasmine* and *White* pencils outward from the curved vertical branches (drawn with Pilot Razor Point), and the dark, shaded needles were drawn with Pilot Razor Point, using the same stroke.

Fig. 4-102

WATER

Still Water, Foreground (4-103 through 4-106)

This illustration was drawn on brownline diazo paper with a toned background.

1 **Apply color to the water last.** Only the foreground vegetation is excluded, because it must be drawn over the completed water (4-103).

Fig. 4-103

2 **Draw in base color for water; outline reflections.** In figure 4-104, *Olive (Olive Green)* marker was used to apply the marker base to the water, stroking horizontally. A medium-value marker color should be used for the marker base so that both dark and light reflections will show, although the hue of the marker color may range from a blue, green, or brown to a gray. *White* pencil was used to draw the outlines of the reflections. After they were initially drawn with straight lines to ensure accuracy, they were then altered to indicate the slight movement of the water.

Fig. 4-104

3 **Draw reflections with color pencil.** Figure 4-105 shows the reflections being drawn with the same color pencils that were used to draw the objects themselves. Use light to medium hand pressure on the pencils; the colors of the reflections should have a slightly lower value and weaker chroma than those of the objects themselves. This happens automatically, because they are drawn over the *Olive (Olive Green)* marker base color. The reflections were flavored with an *Olive Green* pencil to add the effect of the greenish water.

Fig. 4-105

4 **Add sky reflection.** *White* pencil was used to apply the reflected sky color to the water in figure 4-106. It was applied as a slightly wavy line. Note that the reflection becomes brighter toward the horizon, as the angle of the view becomes more oblique. *Greyed Lavender* and *Blue Slate* pencils were used to flavor the reflected sky color.

Fig. 4-106

Still Water, Middle Ground (4-107, 4-108, 4-109)

1 **Apply color to the water's surroundings first.** Figure 4-107 shows the surroundings completely colored.

2 **Draw reflected elements in the water.** The elements touching the water's surface are drawn (in reverse) in the water first (4-108). Note that their reflected image is slightly darker than the elements themselves. In this illustration, the reflections of the stone curb and the stepping stones were drawn with *French Grey 20%, Cool Grey #2 (Cool Grey 20%),* and *Buff (Brick Beige)* markers. The water grasses will be drawn last, as they will be drawn with color pencil; the lilies have no reflection because they lie flat on the water's surface.

The plant materials beyond the water are drawn in next, using a *Dark Olive (French Grey 80%)* marker. The determination of which elements will reflect in the water is established by reversing the image at the point where its base is intersected by an imaginary extension of the plane of the water. For example, the small leaf mass interrupting the triple tree trunks in the center of the illustration is shown reflected in the water. This was established by trial and error, using a pair of dividers with one end located at the approximate intersection of the base of the trunks and the plane of the water while the other end touched the leaf mass. The end of the dividers touching the leaf mass was swung around to see whether it reached the water, while the other end was held stationary. Because it did reach the water, the reverse shape of the leaf mass was drawn in the water with the aforementioned marker. With the use of this quick technique, reflections can easily be established.

3 **Add final touches.** In figure 4-109, *Cool Grey #2 (Cool Grey 20%)* marker was applied to the water, darkening the curb reflection and the formerly white areas. *Cool Grey #3 (Cool Grey 30%)* was used to make the curb reflection adequately dark as compared with the water.

Cloud Blue pencil was used to shift the color of the sky reflection. *Black, Limepeel,* and *Yellow Chartreuse* pencils were used to create the reflections of the water grasses. *Cool Grey 10%* pencil was added to make the ripples around the grasses.

Fig. 4-107

Fig. 4-108

Fig. 4-109

Moving Water (4-110 through 4-113)

Moving water is most easily drawn on a toned paper, whether diazo, trace, or Canson paper. This is because the water can be drawn as added shapes with light-value pencils. You will find the use of photographs of moving water most helpful as references.

This illustration was drawn on brownline diazo paper with a toned background

1 **Draw surroundings first.** In figure 4-110, space was left for both the water jet and the waterfall.

Fig. 4-110

2 **Draw water jet and waterfall.** *White* pencil was used to draw the water forms (4-111), and *Warm Grey 30%* pencil was added to the shaded sides of the water forms. *Blue Slate* pencil (one of the pencils used to draw the sky) was then used to flavor the water forms, indicating reflected sky.

Fig. 4-111

3 **Draw pool surface and splashing water.** *Slate Green* marker was used as a base for the water color in the pool, drawn in carefully around the falling "strings" of water. *Copenhagen Blue* and *Peacock Green* pencils, utilized in the sky, stone, and plant materials as well, were used to flavor the marker color.

White pencil was used to create the effect of the splashing water, with the pencil flicked in short, upward strokes (4-112). *Blue Slate* pencil was then used to flavor the splashing water.

Reflections were added to the less disturbed parts of the water's surface with *Light Peach* and *Dark Umber* pencils. *White* pencil was again used to add ripples to the less disturbed portions of the water's surface.

Fig. 4-112

4 **Add highlights.** Figure 4-113 shows the finished water. Straight lines of white gouache were applied to the straight-moving water forms, and wavy lines were added to the less disturbed areas of the pool. Dots of white gouache were stippled into the areas of the more disturbed water, such as the crown of the water jet and the splashes in the pool.

Fig. 4-113

Rocks (4-114, 4-115, 4-116)

1 **Draw rocks' surroundings.** Rocks usually lie nested in other materials, whether soil, plant materials, or other rocks (4-114), so their bases usually appear flat and/or interrupted by these materials.

Fig. 4-114

2 **Apply base color.** In figure 4-115, these sandstone rock colors were made from a mixture of *Sunset Pink (Deco Pink)* and *Buff (Brick Beige)* markers. Of course, rocks can be a wide variety of colors, so the base colors of the rocks you illustrate should reflect the geologic region of your project.

Fig. 4-115

3 **Add shading, fissures, clefts, and texture.** Figure 4-116 shows the finished rocks. Swipes of *Kraft Brown (Light Tan)* and *French Grey 40%* markers were quickly applied, using the broad edge of the tip, to add shading, clefts, and fissures. A *French Grey 70%* marker was used for the darkest parts of the shading.

A blend of *Willow Green (Lime Green)* and *French Grey 20%* markers was used to dot in lichens on the foreground rocks. A light wash of *Burnt Ochre* pencil on the sunlit faces of the rocks and *French Grey 70%* pencil on the shaded sides give the rocks texture. Stippling was added in the foreground with a Pilot Razor Point.

Fig. 4-116

Landscape Plan Views (4-117 through 4-120)

A plan is an intellectual construct, presenting a view of a place rarely, if ever, seen by most users. It is a tool for communicating conceptual information about that place: information about use areas, their shapes and sizes, and their relationships to each other and to the larger landscape. It can illustrate ideas about circulation, about the relationship between structures and the landscape, and about what materials—both plant and architectural—have a relationship to the ground plane. It can even delineate the distribution of lighting.

Although a plan is not a "real" view of a place, it can still provide some information about its feel and character through the use of color, shade and shadow, pattern and texture. These additional layers of information can expand the plan of an idea from a purely intellectual construct to include some of its experiential qualities as well.

Color not only adds legibility to the functional distinctions of a plan, but can also be used to illustrate the types, patterns, and textures of paving materials, ground covers, shrubs, trees, and vehicles. The addition of shade and shadow to these elements of a plan brings the suggestion of the third dimension. The plan becomes a tool to communicate information *and* experience.

Perhaps most important, however, is that by making the plan more legible through the use of color, pattern, texture, shade, and shadow, the designer invites a wider understanding and participation in the design of the place by fellow designers and nondesigners as well.

There is no one correct approach to color for plans. Almost any combination of colors can be used, provided adequate differentiation between elements and materials can happen when required by the designer. The scheme illustrated here tends toward the medium-to-high-value colors so the lines remain easily visible. Note, too, that through the use of fewer colors in a variety of combinations, the resultant color scheme tends to hold together.

1 **Apply marker base.** In figure 4-117, *Willow Green (Lime Green)* and *Naples Yellow (Eggshell)* markers were applied to the grass areas, and *Olive (Olive Green)* marker was added to the ground cover next to the building. Note that a dark color like olive can be applied to areas where there is no need to see graphic information beneath it.

The marker colors for the wide variety of paving materials were applied next (4-118). The marker base for an area of existing brick paving, located in the lower half of the drawing, was applied with *Redwood (Sienna Brown)* marker. *French Grey 10%* marker was used to represent the existing concrete paving at the upper right and left sides. A blend of *Sunset Pink (Deco Pink)* and *Naples Yellow (Eggshell)* markers was used for the native sandstone transitional pavers and as a base material around the center fountain and the monuments. The walkways in the central part of the project were colored with a *Buff (Brick Beige)* marker, representing a proposed colored concrete.

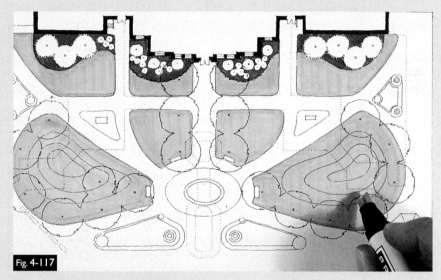

Fig. 4-117

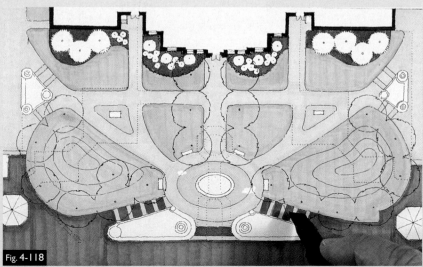

Fig. 4-118

If you are illustrating a plan with a uniform paving material, its color can remain the color of the paper to save time.

In figure 4-119, color was applied to the remaining elements. A combination of *Willow Green (Lime Green)* and *Pale Indigo (Cloud Blue)* markers was applied to the conifer trees on the upper left and upper right; *Pale Indigo (Cloud Blue)* and *Sunset Pink (Deco Pink)* markers were combined on the smallest shrubs, and *Sand (Sand)* and *Flesh (Salmon Pink)* markers were used together for the larger shrubs.

The bluish flowers were made by mixing Derwent *Blue Violet Lake #27* and *Blue Slate* pencils; *Poppy Red* and *Spanish Orange* pencils were used for the remaining flowers.

The trees were colored with *Yellow Green (Limepeel)* marker. Note that transparency is maintained. The base color of the water in the center fountain was made with a combination of *Willow Green (Lime Green)* and *Pale Indigo (Cloud Blue)* markers.

2 **Mute color, add shadows, details, and notes.** You will often find that as a composition of color, your plan must be adjusted once the marker base colors are in place. In figure 4-119, the brick appears too dark and too strong in chroma. Likewise, the trees are also too strong in chroma.

In figure 4-120, greater agreement is established between the values and chromas of the colors. The sunlit brick was muted with a *French Grey 20%* pencil. This weakened the chroma of the base marker color, lightened its value, and created a texture. The shadow on the brick was applied with a *Burnt Umber (Dark Umber)* marker, then flavored with a Derwent *Blue Violet Lake #27* pencil.

The shadows elsewhere on the drawing were first applied with *Pale Indigo (Cloud Blue)* marker, then modified with a variety of color pencils, depending on which surface they fell.

The colored concrete walkway was washed lightly with *Peach* pencil, and the sandstone surfaces with *Peach* and *Burnt Ochre* pencils.

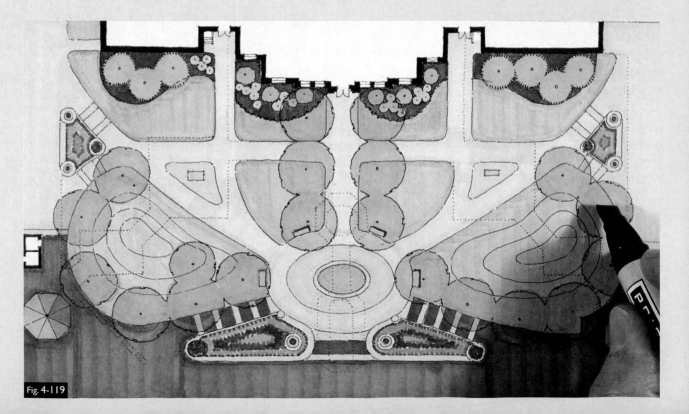

Fig. 4-119

The marker shadows on the colored concrete walks were washed lightly with *Burnt Ochre* pencil, so that the marker still showed through.

The sunlit sides of the large trees were washed with *Light Peach* pencil to both mute and lighten the color of the marker base; the shaded sides were washed with *Olive Green* pencil. The trees were then entirely washed with *Burnt Ochre* pencil.

The grass was washed with *Jasmine* pencil, slightly more heavily where the sides of the berms face the sun. The shaded sides of the berms, as well as the shadows on the grass, were washed with *Olive Green* pencil.

The remaining surfaces and elements, other than the grass, were also washed lightly with *Jasmine* pencil to quickly tie the colors of the plan together and effect a sense of warm light.

The water in the center fountain was made with *Deco Aqua* and *White* pencil in the sunlight, and its shadow was made with Derwent *Blue Violet Lake #27* pencil. The highlights were applied with white gouache.

The notes were added last. Those in capitals were made with a Pilot Razor Point; those in script were written with a Micron 005 pen.

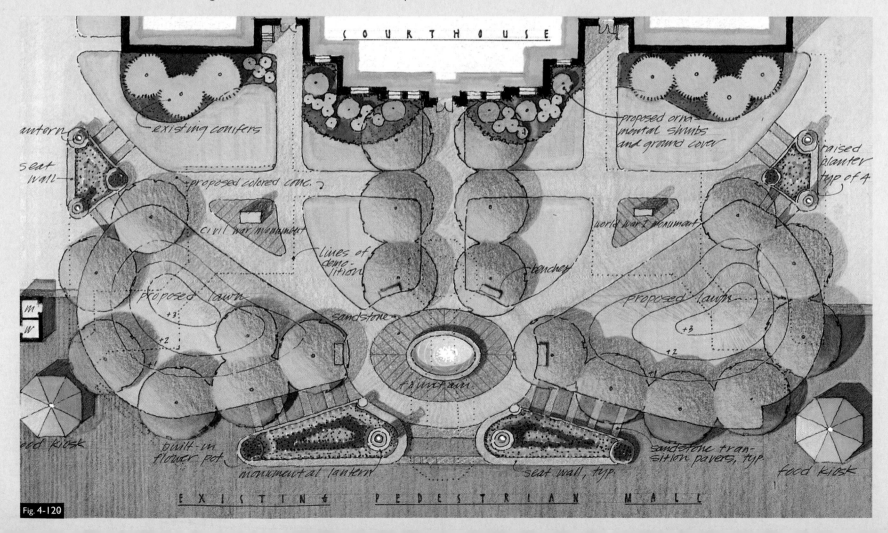

Fig. 4-120

Wall Plane Materials and Windows

You will find that wall plane materials and windows can be most easily created using impressionistic approaches, as the following pages illustrate.

WOOD

Wood wall surfaces are usually finished with paint or stain. Paint finishes, of course, are available in any color. Stains also come in a variety of colors and types and usually, but not always, allow at least some of the natural wood grain to show through. Some stains can make wood appear "weathered" by turning it a silver gray.

The coloration techniques shown for a particular material need not be reserved for that material. For example, the color approach shown here for vertical wood siding can be used for, say, wood shingles to give them a more weathered appearance.

Wood Shingles (4-121, 4-122)

The shingles illustrated here are intended to appear with a semiweathered stain, where a warm gray overtone mutes the new wood. The shingle texture should be subtle so that it does not overwhelm the building details.

1 **Apply marker base.** In figure 4-121, *French Grey 30%* marker was used for the shaded and shadowed areas, followed by *Sand (Sand)* marker. *French Grey 10%* marker was applied to the sunlit surfaces, followed by *Buff (Brick Beige)* marker. The markers were stroked horizontally to apply the color.

2 **Add pencil details.** Figure 4-122 shows the finished shingles. *French Grey 70%* pencil was used to create the continuous horizontal shadows made by the butt ends of the shingles. This line is kept quite thin.

Peach and *French Grey 30%* pencils were used to quickly add the spots of color between the horizontal lines. A .5 mm pencil with a 2H lead was used to add the random vertical marks between the horizontal lines.

Fig. 4-121

Fig. 4-122

Vertical Wood Siding (4-123, 4-124)

The base color of this siding was created similarly to that of the shingles. However, different pencils were added in the final steps to give it a more weathered look.

1 **Apply marker base.** Figure 4-123 shows *French Grey 30%* and *Sand (Sand)* markers applied to the shaded areas as well as the shadows that diagonally cross the sunlit surface. The sunlit surface received an application of *French Grey 10%* marker, followed by *Buff (Brick Beige)* marker. These markers were applied with vertical strokes.

2 **Add pencil detail.** Because certain boards are slightly darker or lighter than others, streaks of *French Grey 50%, 30%,* and *10%* pencils were applied with a straightedge (4-124).

The entire surface, in both sunlight and shade, was washed lightly with *Celadon Green* pencil. The surfaces in shade, as well as the shadows, were lightly washed with Derwent *Blue Violet Lake #27* pencil.

A straightedge was used to add light vertical lines, drawn with a .5 mm pencil with a 2H lead. Note that these lines need not be added to every board. The same pencil was used to apply some stipple texture to the wood.

Fig. 4-123

Fig. 4-124

Board and Batten and Lap Siding, Painted (4-125, 4-126)

1 **Apply marker base.** Figure 4-125 shows *Sand (Sand)* marker applied to the sunlit surfaces of the board and batten building in the background. *Mocha (Light Umber)* marker was added to its shadow and shaded surfaces.

The sunlit surface of the foreground lap-sided building was colored with *Buff (Brick Beige)* marker, followed by *Light Ivy (Putty + Cream)* marker. *Kraft Brown (Light Tan)* marker, followed by *Willow Green (Lime Green)* marker, was used for the shadow.

Note that the light "help lines" for the battens and lap siding are used to guide the marker strokes and subsequent detailing.

2 **Add pencil detailing.** In figure 4-126, a *Yellow Ochre* pencil wash was applied over the sunlit, shaded, and shadowed surfaces of the board and batten siding. A *Cream* pencil was used to "force" the shadow at the top of the sunlit surface. The painted battens were added with *Terra Cotta* pencil and a straightedge. The battens are sufficiently dark that no shadow is necessary. However, if the battens were painted the same color as the boards, a shadow line with a *Sepia* pencil, added to the right of each batten, would help make them visible.

The lap siding was washed with a *Celadon Green* pencil, and its shadow too was forced with a *Cream* pencil. *Yellow Ochre* pencil was then used to flavor the surface, providing a degree of color "agreement" with the board and batten color.

Horizontal shadow lines, beneath the heel of each piece of lap siding, were applied with a *Cool Grey 70%* pencil.

Derwent *Blue Violet Lake #27* pencil was used to flavor the shade and shadow on all surfaces.

Note that the telltale profile edge of the lap siding was added at the lower outside corner and where it abuts the window trim. This edge was added with a Micron 005 pen.

Fig. 4-125

Fig. 4-126

MASONRY

Stucco and Concrete Block (4-127, 4-128)

Stucco can be natural—made of portland cement, lime, and sand—or synthetic, often referred to as "EFIS" (Exterior Finish Insulating System). Natural stucco is available in many textures and colors, but the colors are typically muted and can appear mottled when dry. Synthetic stucco usually appears more uniform (no mottling) and is available in almost any color—some quite strong—as well as textures similar to those of natural stucco.

Concrete block is also available in a variety of colors—again, usually weak in chroma, depending on the colors of the aggregate and portland cement used to make it. It too comes in a wide choice of textures, such as the usual plain-face, split-face, and ground-face finishes.

In the masonry finishes illustrated here, the concrete block is a warm color with a plain-face finish. The foremost building forms behind are intended to be natural stucco, and the green-yellow and yellow-red forms are colors more likely achieved with synthetic stucco.

1 **Apply marker base.** Figure 4-127 shows *French Grey 10%* marker applied to the sunlit faces of the portal and *French Grey 50%* marker used for the shaded faces. The capitals of the columns and the staircase were colored with *Pale Sepia (Goldenrod)* marker.

Warm Grey 50% and *10%* markers were used on the shaded and sunlit faces, respectively, of the purplish building form. The green-yellow form was colored with *Dark Olive (French Grey 80%)* marker on the shaded surface and *Olive (Olive Green)* marker on the sunlit surface. On the most distant building form, *Redwood (Sienna Brown)* and *Pale Cherry (Mineral Orange)* markers were used to color its shaded and sunlit sides, respectively.

2 **Add modifying colors and details.** In figure 4-128, the sunlit surface of the foreground building form was rubbed with *Indian Red 347.9* stick pastel. Then both its sunlit and shaded surfaces were dabbed with an electric eraser to remove some of their color to give them a mottled appearance.

The sunlit surface was then spotted with the side of a *Yellow Ochre* pencil, and the same was done to the shaded side with a *French Grey 30%* pencil, increasing the mottled effect.

The remaining left-facing surfaces (in shade) in the illustration were washed lightly with Derwent *Blue Violet Lake #27* pencil, suggesting the reflection of north light. The right-facing, illuminated surfaces were washed with *Yellow Ochre* and *Jasmine* pencil, simulating the effect of low sun.

Horizontal mortar joints were added to the sunlit surfaces of the concrete block with a .5 mm pencil using a 2H lead. The mortar joints on the surfaces in shade were supplied with a *French Grey 10%* pencil. Note how the vertical mortar joints gradually disappear as the portal recedes into the distance.

Note how both the foreground concrete block and foreground stucco are stippled for additional texture. The sunlit surfaces are stippled with the .5 mm pencil mentioned earlier, and the shaded surfaces are stippled with both a *French Grey 10%* pencil and a Micron 005 pen.

Fig. 4-127

Fig. 4-128

Brick, Middle Range (4-129, 4-130)

1 **Apply marker base.** *Kraft Brown (Light Tan)* marker was applied to the entire brick surface in figure 4-129. *Burnt Umber (Dark Umber)* marker was used to draw the shadows and darken the shaded surfaces.

A *Light Peach* pencil wash was applied over the sunlit surface at medium hand pressure. Less pressure was used to apply a *Peach* pencil over the shadows and shaded surfaces.

2 **Add mortar joints.** In figure 4-130, a *French Grey 10%* pencil was applied with a straightedge to draw thin, evenly spaced lines toward the same vanishing point used to draw the building.

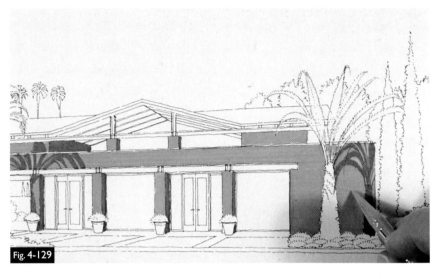

Fig. 4-129

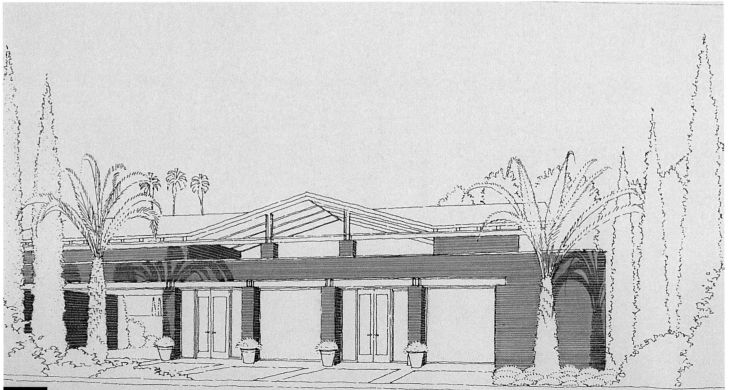

Fig. 4-130

Stone, Uncoursed and Roughly Squared (4-131, 4-132, 4-133)

Stone is available in a wide variety of types and "earth" colors, ranging from grays and blues to yellows and reds. Your choices of types and colors will depend on the budget for and location of your project. The stone can be jointed in many different ways, from completely random to coursed and bonded. The stone shown here, like most stone finishes, is used as a facing over a substrate.

The "roughly squared" stone illustrated here, although not laid up in contiguous rows, is still arranged as approximately level.

1 Apply marker base. In this particular illustration (4-131), *Sand (Sand)* marker was applied as a base color for the stone in shade and shadow, and *Buff (Brick Beige)* marker was used for the base color in sunlight.

Note the horizontal help lines, added with pencil. Although the stone is rough, these help lines assist in keeping the stones in perspective when the marker colors are applied and the joints drawn in subsequent steps.

2 Add stone coloration. In figure 4-132, touches of *French Grey 20%* and *Light Ivy (Putty + Cream)* markers were used to add stone colors to the wall in the sunlit areas. *French Grey 50%* marker was used to add darker stone colors in the shade and shadow. Note how some of the marker strokes turn the corners in the same way as credible stone masonry.

Raw Sienna 234.9 stick pastel was rubbed randomly onto the sunlit parts of the stone, and *White* stick pastel was applied to the sunlit surface where it meets the shadow, "forcing" the shadow.

Smudges of Schwan Stabilo *#620* and *#600* pencil pastels were randomly applied to both sunlit and shaded surfaces. A light wash of Derwent *Blue Violet Lake #27* pencil was applied to those shaded surfaces that "see" the sky.

Fig. 4-131

2 **Add joints.** Figure 4-133 shows the finished illustration after the joints have been added. In the surfaces in shade and shadow closest to the viewer, *Black* pencil was used to make the joints, with light but varying hand pressure. This makes the joint lines slightly lighter in some places and darker in others, quickly simulating joints of varying widths. On the sunlit surfaces, as well as the more distant stones in both sun and shadow, a .5 mm pencil with a 2H lead was used the same way for the same purpose.

The stone pattern can be invented as it is drawn. The pencil is rarely lifted from the page. Note, too, that every single stone need not be drawn. Rather, only enough must be drawn to ensure the impression of the stone units.

Some stippling was added to the foreground stones with a Pilot Razor Point.

Fig. 4-133

Fig. 4-132

Stone, Dimensioned in a Running Bond (4-134, 4-135)

1 **Apply marker base.** The use of a series of gray markers *(Warm, Cool, French)* can create the impression of stone quite easily, as many kinds of stone have subtle (very weak chroma) color and the values can be easily controlled.

In figure 4-134, *French Grey 10%* marker was applied to the sunlit surfaces, and *French Grey 50%* marker was used on the surfaces in shade and shadow. The surfaces angled 45° toward the sun were left white, and those angled away from the sun were colored with a *French Grey 20%* marker.

The header stones and base course are intended to be slightly darker in value than the rest of the stone. Thus, the marker sequence applied to them was likewise slightly darker. *French Grey 20%* was used on the sunlit surfaces, and *French Grey 10%* marker was applied to those surfaces angled toward the sun. *French Grey 30%* marker was used on the surfaces angled away from the sun.

Additional strokes with the broad edge of the *French Grey 10%* marker were applied to the sunlit surfaces to create the impression of stone units slightly darker than the others.

Fig. 4-134

2 **Add color and detail.** The subtle coloration of the stone will depend on the kind of stone you intend to imitate. In figure 4-135, *Indian Red 347.9* stick pastel was applied randomly and rubbed lightly by finger over the marker base. Schwan Stabilo *#692* and *#620* pencil pastels were also applied the same way, then lightly wiped with a chamois.

The surfaces in shade and shadow were flavored with a Derwent *Blue Violet Lake #27* pencil.

The joints were added by lightly applying a .5 mm pencil, using a 2H lead, with a straightedge. The joints in shadow were applied with a *French Grey 10%* pencil.

Fig. 4-135

Precast Concrete (4-136, 4-137)

Precast concrete is an architectural finish material that can be cast in virtually any shape with a wide variety of textures and can be colored with a variety of concrete colorants. It can be cast in sizes up to certain economical maximums, so the precast concrete finish of a project is characterized by its precise shapes and the joints between them.

The precast concrete illustrated here has two colors and two textures.

1 **Apply marker base.** *Buff (Brick Beige)* and *French Grey 20%* markers were applied in alternating stripes on the piers and retaining walls of the bridge (4-136); *Buff (Brick Beige)* marker alone was used for the precast of the arch. *French Grey 30%* marker was used for the shade and shadow on the gray color, and *Sand (Sand)* marker was used to make the shade and shadow on the buff color.

Fig. 4-137

Fig. 4-136

2 **Add detail and finishing touches.** In figure 4-137, a Schwan Stabilo #680 pastel pencil was used to enhance the color of the *French Grey* stripes. The close-range portion of this darker precast concrete was also stippled with the fine-point end of a *Light Tan* Prismacolor marker to impart a subtle texture effect. The lighter color was given a much finer stipple texture with a .5 mm pencil using a 2H lead.

The surfaces of the darker color that are in shade and shadow were lightly washed with a *Burnt Ochre* pencil. The colors of the corresponding surfaces on the lighter precast concrete were enhanced with flavorings of *Yellow Ochre* and *Peach* pencils. The recessed joints between the panels of the foreground precast concrete were first darkened with a *Burnt Ochre* pencil, then edged with a .5 mm pencil using a 2H lead.

METAL

Corrugated Metal Siding (4-138, 4-139)

Corrugated metal siding is seen most often with its typical galvanized finish. As such, it is semireflective and tends to display faint but noticeable diffuse reflections of the colors that surround it. It can also display white highlights which, close up, have diffuse edges.

Any combination of gray markers can be used to successfully illustrate galvanized metal. The combination you select will depend on your intentions for the overall scheme of colors you have for your design illustration.

1 **Apply marker base.** In figure 4-138, *Cool Grey #5 (Cool Grey 50%)* marker was used for the shadows on the foreground building, and *Cool Grey #3 (Cool Grey 30%)* marker was applied for the shadow on the background building.

The foreground building's sunlit surface grades horizontally from *Warm Grey #3 (Warm Grey 30%)* marker at the doors to *Warm Grey #2 (Warm Grey 20%)* through *Warm Grey #1 (Warm Grey 10%)* markers behind the red chair. The sunlit wall on the background building was colored with *Cool Grey #1 (Cool Grey 10%)* marker.

Color was added to the chairs to show the reflectivity of the siding. An easy way to introduce reflected color to the siding is by rubbing it lightly with pastel colors that are related to colors close by. In this example, part of the background siding was rubbed with Schwan Stabilo #692 pencil pastel (the color reflected is not shown). The wall behind the red and blue chairs was rubbed with #310 and #430 pencil pastels respectively.

2 **Add detail.** *White* pencil and a straightedge were used to apply the horizontal highlights on the foreground building (4-139).

In the shadows on both buildings, *Cool Grey 70%* pencil was applied in the same fashion to add shading in the recesses of the corrugations. *Cool Grey 50%* pencil was applied in the same way to add texture to sunlit surface of the background building.

The shadows on both surfaces were flavored with *Copenhagen Blue* pencil.

Fig. 4-138

Fig. 4-139

Architectural Metal Panels (4-140, 4-141)

Architectural metal panels are available in virtually any color and many types of finish, ranging from gloss to matte and smooth to textured. They are usually custom fabricated in modular form for a project and therefore have joints of varying widths. These joints can appear very light to very dark, depending on the angle of light.

A typical medium-finish panel, illustrated here, often displays gradations of light and color as well as diffuse highlights.

1 **Apply marker base.** In figure 4-140, *Pale Cherry (Mineral Orange)* marker was applied to the entire column, and *Kraft Brown (Light Tan)* marker was used for its shadow. The shadow was pronounced near its top with a *Redwood (Sienna Brown)* marker. The chroma of the sunlit portion of the column was reduced slightly with a *French Grey 10%* marker.

Cool Grey #5 (Cool Grey 50%) marker was applied as a shadow on the building panels, and a gradation of *Cool Grey #1* and *#2 (Cool Grey 10%* and *20%)* markers was applied from the bottom upward toward the shadow. The entire wall was then washed with a *Celadon Green* Prismacolor marker.

2 **Add pastel and detail.** Figure 4-141 shows that pastel was applied to modify the panel colors. Pastel was used because it appears smooth and does not pick up the grain of the paper.

White stick pastel was added to the upper portion of the sunlit face of the column, as well as the wall, to force the shadow. Schwan Stabilo *#430* pencil pastel was applied to the shadow on the wall.

Reflections and highlights were applied with color pencil. A *White* pencil was used to add diffuse highlights to both the front and back of the column, with the stronger highlight on the front. Note that these highlights were drawn over the joints so that they remain smooth and consistent. Highlights were also applied to the edges of the panels with a straightedge, again using a *White* pencil. Diffuse reflections from the ceiling and guardrail were added by light application of *White* and *Burnt Ochre* pencils to the wall panels.

A final touch of *Cool Grey 70%* pencil was added to darken the joints and to interrupt the highlights and reflections drawn in the previous steps.

Fig. 4-140

Fig. 4-141

WINDOWS

Windows have been called the "eyes" of a building and play an important role in its animation.

1 **Add color to the window's surroundings first.** In figure 4-142, color was added to everything except the window surface and the objects seen through it. The trees will be completed, along with the shrubs, after the reflections are drawn, inasmuch as these plant materials will interrupt the view of the reflections.

Fig. 4-142

2 **Apply marker to everything seen through the window.** Marker *only* is applied at this stage (4-143), with the use of colors appropriate to the objects. *Cool Grey #9 (Cool Grey 90%)* was used to darken the interior beyond.

Fig. 4-143

3 **Add reflections with color pencil.** Figure 4-144 shows that *White* pencil was used to lightly lay out the reflections, drawn directly over the objects seen through the window. Color pencil was used to add color to the reflections, the designer making sure that the reflections were slightly darker and slightly weaker in chroma than the colors of the reflected objects themselves. Care was taken to apply these colors *lightly* and smoothly, so that the objects *in* the window could still be seen after the reflection was completed.

To avoid confusion, the reflections of objects closest to the window surface were drawn first, then the objects progressively farther away from the window were drawn. Thus, the undersides of the awnings were drawn first, then the stone forming the left window jamb, the figures, the green car on the left, the streetlight, the brown car on the right, and so forth.

Fig. 4-144

4 **Add reflected background if necessary.** Once the reflections of the objects seen in the picture in front of the window were drawn, a simple background reflection was added, as shown in figure 4-145. Because the environment appears to be urban, building reflections were added with *Terra Cotta, Burnt Ochre,* and *Dark Umber* pencils. *White* pencil was applied over *Light Cerulean Blue* pencil to create the reflection of the sky.

5 **Add trees and shrubs, their reflections, and finishing touches.** The tree reflections were drawn over the other reflections, using a *Cool Grey 70%* pencil with touches of *White* pencil on the sunlit edges. The shrub reflections were added, followed by the trees and shrubs themselves. The items in the windows, such as the manikins, were reoutlined with a Pilot Razor Point so that they would appear more solid than the reflections.

Fig. 4-145

Daytime Windows, Middle Ground (4-146, 4-147, 4-148)

Rather than simply making the openings black, a designer can make daytime windows more lifelike and animated. They typically have three components: street-level window detail (those elements seen *through* the windows), the upper-level reflection mass, and the reflection of the sky.

1 **Draw those elements seen through street-level windows; add upper-level reflection mass.** The street-level elements in figure 4-146 are manikins in the window of a retail store. Directly behind the manikins, the low wall and other subordinate details are colored with markers of medium value. In this case, a *Cool Grey #6 (Cool Grey 60%)* marker was used.

The far background at the first level, as well as the upper-level reflection mass, should be colored with a marker that is quite dark in value—a low-value gray to black. In this example, a *Cool Grey #9 (Cool Grey 90%)* marker was used. The term "reflection mass" indicates that the buildings and trees reflected into the (usually tinted) upper-level glass are so dark that they appear as a single mass whose only clear distinctions are the spaces between them and the silhouette of their top edge.

Note that this dark marker is applied directly over the window muntins. This is faster than attempting to avoid each muntin with the marker, and the muntins can be redrawn with pencil in a later step.

2 **Add pencil detail.** In figure 4-147, the manikins have been toned down with a *Cool Grey #3 (Cool Grey 30%)* marker. They were then lightly washed, just enough to give them some hue, with pencil. In this case *Celadon Green*, *Jasmine*, and *Blush Pink* pencils were used. The sky reflection was lightly washed with *Light Cerulean Blue* pencil.

Fig. 4-146

Fig. 4-147

3 **Add details and muntins.** The fluorescent ceiling lights of most commercial buildings are visible from the outside even during the day. In figure 4-148, these lines of lights are drawn with a *White* pencil and a straightedge aimed toward a vanishing point. It usually does not matter toward which vanishing point, in a typical two-point perspective, the rows of lights are aligned. The display lights in the retail windows on the first level are dotted in with white gouache.

The muntins and frames of the windows should be trimmed to consistently "read" against the glass and its reflections. They can be darker or lighter than the glass and its reflections, or they can be both, so that they read against all combinations of value. In figure 4-148, a *White* pencil was first applied to the frames and muntins of the windows with a straightedge. Then, where necessary, the shaded sides of those frames and muntins were edged with a *French Grey 90%* pencil in the same way.

Fig. 4-148

Dusk Windows (4-149 through 4-153)

Windows at dusk are very easy to illustrate. The advantage of showing a building at dusk is that although the exterior of the building (with its materials and finishes) is still visible, additional information about the interior of the building—its uses, spaces and the character of its lighting—can also be revealed.

Dusk windows are most easily illustrated on white roll tracing paper, using the retrocolor technique (see figures 7-63 through 7-66).

1 **Apply color to those elements seen through the street-level windows.** Your entire building will have more appeal if the street-level windows display goods and appropriate activity instead of remaining blank. Draw those elements—whether retail, restaurant, office, or other types—one might see through such windows. In this example, pencil was used so as to keep the outlines of the elements from being too visually assertive. Note that they are drawn simply and detail is kept to a minimum.

The color is applied to the back of the drawing with a variety of color pencils. Figure 4-149 shows the drawing on white tracing paper with brown kraft paper placed behind it.

2 **Add window illumination.** Figure 4-150 shows the back side of the illustration after color pencil was applied to the windows. *Jasmine* pencil was applied first, with medium hand pressure, followed by *White* pencil at heavy hand pressure. These two pencils were applied quickly and loosely. Although some of the pencil spilled outside the lines, the mistakes are not noticeable, because when the illustration is turned right-side-up, the lines are not occluded by the pencil. This effect applies to the window muntins as well, also colored over on the back side but perfectly visible from the front of the drawing.

The figures standing in front of the window were darkened with *French Grey 90%* marker. Because the foreground elements were made to appear in silhouette, the windows appear brighter owing to the value contrast.

Note that glowing windows also throw light on soffits, column edges, sidewalks, and so on, not only helping to reveal further information about the building, but adding drama and interest to the illustration as well.

Fig. 4-149

Fig. 4-150

3 **Add final touches.** Figure 4-151 shows touches of white gouache added for lights and sparkle in the street-level windows. Color has also been added to the foreground figures which, although they remain in silhouette, gives them a touch more character.

Fig. 4-151

4 **Then color photocopy.** Notice, in figure 4-152, how the dusk-window effect is intensified by a color photocopy, which was made with the brown kraft paper still behind the drawing. A dusk scene can be turned into a night scene by substituting a very dark blue paper (Crescent, Canson, or Pantone paper, etc.) for the brown kraft paper (4-153). Both color photocopies were made with the machine's "lightness-darkness" at a darker than normal setting.

Fig. 4-152

Fig. 4-153

Night Windows (4-154, 4-155, 4-156)

1 **Make a dark blackline diazo print.** A blackline diazo print was made of the line drawing, which was run through the diazo machine at a much faster than usual speed. You can see, in figure 4-154, that the background is quite dark but the linework of the drawing is still visible.

2 **Draw street-level window elements.** A line drawing of the elements in the street-level windows was made with a Micron 005 pen. In figure 4-154, the manikins are colored with pencil as brightly as possible. The lower part of the window display area is colored with *White* pencil to simulate the high illumination of the horizontal surfaces from the display lighting above.

The background ambient glow was added, as shown on the left, with a *Deco Orange* pencil, blending into the area colored with the *White* pencil in the lower part of the window.

Although the manikins are recognizable as such, note that the juxtapositions of colors and forms can make the overall effect somewhat abstract. Care was taken not to spend too much time making the window display unduly realistic or detailed, as its role in the illustration is secondary. Note, too, that as the street-level window images were colored, the silhouetted figures in front of the windows were carefully outlined by the colors and remain the tone of the paper.

3 **Add window illumination.** *Jasmine, Deco Orange,* and *White* pencils were used to fill in the upper window apertures with light. In figure 4-155, these pencils were used to create subtle shifts in color temperature, suggesting various locations of the sources of light. The fact that the entire interior of the building is also unevenly illuminated helps to create a more realistic lighting scenario.

In this step it was much easier to apply the color right over the window muntins. They were quickly drawn back in the subsequent step.

Fig. 4-154

Fig. 4-155

4 **Add details.** Figure 4-156 shows "spill light" added to the surrounding surfaces. The light on the soffits, sides of columns, and various edges was applied with a *Deco Orange* pencil. The light on the sidewalk was added with a *White* pencil.

The window frames, muntins, and balcony railings were redrawn with a *Black* pencil. Lights and highlights were dotted in with touches of white gouache.

Fig. 4-156

Daytime Windows, Large Buildings (4-157, 4-158, 4-159)

The daytime windows in large buildings have many of the same components as those in smaller buildings. There are a reflection mass and a sky reflection. You can even see the ceiling-mounted fluorescent lights. Usually, however, the viewer is far enough away from the drawing so that details to street-level windows are unnecessary.

In many tall buildings, you will notice that the sky reflection often grades to a brighter value as the building goes higher. This is because, relative to the viewer's sight line, the angle of the building's surface relative to the sky reflection becomes progressively more oblique. In addition, the values of the reflections in the windows can become much darker or lighter as the building surfaces change direction, such as in turning a corner. As the orientation of a surface changes, what that surface is reflecting suddenly changes as well. The reflections in the windows of a building often have a *darker average value on its sunlit faces and appear to have a lighter average value on the faces in shade.*

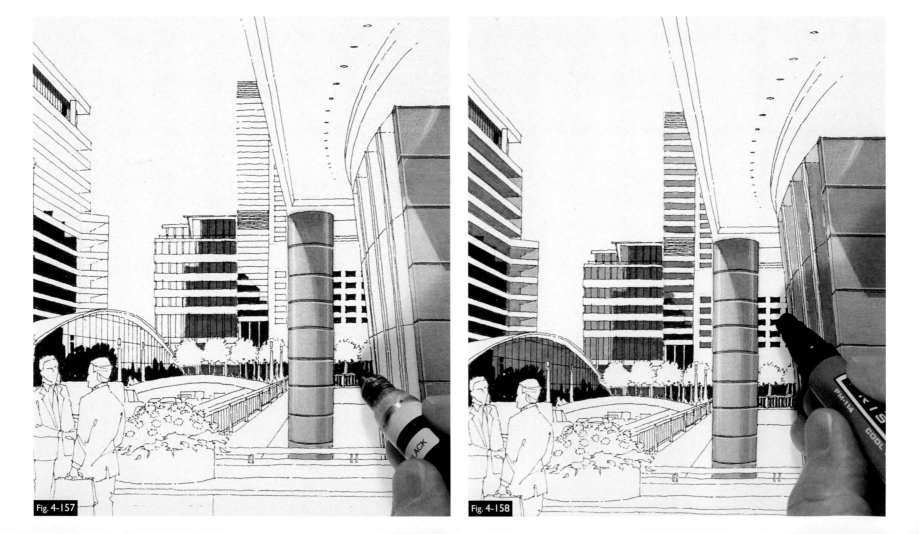

Fig. 4-157

Fig. 4-158

1 **Estimate and draw size and shape of reflection masses.** The reflections of objects (trees, other buildings) were quickly estimated and drawn on the faces of the buildings shown in figure 4-157. These rough, approximate reflections even included buildings not shown in the picture.

The reflection masses are typically drawn with a black marker or a very dark cool gray marker. Distant reflection masses, including those appearing where the building faces change direction, can be drawn in a slightly lighter gray. In this example they are drawn with a *Cool Grey #8 (Cool Grey 80%)* marker.

2 **Add marker base for sky reflection.** In figure 4-158, the sky reflections were filled in with a variety of cool gray markers. In the case of the low building with the parabolic roof, as well as the large building just behind it, the remaining windows facing to the right were filled in with *Cool Grey #7 (Cool Grey 70%)* marker.

The bays and windows facing other directions were filled in with *Cool Grey #5, #3,* and *#2 (Cool Grey 50%, 30%,* and *20%)* markers. Note that the see-through corners were made slightly lighter than the gray on the adjacent ceilings.

3 **Apply color washes, clouds, mullions, and lights.** Figure 4-159 shows that the sky reflections *only* were washed with *Blue Slate* pencil. Progressively more *White* pencil was added over the *Blue Slate* pencil as the buildings increase in height. A mixture of *Celadon Green* and *Deco Aqua* pencils were applied in a light wash over the windows at the see-through corners.

Some streaks of *White* pencil were added for clouds in the upper windows of the building on the left.

Ceiling-mounted fluorescent lights were added, using a *White* pencil and a straightedge aimed toward the vanishing points. Note that these white dashes were applied over the darker reflection masses and the lighter sky reflections alike.

The window mullions were added last. *Black* pencil was used with a straightedge to apply the mullions to the lighter areas of the windows, and *White* pencil was applied over the darker areas.

Fig. 4-159

TREES

Trees help to shape, animate, and soften the wall planes of outdoor places. The architecture of tree forms is as critical to the successful creation of the character of these places as is the architecture of their built forms. Thus, the designer's attention to the size, proportion, and massing of trees in design illustrations is as important as that given to the building elements.

The rules of light, shade, and shadow apply to the development of tree forms every bit as much as they do to architectural forms. The canopies of trees in foliage have an illuminated side, a shaded side, and usually a bottom or underside that is also in shade. Their shadows can be seen on the ground, usually punctuated with oblong penetrations of sunlight.

The branches of bare trees, as well as those seen in leafy tree canopies, can contrast with their backgrounds in order to maintain legibility. If part of a background is dark, the branches can be made lighter; if the background is light, the branches can be darker—all on the same trees. Details can often help to make a tree sufficiently convincing. For example, a tree can easily be made to appear more "leafy," less heavy and opaque, by allowing more sky to be visible through its canopy. Likewise, bare trees often appear with the shadows of their branches on other branches and spiraling down their trunks.

Bare Deciduous Trees, Foreground (4-160, 4-161, 4-162)

In most illustrations a foreground tree is only partially visible. The tree, as well as its shadow, is usually used as a way to "frame" the middle-ground view.

1 **Draw trunk and main branches.** As figure 4-160 shows, only the trunk, main branches, and a light outline of the canopy edge were used to begin the drawing. The rest of the branching will be added in a later step. If necessary, use a photograph of a tree as a reference when drawing this significant component of a design illustration.

The background and surroundings of the tree were added next. The sky was applied with pastel, and the sidewalk and grass were added with marker.

Marker was then added to the trunk and main branches. *French Grey 70%* marker was applied to the shaded sides of the trunk; *French Grey 50%* marker was added to the sunlit side.

Fig. 4-160

2 **Add fine branching, shadows, and texture.** Once the larger branches and trunk were drawn with marker, the smaller branches were extended to the predetermined outline edge with a *French Grey 70%* pencil. In figure 4-161, these branches were drawn by applying more pressure to the pencil at each branch's point of origin, then easing pressure on the pencil to make the branches thinner near the edge of the canopy. Note that the fine branches at the edge of the canopy were lightly washed with the side of the *French Grey 70%* pencil to quickly replicate the density created by the mass of even smaller branches.

When the small branches were completed, shadows were applied to the large branches and trunk with a *French Grey 70%* marker. A *French Grey 10%* pencil was used to wash the sunlit portion of the trunk. Thin, wavy lines of *Black* and *French Grey 10%* pencil were drawn along the main branches and trunk to create a bark texture. The trunk and fine branch masses were stippled with a Pilot Razor Point.

Fig. 4-161

3 **Add ground shadow.** A bare tree is accompanied by a shadow that has two separate components. The trunk and main branches cast darker, more distinct shadow, and the finer branches create areas of lighter, diffuse shadow.

In figure 4-162, *Yellow Green (Limepeel)* marker was used as a base color for the grass, and *Olive (Olive Green)* marker was used as a base color for the shadows of the trunk and main branches. *French Grey 40%* marker was used to continue these shadows onto the concrete sidewalk.

Sunset Pink (Deco Pink) marker was added to the grass to mute the green slightly. *Celadon Green* pencil was applied to portions of the grass to make it more bluish green.

Copenhagen Blue pencil was applied lightly over the shadow on the grass to add the lighter, diffuse shadow. *Blue Slate* pencil was used for the same purpose on the sidewalk.

Fig. 4-162

Bare Deciduous Trees, Middle Ground and Background

(4-163, 4-164, 4-165)

The preliminary line drawings for bare trees in the middle ground or background of a design illustration are prepared similarly to those for bare foreground trees. The trunks, main branches, and penciled canopy outlines are drawn first.

1 **Apply color to the background.** In figure 4-163, color was first applied to those elements seen *through* the closer trees. *French Grey 30%* marker was applied to the canopies of the line of trees in the middle of the drawing. *French Grey 10%* marker was added to the next more distant layer of trees. *Cool Grey #1 (Cool Grey 10%)* marker was applied over the *French Grey 10%* marker as well as to the most distant tree/hill forms.

The sky is a blend of Schwan Stabilo #430 pencil pastel (top) and *Light Oxide Red 339.9* (middle) and *Ultramarine Deep 506.9* (lower) stick pastels. The sky near the horizon was left white.

Color was added to the building, with care taken to keep its value relatively light and the contrast minimal between its sunlit and shaded surfaces.

2 **Add the trunks, main branches, and shadows beneath the trees.** The shadows beneath the middle row of trees, as well as the trunks and main branches visible against the lighter backgrounds, were added with *French Grey 70%* and *50%* markers (4-164). The trunks visible against the darker backgrounds were left white, then toned with a *French Grey 10%* marker.

The shadows of the middle-ground trees on the right were first applied with *French Grey 50%* marker—for the trunks and main branches—followed by a wash of *French Grey 10%* marker for the diffuse shadows of the smaller branch masses.

Touches of *Olive (Olive Green)* marker were added for evergreen shrubs beneath the middle row of trees; the embankment beyond the distant fence was washed with a blend of *Willow Green (Lime Green)* and *Buff (Brick Beige)* markers.

Fig. 4-163

Fig. 4-164

3 **Add fine branching.** In figure 4-165, the finer branches were added with a *French Grey 70%* pencil. The finest branching, of course, is located at the outer edge of the tree canopies. These branch masses were added with the side of *Burnt Ochre* and *French Grey 50%* pencils.

The trunks of the middle row of trees were lightened and darkened with very light touches of *French Grey 10%* and *90%* pencils, respectively. *Jasmine* pencil was used to brighten the sunlit sides of the trunks. Pilot Razor Point was used to stipple the closest tree canopies.

Fig. 4-165

Bare Deciduous Trees, in Front of Graded Background
(4-166)

Use a light-value color pencil when drawing bare trees or shrubs in front of dark values such as shadows, windows, or darkened skies. In figure 4-166, *Cream* pencil was used to draw the part of the shrub that is in front of the part of the wall in shade. *Warm Grey 20%* pencil was used to draw the tree in front of the darkened sky on the right, and *Warm Grey 50%* pencil was used to draw the bare tree on the left. This technique works best when there is little or no color pencil on the surface over which you intend to draw these plant materials.

Fig. 4-166

Deciduous Trees in Foliage, Foreground (4-167, 4-168, 4-169)

This illustration was drawn on blackline diazo print paper.

A foreground deciduous tree in foliage, like its bare counterpart in figure 4-162, is rarely shown in its entirety. Note that the larger branches are drawn first, but darkened in later steps.

1 **Draw foliage with marker.** The outline of the tree canopy was delineated with a thin pencil line to serve as a guide for the marker application. In figure 4-167, *Yellow Green (Limepeel)* and *Olive (Olive Green)* markers were used to begin the foliage, stroked diagonally with the broad side of the marker tip. (Autumn foliage can also be drawn as easily, beginning with such markers as *Brick Red (Cherry)*, *Pale Cherry (Mineral Orange)*, and *Pale Sepia (Goldenrod)*.

2 **Complete foliage, draw branches, begin shadows with marker.** As figure 4-168 shows, *Dark Olive (French Grey 80%)* and *Cool Grey #9 (Cool Grey 90%)* markers were added to complete the foliage.

A pointed-nib Design Marker was used to darken the smaller branches. This resulted in a series of broken, rather than continuous, lines, because the view of the branches is interrupted by the leaf clusters.

After the marker base colors for the grass were applied, *Dark Olive (French Grey 80%)* marker was applied in a series of close *horizontal* strokes. The same type of stroke was used to apply *Cool Grey #5 (Cool Grey 50%)* marker for the sidewalk shadows. *Burnt Umber (Dark Umber)* marker was applied with a *diagonal* stroke to the brick wall.

3 **Add highlights, detail, and finishing touches.** In figure 4-169, *Cream* pencil was applied over the foliage drawn with the *Yellow Green (Limepeel)* marker. *Light Cerulean Blue* pencil, with *White* pencil applied over it, was used to add the bits of sky visible through the canopy of the tree.

Cool Grey #5 (Cool Grey 50%) marker was used to draw the shadows on the trunk. *Cream* and *White* pencils were used to wash the sunlit areas between the shadows. A light wash of *Burnt Ochre* pencil was then applied

Fig. 4-167

Fig. 4-168

over the entire trunk. Further trunk texture was applied with a Pilot Razor Point, by stippling and adding diagonal strokes to the shadow areas.

A wash of *Olive Green* pencil was applied over the marker shadows on the grass, followed by a vertical texture added with a Pilot Razor Point. *Cream* pencil was used for adding a similar texture to the sunlit portions of the grass.

Peach pencil was used to flavor the marker shadows on the brick wall, and a wash of *Peach* and *White* pencil was added to the sunlit portion. The mortar joints were added with a *White* pencil and a straightedge to give the shadow a transparent quality.

Copenhagen Blue pencil was used to flavor the shadows on the sidewalk; *White* pencil, flavored with *Peach* pencil, was used to enhance the sunlit areas.

Fig. 4-169

Deciduous Trees in Foliage, Middle Ground (4-170, 4-171, 4-172)

This illustration was drawn on brownline diazo print paper.

1   **Apply marker base.** In figure 4-170, *Yellow Green (Limepeel)* marker was used for sunlit foliage, *Olive (Olive Green)* marker for foliage in middle light, and *Dark Olive (French Grey 80%)* marker for foliage in shade and shadow. Note that the lines of the buildings still show through the foliage in places and act as a guide for applying color to those surfaces behind the trees.

2   **Create shadows with marker.** A variety of markers were used in figure 4-171 to create the shadows cast by the trees—darker values on dark surfaces, lighter values on light surfaces. *Horizontal* strokes were used for shadows on the ground, and *diagonal* strokes were used to make the shadows on the vertical surfaces parallel to the direction of the sunlight.

3   **Add color to surfaces seen through the trees.** The appropriate colors were applied to those surfaces not touched by the markers used to create the foliage. These colors were applied with color pencil to the building surfaces and the sky.

4   **Apply highlights, details, and finishing touches.** In figure 4-172, a mixture of *Jasmine* and *Cream* pencils was applied over the sunlit side of the trees. Branches were added with a pointed-nib Design Marker and a Pilot Razor Point, with the use of intermittent strokes. *Cool Grey #9 (Cool Grey 90%)* marker was used to stipple some even darker areas of the leaf masses. Details, highlights, and flavorings were added to the surrounding sunlit and shadowed surfaces.

Fig. 4-170

Fig. 4-171

Fig. 4-172

Deciduous Trees in Foliage (Abbreviated Technique)

(4-173, 4-174, 4-175)

1 **Apply sky, distant objects, and marker base.** In figure 4-173, color was applied to the sky and the building in the distance, similarly to the way it was done in figure 4-163. However, in this example there is no need to extend the color of the background building very far below the outline of the tree canopies, inasmuch as it will be blocked by the dense foliage.

Yellow Green (Limepeel) marker was applied to the upper sunlit sides of the trees with the broad *edge* of the tip. Note how the strokes were oriented outward from the center of the trees. *Olive (Olive Green)* marker was carefully applied between these lighter strokes on the *shaded* side of each tree. You can see how the trees within the mass repeat the light-dark pattern, one against the other, individuating trees within the mass. The darker marker was also applied to the *bottom* of each canopy, forming a rough, continuous line of dark value between the canopies and trunks.

2 **Develop tree forms, colors, and shadows.** *Black* marker was applied to the darkest areas beneath the trees in figure 4-174. As it was worked upward into the tree canopies, the *Black* was dotted in with the marker tip.

Black marker was also used on the left side of the middle-ground tree to the right. *Olive (Olive Green)* marker was used to pick up where the black left off as the color progressed toward the sunlit side.

Olive (Olive Green) marker was also used to apply the shadow of the tree on the ground as well as the long shadows in the field beyond. *Yellow Green (Limepeel)* marker was used on the sunlit portions of the field.

The sunlit sides of the trees and fields were muted with *Sunset Pink (Deco Pink)* marker, and *Willow Green (Lime Green)* marker was used as a transition color between the sunlit and shaded sides of the tree canopies.

The most distant hills, near the horizon, were colored with *Cool Grey #1 (Cool Grey 10%)* marker; *Cool Grey #3 (Cool Grey 30%)* marker was used on the next closest "layer" of trees. The layer of trees just in front of these were drawn with *Cool Grey #1* and *#3 (Cool Grey 10%* and *30%)* markers, then washed with *Willow Green (Lime Green)* and *Naples Yellow (Eggshell)* markers.

Fig. 4-173

Fig. 4-174

3 **Add details.** You may frequently find that when you have applied the marker base to a tree canopy in foliage that is seen against the sky, you have not left adequate "white spaces" showing. As a result, the canopy can appear too opaque and heavy. This was the case with the closest trees in figure 4-175. To remedy the situation, *White* pencil was added to the upper parts of the canopies of the trees on the left and right to "open them up."

Peach pencil was used to flavor the sunlit sides of the tree canopies and their trunks, helping to create the effect of morning or late afternoon sun. If you want the light to appear as if it is occurring later in the day, use *Jasmine* pencil or no pencil flavoring at all.

Fig. 4-175

Evergreen Trees, Foreground (4-176, 4-177, 4-178)

The evergreen trees illustrated in this sequence of steps are typical of the many kinds of evergreen found throughout the world. Tree (1) is a sprucelike tree. By using the stroke shown in the inset you can, by varying the form, draw trees similar in form to that of the spruce (genus *Picea*), such as the hemlock *(Tsuga)*, fir *(Psuedotsuga* and *Abies)*, larch *(Larix)*, and cedar *(cedrus)*. Tree (2) is a pinelike tree, and the stroke *(inset)* can be used for drawing the many types of pines *(Pinus)*. Tree (3) is a cypresslike tree *(Chamaecyparis)*, and the stroke used to draw it may be applied to similar tree forms, such as the juniper *(Juniperus)* and the yew *(Taxus)*.

1 **Apply marker base to foliage.** In figure 4-176, *Slate Green (Teal Blue)* marker was applied to the sprucelike tree, using the stroke shown in the inset. In this particular example, a Colorado blue spruce *(Picea pungens glauca)* tree form was created.

A *Cool Grey #7 (Cool Grey 70%)* marker was used for the pinelike tree, following the stroke technique shown in the inset. For best results, use a marker that is slightly dry to create the feathered edge at the end of the stroke. The tree form in this example is a ponderosa pine *(Pinus ponderosa)*.

A *Slate Green (Teal Blue)* marker was also used, following the stroke shown in the inset, to begin the cypresslike tree.

Fig. 4-176

1

2

3

2 **Develop color, shading, and trunks with marker.** In figure 4-177, *Cool Grey #9 (Cool Grey 90%)* marker was stippled on the underside of the foliage masses of the sprucelike tree. It was also used to darken the tips of the masses on the shaded side of the tree.

Olive *(Olive Green)* marker was applied over the *Cool Grey #7 (Cool Grey 70%)* marker base of the pinelike tree. *Cool Grey #9 (Cool Grey 90%)* marker was used on the underside of the foliage masses to develop their shading. The trunks were drawn with *Redwood (Sienna Brown)* marker, with *Cool Grey #9 (Cool Grey 90%)* marker used on the shaded sides.

Olive *(Olive Green)* marker was applied over the *Slate Green (Teal Blue)* marker base of the cypresslike trees, with the same stroke as that shown for that tree in the inset in figure 4-176. *Cool Grey #9 (Cool Grey 90%)* marker is stippled on the shaded sides of the trees, in gradually diminished amounts as it progresses toward the sunlit side.

Fig. 4-177

1

2

3

3 **Add highlights and final touches.** Figure 4-178 shows that *Olive Green* pencil was used to wash the entire sprucelike tree and *White* pencil was applied to the sunlit foliage masses with an upward stroke. Touches of *Burnt Ochre* pencil were added to indicate dead foliage.

Jasmine pencil was used to highlight the sunlit tops of the foliage masses of the pinelike tree. *Olive Green* pencil was added to its shaded areas to bring out their color. Pilot Razor Point was used to add a needlelike texture to the shaded sides of the foliage masses. Again, touches of *Burnt Ochre* pencil were used to add dead foliage. *Cream* and *White* pencils were applied to the sunlit parts of the trunks for highlights, and *Dark Umber* and Derwent *Blue Violet Lake #27* pencils were added to the shaded areas.

Jasmine and *Cream* pencils were applied to highlight the sunlit areas of the cypresslike tree. Note the small fan-shaped texture patterns created with these pencils.

Fig. 4-178

Evergreen Trees, Middle Ground and Background

(4-179, 4-180)

1 **Draw middle-ground trees first.** A pointed-nib Design Marker can be used to draw the middle-ground trees, with a simple slanted stroke over a vertical trunk line. The example in figure 4-179 shows a Sanford Sharpie—a felt-tipped pen with a similar tip—is being used for this step. As the inset shows, the stroke is slanted in opposite directions on opposite sides of the trunk.

The closer trees, drawn on the extreme left and right, were created by stippling a *Cool Grey #9 (Cool Grey 90%)* marker over a vertical trunk line. These trees will remain dark, because they are silhouetted by the lighter trees in the background.

2 **Add trunks.** *Warm Grey 20%* pencil was used to draw the trunks of the trees with intermittent lines.

Fig. 4-179

3 **Draw distant trees.** Once the middle-ground trees were drawn, the point of an *Olive (Olive Green)* marker was used to add the distant trees—the marker was repeatedly flicked upward, quickly producing a simple evergreenlike shape with a wider bottom and narrower top (4-180).

The same stroke was used in applying a Pilot Razor Point to suggest both tree-mass texture and shading. These lines were drawn more densely at the crest of the hill so that it would contrast more strongly with the mountain beyond.

Jasmine pencil was applied, with the same stroke, to create a low-sun effect on the trees.

Note that *Blue Slate* pencil was used just behind the middle-ground trees to create greater contrast with the distant tree mass.

Fig. 4-180

Palm Trees (4-181, 4-182)

An important element in the illustration of palm trees is the accuracy with which the shape and proportion of the trees are created.

1 **Color the sky; apply marker base to the tree canopies.** In figure 4-181, *Yellow Green (Limepeel)* marker was applied to the sunlit portion of the tree canopies, and *Olive (Olive Green)* marker was applied to the shaded side. The markers were applied with the tip of the point, flicking outward from the center of the canopy. This gives a pointed end to the marker strokes. *Willow Green (Lime Green)* marker was used as a wash over both base colors to shift their colors.

2 **Apply color to trunks; add details.** *Kraft Brown (Light Tan)* marker was added to color the trunks, dead fronds just beneath the tree canopies, and dying fronds within the canopies themselves (4-182).

French Grey 70% marker was used to darken the shadows on the trunks. Light washes of *Cool Grey 30%* pencil were applied to the tree canopies, becoming slightly heavier washes as the trees progressed into the distance. This both lightened the value and weakened the chroma of the canopy colors, creating a sense of atmospheric perspective.

Burnt Ochre and *French Grey 70%* pencils were crosshatched to create a texture on the trees closest to the viewer.

Fig. 4-181

Fig. 4-182

Climbing Vines (4-183, 4-184)

1 **Apply color and shadows to climbing surface.** Color was first added to the stone bridge, including those parts seen through the openings in the plant material. Shadows cast by the vine mass were added below and to the left of each part of the mass.

2 **Apply marker base to vine mass.** *Willow Green (Lime Green)* and *Yellow Green (Limepeel)* markers were applied to the vine mass. Figure 4-183 shows *Olive (Olive Green)* marker being applied to the recesses and parts of the vine mass in shade.

3 **Add pencil wash.** In figure 4-184, a *Dark Green* pencil was applied as a light wash, using the side of the point. This not only shifts the color of the vine mass, but quickly adds an appropriate texture as well.

Fig. 4-183

Fig. 4-184

BACKGROUNDS

Urban Backgrounds (4-185, 4-186)

There are some distinct guidelines that will help you to easily create urban backgrounds: As the distance increases in an urban background, increase the value of the colors and decrease the value contrast *between* colors. The chroma of the colors should become weaker, and the hues should tend more toward the bluish range. Less detail should be shown on the buildings.

1 **Apply marker base.** Because colors in the outdoor urban landscape are predominantly weak in chroma, gray markers were used as the base (4-185). *Cool Grey #7 (Cool Grey 70%)* was the dominant marker used in the foreground, along with touches of *Cool Grey #9 (Cool Grey 90%)* and *Black* markers. Successively lighter cool gray markers were applied to the buildings as the distance increased.

2 **Flavor walls of buildings with pencil.** In figure 4-186, the walls of the closest buildings were flavored with warm-hued pencils, including *Terra Cotta, Peach, Jasmine, Mineral Orange, Burnt Ochre, Dark Umber,* and *Light Peach. White* pencil was used for highlights.

Fig. 4-185

The buildings in the middle-to-far distance were flavored with *Light Peach* pencil on their sunlit sides and *Light Cerulean Blue* pencil on their shaded sides. *White* pencil was also added to the most distant building surfaces to increase the value and decrease the chroma of the pencil flavorings. The entire distant part of the drawing, including buildings, was flavored with *Jasmine* and *Cream* pencils to create the effect of haze.

3 **Add window treatments.** A Pilot Razor Point was used to darken the windows on the sunlit sides of the closest buildings. A *Cool Grey 70%* pencil was added to windows on buildings farther in the distance. A mixture of *Light Cerulean Blue* and *White* pencils was used to create the effects of reflected skylight on the windows of the shaded sides of the closest buildings. A Pilot Razor Point was used to draw the muntins, frames, and shaded recesses.

Fig. 4-186

Rural Backgrounds (4-187, 4-188, 4-189)

The color phenomena exhibited in urban backgrounds are similar in rural backgrounds. The chroma of the colors becomes weaker, their values increase, and the apparent textures diminish as the distance increases. However, the hues seen in rural backgrounds generally form a clockwise progression around the color wheel, from green yellows in the foreground to purple blue or purple in the far distance.

1 **Apply marker base to the foreground.** In figure 4-187, *Cool Grey #9, #7, and #5 (Cool Grey 90%, 70%, and 50%)* markers were used to create a dark foreground mass of trees, producing a more dramatic effect of distance through value contrast. *Burnt Umber (Dark Umber)* marker was used for the roof and deck of the building.

2 **Add help lines; create distant trees and fields with marker.** In figure 4-188, rolling help lines were introduced to help guide the addition of distant fields, roads, and land contours. *Cool Grey #5 (Cool Grey 50%)* marker was used to stipple in the trees on the first ridge, in the middle of the drawing. Shade and shadows were added with a *Cool Grey #7 (Cool Grey 70%)* marker.

Light Ivy (Putty + Cream) and *Buff (Brick Beige)* markers were added to the fields, along with touches of *Yellow Green (Limepeel)* marker.

The trees on the hill beyond the first ridge were stippled in with a *Cool Grey #3 (Cool Grey 30%)* marker. *Cool Grey #1 (Cool Grey 10%)* marker was applied to the farthest hillside.

Fig. 4-187

Fig. 4-188

3 **Apply pencil.** In figure 4-189, *Olive Green* pencil was used to wash the foreground trees as well as the trees on the first ridge. The foreground trees were then stippled with a Pilot Razor Point.

Olive Green and *Peacock Green* pencils were used to flavor the trees on the next ridge. *Peacock Green* pencil only was used to flavor the next ridge beyond.

Peacock Green and *Blue Slate* pencils were used on the ridge beyond that, and *Blue Slate* and *Greyed Lavender* pencils were used to flavor the last ridge before the mountain. A mixture of *Greyed Lavender* and *White* pencils was lightly applied to the mountain.

Fig. 4-189

SLOPING ROOFS

Shingle Roof (4-190, 4-191)

The Overhead Plane: Roofs and Skies

Sloping roofs and skies work together in a design drawing. Roof materials can be represented with a variety of media. They should be appropriately subtle and follow the rules of perspective. Skies can add a level of finish and even be a source of drama in a design drawing.

The shingle techniques shown in these illustrations can, depending on your color selections, be used for asphalt, wood, slate, or concrete shingles. The shingles illustrated in this example are wood shingles.

1 **Apply marker base.** First, an assumption was made that the light was coming from the left, determining which parts of the roof would be in shade and shadow. In figure 4-190, *French Grey 10%* marker was applied to the more directly illuminated surface, and *French Grey 30%* marker was used on the right-facing roof surface.

Note the light pencil help lines drawn on the roof. These lines radiate from the vanishing points and help guide the marker strokes. Streaks of *Buff (Brick Beige)* were added to the roof, stroked along these lines.

The dappled tree shadow to the left was made with *French Grey 70%, 50%,* and *30%* markers.

Fig. 4-190

2 **Add pencil texture.** As figure 4-191 shows, a .5 mm pencil with a 2H lead was used to draw the shadows of the butt ends of the shingles on the lighter slope of the roof. These lines were guided by the aforementioned help lines and were drawn with a short, choppy, back-and-forth motion along a straightedge. This motion imparts an uneven density to the line. Because this pencil does not show in the shadow on the left, a *Light Peach* pencil was used to continue the same line into the shadow. Note that a few individual shingle lines were added *along* the roof slope as well, with the use of both pencils.

A Micron 005 pen was used with the same kind of back-and-forth stroke to make the lines on the darker roof slope.

Fig. 4-191

Metal Roof, Standing Seam (4-192, 4-193)

1 **Apply marker base.** Metal roofs can be any color, but are typically muted. In figure 4-192, *Cool Grey #3 (Cool Grey 30%)* marker was applied to the more directly illuminated roof surfaces, and *Cool Grey #5 (Cool Grey 50%)* marker was used on the surfaces receiving less light. *Willow Green (Lime Green)* marker was then used to wash all roof surfaces.

To shift the color slightly, *Sand (Sand)* marker was added to the darker parts of the roof, and *Buff (Brick Beige)* marker was applied to the lighter surfaces.

Note the pencil help lines, once again added to keep the marker strokes—and subsequent pencil strokes—aligned toward the vanishing points for the sloping roofs.

Fig. 4-192

2 **Add pencil detail.** Figure 4-193 shows the completed roof. *French Grey 70%* pencil was applied with a straightedge to create the standing seams on the lighter roof surfaces, and side-by-side lines of *French Grey 10%* and *French Grey 70%* pencil were added to the darker roofs.

Notice that the standing seam lines are evenly spaced and each aims toward the respective vanishing points for the sloping roofs.

Fig. 4-193

Tile Roof (4-194, 4-195)

1 **Apply marker base; modify color with pastel.** *Kraft Brown (Light Tan)* marker was applied to the sunlit portion of the roof, and *Burnt Umber (Dark Umber)* marker was used for the shadow.

A random application of Schwan Stabilo *#620*, *#675*, and *#690* pencil pastels was blended by finger on the sunlit portions of the roof. The excess was brushed away with a drafting brush.

2 **Add pencil detail.** In figure 4-194, *Black* pencil was added to the dark spaces between the rows of tiles. Note that each of these lines radiates from the roof's vanishing point, shown lightly in pencil above the roof.

Fig. 4-194

3 **Apply finishing touches.** Figure 4-195 shows the rest of the black lines added to the roof. Note that not every line need be applied. *French Grey 30%* pencil lines were lightly added to the shadowed parts of the roof.

Dashes of *Terra Cotta* and *Light Peach* pencil were applied to give additional texture. A pointed-nib Design Marker was used to dot in the dark tile ends at the eaves.

SKIES

Daytime Sky (4-196, 4-197, 4-198)

A daytime sky often appears as a gradation of color and, under normal, clear weather conditions, is usually lighter at the horizon and grades to a darker blue toward the zenith. Daytime skies—even those on large drawings—can be created very quickly and easily with pastel.

1 **Apply pastel.** You will find it easier, when planning a design illustration, to apply the sky first, before color is added to the roofs and treetops. When sky color spills onto these adjacent surfaces, it can be erased without disturbing their color.

In figure 4-196, *Ultramarine Deep 506.9* stick pastel was applied quickly and roughly in the area closest to the horizon, with care taken to leave the white of the paper just above the horizon. Higher in the sky, a Schwan Stabilo

Fig. 4-195

Fig. 4-196

#430 pencil pastel was also quickly applied as a transitional color to the darker *Cobalt Blue 512.5* stick pastel, added to the top part of the sky.

2 **Mix pastel with fingers or facial tissue.** Figure 4-197 shows the three pastels being mixed with a facial tissue to form a graded blue sky. If the gradation is not consistent when the excess is brushed away, additional pastel or color pencil can be applied to create consistency.

3 **Apply finishing touches.** The finished sky is shown in figure 4-198. To keep the sky gradation consistent, it was wiped with a chamois only at the bottom, near the horizon. The rest was simply brushed with a drafting brush. Pastel that found its way into the trees was erased away with an electric eraser using a soft white erasing strip.

Protect the original illustration with a layer of tracing paper, because it can smear easily. Use a color photocopy or a color bubble-jet copy of the illustration for review and presentation purposes. Use a spray fixative only if you must, because fixative tends to mute the colors of the pastel.

Fig. 4-197

Fig. 4-198

Dusk (or Dawn) Skies (4-199 through 4-202)

There are two easy ways to make dusk or dawn skies. Both use toned paper techniques and work well in illustrations in which the windows will be illuminated.

A. On white tracing paper (4-199, 4-200, 4-201)

1 **Apply sky colors to the back of the tracing paper.** In figure 4-199, *Pink*, *Blush Pink*, and *Deco Orange* pencils were applied near the horizon and faded into the color of the paper. *Cobalt Blue 512.5* stick pastel was applied to the part of the sky farthest from the setting (rising) sun and will also be faded onto the paper color from the opposite direction.

Note that the illustration is created with brown kraft paper placed beneath the tracing paper so that the effect of the light colors is more obvious.

Fig. 4-199

2 **Blend colors.** The pastel was rubbed into the paper and smoothed with the fingers. *Blush Pink* and *Deco Orange* pencils were also added to the *front* of the paper for the purpose of adding streaks of pink and orange *over* the blue sky color.

3 **Add finishing touches.** Figure 4-200 shows that the pastel was erased from the trees. A few stars were added, with white gouache, to the front of the illustration. Elements that abut the sky, in this case deciduous and evergreen trees, can be silhouetted against the sky by filling in their forms with a *Black* marker on the front side of the illustration. This makes the sky appear still more luminous by contrast. Figure 4-201 shows the intended final form of the illustration—as a color photocopy.

Fig. 4-200

Fig. 4-201

B. On blackline diazo print paper (4-202)

A dusk or dawn sky is very easy to create on dark diazo paper, because the effect requires that the sky be only partially colored.

1 **Make a dark blackline or blueline print of your line drawing.** This print should be run at a machine speed that is much faster than usual. The print shown in figure 4-202 was graded in value, from darkest at the upper left to lightest on the lower right, by varying the machine speed as the print was run.

2 **Apply color pencil in a progression of graded washes.** *Deco Orange, Blush Pink, Pink, Light Cerulean Blue,* and *Copenhagen Blue* pencils were applied, in the order listed, from the horizon up. Each pencil color was graded one into the other, the sides of the pencil points were used, which yielded a wider and smoother stroke. Horizontal clouds, appearing as streaks of color, were added with *Pink* and *Deco Orange* pencils.

Note that the colors used form a progression around the color wheel, from yellow red at the horizon to purple blue. The purple blue in this example, *Copenhagen Blue* pencil, was, in turn, faded into the paper color.

Pastel was not used in this example because when erased it can lift the dark coating from the paper, resulting in unwanted streaking.

3 **Add touches of white gouache for stars.**

Fig. 4-202

Daytime Skies with Clouds (4-203, 4-204)

Clouds are easy and fun to create. For this reason, however, they can easily be overdone, becoming portentous, fussy, and a distraction from the original purpose of the illustration. Clouds should remain as background, helping to create the context for your design ideas.

1 **Make a daytime sky.** Use the same materials and techniques for creating a daytime sky as those illustrated in figures 4-196 through 4-198.

2 **Erase away sky to create clouds.** An electric eraser with a soft white erasing strip is used in figure 4-203 to create the cloud forms by erasing away the pastel base used to make the sky. These forms can be virtually any shape and oriented in any direction, depending on the sky effect you want. Use photographs of cloud forms to guide your efforts.

3 **Add final touches.** You can simply stop after step 2 and have very satisfactory clouds for the purposes of most design illustrations. If you wish, you can add some color to the clouds, inasmuch as they are often tinted by the color of the sky—as during sunsets, for example.

In this instance (4-204), *Light Oxide Red 339.9* stick pastel was mixed with *White* stick pastel on the sunlit sides of the cloud forms, then rubbed with a facial tissue and brushed with a drafting brush. Other very light pastel colors can also be used for tinting clouds

Fig. 4-203

Fig. 4-204

SCALE ELEMENTS: FIGURES AND AUTOMOBILES

The inclusion of human figures and automobiles in your color design drawings gives the viewer of those drawings a comparative reference by which the sizes of all parts of the ideas expressed can be quickly judged. They also add a welcome and necessary level of human activity to the illustrations of the places you design.

However, there is an irony in introducing these scale elements into your drawings. On one hand, these "hard-to-draw" elements seem to be a time-consuming bother as compared with the "real work" of illustrating the ideas themselves. On the other hand, they are precisely the point. By introducing these elements—people and, where appropriate, the cars they drive—into all design drawings, from conceptual sketches to presentation drawings, you keep those for whom these places are created in the forefront of your attention.

Nevertheless, it is important to not belabor these elements by spending too much time in their creation or by allowing them to attract undue attention. Although designers are in many ways inventors, remember that your task does not include the design of people and cars. Trace and copy these elements whenever it is opportune to do so. Keep them simple and use a level of detail appropriate to the drawing.

DRAWING FIGURES IN COLOR

Your lifelong experience with your fellow humans allows you to estimate the relative sizes of the forms, spaces, and elements that surround them. Their presence in a place helps you to judge how big or small something is. Likewise, the addition of human figures to design drawings adds a critical element of *scale,* as well as animation and vitality, to your design ideas (5-1). However, because of this very familiarity, the figures in a design drawing can sometimes attract the viewer's attention unnecessarily. Poorly drawn or visually demanding figures can distract the viewer from the purpose of the drawing and, worse, can detract from otherwise good design ideas. Human figures should blend into the design drawing and act as a subtle reference for the viewer.

Fig. 5-1

Fig. 5-1 Although only a few figures would have sufficed for scale, the multitude of figures here adds vitality to this redesigned entertainment complex. Note how simply the figures are drawn because they are relatively distant in the illustration. See the enlargement in figure 5-7.

Trace Files

Because your task as a designer is to design our surroundings but not the people who occupy them, you may wish to trace figures from photographs or one of the many "entourage" books available. This is always best when the opportunity arises—just the right figure or an automobile at precisely the angle you need. But reliance on tracing can be more time consuming than it may appear. First, the right figures must be located—that is, appropriate in dress and activity for the project type and location. Second, figures are more effective if you can engage them in the place you are making: sitting on the bench, facing a particular way, relaxing in a seating area, or window shopping at a certain storefront. These requirements can narrow the field of suitable candidates for traced figures considerably. When appropriate figures *are* located, they must then be enlarged or reduced on a photocopier, usually a number of times, to achieve the right scale. Even when the drawing is complete, the figures can have an awkward look (facing or walking in odd directions, too much clothing detail, etc.) that often accompanies those imported from a different context.

Simple, Believable Figures

You may find it easier and faster to learn to draw simple, believably proportioned figures to use where and when necessary (5-2, 5-3). By learning to draw acceptable figures that are standing, sitting, and walking, you will have most all the positions of the human figure you need for your design work. You will also find the design drawing process more fluid if you do not have to stop to search for figures from photo references. Instead, use photographs and entourage books for clues about clothing types, postures, and accessories as you position and draw your own figures.

Fig. 5-2 These simple standing and walking figures add scale to a street section drawn at 1" = 10'.

Fig. 5-2

Fig. 5-3

Fig. 5-3   These seated figures do not have to be highly detailed to animate this semienclosed restaurant.

What constitutes a well-drawn scale figure? The most important quality of a scale figure is the naturalness of its proportions. That is, the relationships of the parts of the figure to one another should look about right (5-4). Well-proportioned figures, even as outline shapes in a drawing, are very useful not only for the viewer of a design illustration, but for the designer as well. You use figures as an instant comparative scale, during the drawing process, for making the parts of the design an appropriate size. Once you have a feel for drawing outline figures that are believably proportioned, attempt simple clothing and acces-

sories on an overlay of tracing paper (5-5). These elements need not be elaborate or highly detailed, but the clothing you draw on your figures should be appropriate for the type of place you are creating and its climate (5-6). Remember, too, that the more distant a figure is in a drawing, the *simpler its clothing and level of detail should be* (5-7). The colors and details of the clothing on your figures can be any that appear believable (5-8). One of the best ways to choose colors for the clothing of your figures is to recombine colors already in use elsewhere in the drawing. Figures are good agents of repetition and can help create a color rhythm by distributing selected colors throughout the illustration.

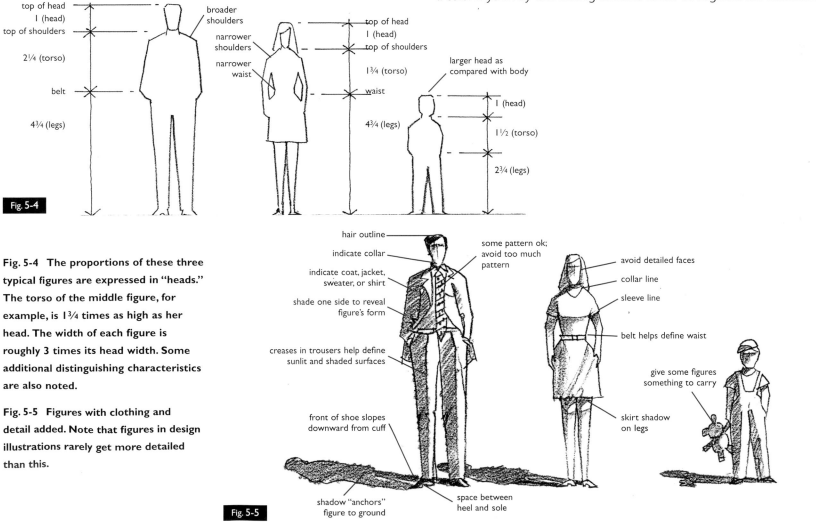

Fig. 5-4

Fig. 5-5

Fig. 5-4 The proportions of these three typical figures are expressed in "heads." The torso of the middle figure, for example, is 1¾ times as high as her head. The width of each figure is roughly 3 times its head width. Some additional distinguishing characteristics are also noted.

Fig. 5-5 Figures with clothing and detail added. Note that figures in design illustrations rarely get more detailed than this.

Fig. 5-6 The walking figure is appropriately dressed for the New York location of this store.

Fig. 5-7 A detail of the illustration shown in figure 5-1. All of the figures in 5-1 appear quite distant because of the scope of this multiple-vanishing-point view. The standing figures vary in size according to their location in the illustration, but are about ¼" high in the original 11" x 12" illustration.

Fig. 5-8 The full colored figures shown in figure 5-5. The shade and shadow were applied to the front of the white tracing paper, and the pencil colors indicated were applied to the back.

Fig. 5-6

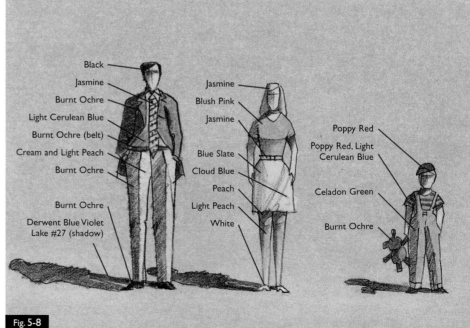

Fig. 5-8

Fig. 5-7

Introducing Figures into the Design Drawing Process

Once you are comfortable drawing a well-proportioned generic figure, practice drawing figures in the early stages of your design drawings, in both elevation and perspective. In a typical eye-level perspective, the heads of all standing figures will be on or near the horizon line. Larger figures will appear closer to the viewer, and smaller figures appear farther away (5-9).

A typical design drawing process is shown in figures 5-10 through 5-16. Note how figures are used during the inception of the design drawing to estimate the dimensions of its forms and spaces. These figures are not necessarily those used in the later stages of the drawing to provide scale and animation. Once a rough perspective view of the place is developed (5-10, 5-11), quickly drawn figures are introduced on a subsequent layer of tracing paper for location and action (5-12), then refined (5-13) by being given better proportions, clothing, and detail. After this stage, the *entire* line drawing is again edited as it is refined. It is then ready to receive shade, shadow, and color (5-14). Note that color is first applied to everything *but* the figures (5-15). Once the colors for the design are determined and applied, the same palette is then used on the figures in various recombinations (5-16).

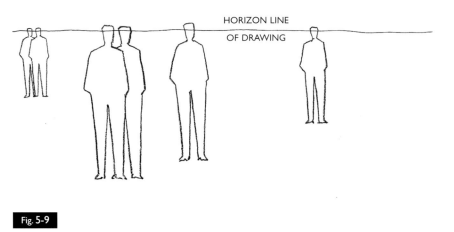

HORIZON LINE
OF DRAWING

Fig. 5-9

Fig. 5-9 Outline figures at various distances from the viewer. To begin drawing one of these figures, determine where you want its feet to be. Then use the proportions shown in figure 5-4 to help you draw a well-proportioned figure between the horizon line and the desired location of its feet. After some practice, you will be able to draw these figures quickly.

Fig. 5-10 The beginning of a design study in perspective. The figures are used to quickly determine comparative sizes of nearby forms and spaces.

Fig. 5-10

Fig. 5-11

Fig. 5-11 An additional layer of design exploration. The figure was used to help approximate the correct size of the decorative pots.

Fig. 5-12

Fig. 5-12 Gestural figures are located and manipulated to determine how they may best interact with the surroundings.

Fig. 5-13

Fig. 5-14

Fig. 5-15

Fig. 5-13 The figures are refined in proportion, gesture, clothing elements, and detail on a subsequent layer of tracing paper.

Fig. 5-14 The layer of tracing paper with the rough gestural figures was removed, and the combination was traced a final time with a **Micron 005** pen. The image was refined and edited in the process, with all the information on one sheet of white tracing paper.

Fig. 5-15 Shade and shadow were applied to the front of the final line drawing, and pastel and color pencil were first applied to the designed elements on the back of the sheet.

Fig. 5-16 The completed drawing. The palette of colors used for the designed elements was also used for the figures.

Fig. 5-16

AUTOMOBILES

Architects and landscape architects frequently find themselves in the position of having to draw automobiles. Being able to do so is an indispensable skill when design ideas must be illustrated within realistic outdoor contexts.

Cars are not difficult to draw. Begin by taking care of first things first. An automobile traced from a photograph frequently does not look "quite right" because the car does not conform to the perspective of the drawing it is traced into. When drawing an automobile from scratch, draw a scale person or persons directly beside or in front of the place where you intend to locate an automobile. Then, when you draw simple box shapes that are the approximate sizes of the lower and upper parts of the automobile, you can both judge (by referencing the figure) how large the automobile should be *and* make sure that it conforms to the perspective of the drawing (5-17). You can do this by drawing the boxes using vanishing points that are located on the drawing's horizon line. The scale figure(s) also allows you to estimate the proportions of the automobile— width to length to height—as well as approximate the distance between the front and back wheels.

Once the basic box shapes are in place, draw an automobile shape that stays within the confines of the boxes (5-18). You will find it much easier to draw using photographic references to help you with the proportions of the basic shapes, rather than attempting to rely on memory. If your drawings of automobiles are large enough, you can create their final version freehand. However, if the drawings are small, a french curve and ellipse templates can be helpful when drawing them in their final version (5-19), as lines that are too shaky can make the cars appear wrinkled and dented. Remember to use a minimum of detail on the cars, so the attention of the viewer remains on the designed elements within the drawing.

An illustrated step-by-step process for drawing automobiles in the middle ground is shown in figures 5-17 through 5-21. The steps used to draw more distant automobiles are shown in figures 5-22 through 5-24.

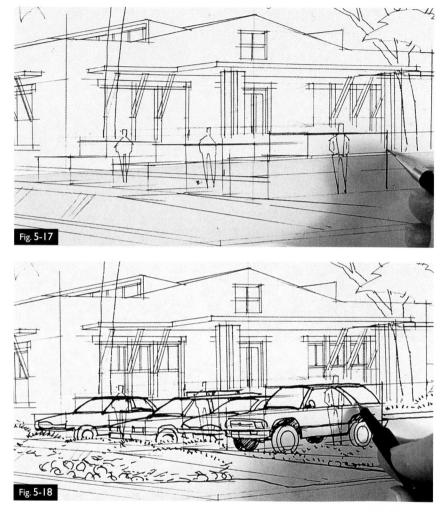

Fig. 5-17

Fig. 5-18

Fig. 5-17 To begin, the automobiles were laid out along with the layout of the design ideas. Human figures were placed at the proposed locations of the automobiles, so a comparative element could be used to quickly size them. The upper and lower forms of the automobiles were initially drawn as simple stacked boxes. The vanishing points for the vehicles were located on the same horizon line used for the rest of the drawing. In fact, in this illustration the vanishing points for the automobiles are the same as those used to draw the building.

Fig. 5-18 The automobiles were quickly shaped from the box-shaped guides. Photographs were used—not traced, but for information—to guide the creation of the shapes.

Fig. 5-19

Fig. 5-19 On a fresh sheet of white tracing paper, the final line drawing was made. In this illustration, the trees, building, and plant materials were drawn freehand with a Micron 005 pen. However, the cars were traced using a french curve and a straightedge. This makes the subtle curved lines of a car much easier to draw and gives it a smoother, more machinelike look. As few lines as possible were used. The wheels were drawn with a small-ellipse template (Pickett, No. 12631), because credible wheels are difficult to draw freehand.

Fig. 5-20

Fig. 5-20 The final line drawing was photocopied onto Bristol paper. *Cool Grey #3 (Cool Grey 30%)* marker was used for the windshields, and *Black* marker was used for silhouetted seats, headrests, and the heavily tinted back windows of the foremost vehicle. Marker base colors were then applied to the car bodies. Any believeable color will do. Often, the body colors of automobiles are the same as those used elsewhere in the illustration so that the cars appear to "belong" to the color scheme when the illustration is complete.

Fig. 5-21

Fig. 5-21 *Black* marker was applied to the lower parts of the plastic bumpers, the wheel wells, and the far tires (seen in silhouette) of the closest vehicle. *Cool Grey #7 (Cool Grey 70%)* marker was applied to the closer tires.

Cool Greys #9, #5, #3, and *#1 (Cool Greys 90%, 50%, 30%,* and *10%)* markers were used to create the diffuse shadows beneath the vehicles. A *Cool Grey #1 (Cool Grey 10%)* marker was also applied to the asphalt parking lot surface, then flavored with a *Cloud Blue* pencil.

The concrete curb in the background and the foreground walkway were colored with *French Grey 10%* marker and flavored with a *Light Peach* pencil.

Swipes of *White* pencil were applied to the upward-facing surfaces of the cars—hoods, roofs, and windshields. A *Deco Aqua* pencil was then used to lightly wash the windshields, followed by the *White* pencil for highlights.

Fig. 5-22 Fig. 5-22 Once the surroundings were drawn for these distant automobiles, figures were positioned where automobiles were to be located. The figures and the automobiles use the same horizon line (and, again in this case, the same vanishing points) as used for the buildings. This ensured that the automobiles would appear "level" and in visual agreement with the building. The figures were used for comparative scale in drawing the first forms of the cars. Note that the foremost cars (light red) were fully drawn, from roof to wheels. The cars beyond, however, were only partially drawn—mostly as roofs and windows. Photographs were used for reference as necessary.

Fig. 5-23 Fig. 5-23 The roughly drawn automobiles were traced onto the overlay, edited for perspective, and simplified. Because these cars are more numerous and more distant than the middle-ground cars, they were drawn freehand with a Micron 005 pen. As few lines as possible were used, and the strokes were made quickly to keep the lines smooth.

The finished illustration was photocopied onto Bristol paper. *Cool Grey #3 (Cool Grey 30%)* marker was used for the windshields, and various marker base colors were applied to the bodies. Note that the colors were kept somewhat muted so the viewer's attention would be drawn to the designed elements.

Fig. 5-24

Fig. 5-24 *Cool Grey #7 (Cool Grey 70%)* marker was applied to the illuminated tires, and *Black* marker was added to the wheel wells, seats, headrests, and those tires that appear in silhouette. *Cool Grey #9 and #5 (Cool Grey 90% and 50%)* markers were used to add diffuse shadows beneath the cars. Note how this shadow "anchors" the cars to the ground.

Streaks of *White* pencil were applied to upward-facing surfaces and wind-shields. *Poppy Red* pencil was added to the taillights. *Celadon Green* pencil was used to flavor the color of the window glass. The widespread use of this color helps to tie the cars together visually, as a mass.

Pale Indigo (Cloud Blue) marker was

added to the hubcaps, and a blend of *French Grey 10%* and *Cool Grey #1 (Cool Grey 10%)* markers was used to create the mottled color of the asphalt parking lot.

PRESENTATION

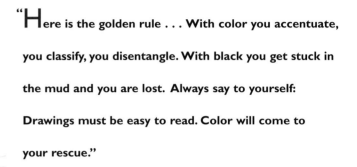

"**H**ere is the golden rule . . . With color you accentuate, you classify, you disentangle. With black you get stuck in the mud and you are lost. Always say to yourself: Drawings must be easy to read. Color will come to your rescue."

| *Le Corbusier*

COLOR AND COMPOSITION IN ILLUSTRATION

When you begin to think about how to use color as part of the *composition* of an illustration, it should be considered in two ways. First, consider how the colors can be related to one another. Then consider what role color plays in the composition as a whole. As you will see in this chapter, these two ways of thinking about color are both important when you attempt a color presentation drawing.

You may also notice that there are no extended discussions of color "schemes" in this chapter. Such schemes of color as "complementary," "analogous," "triadic," and so on are actually predicated on arrangements of hues only. It is rare that the designer has the luxury of selecting the hues for a project—or its illustration—without constraint. In most situations, at least some of the hues you must work with on a project are usually pre-selected, owing to the range of color found in the natural materials destined for the project, the preferences of the client, or perhaps because certain colors already exist in the project, as often happens with remodel work.

This chapter introduces you to the idea that *any* arrangement of hues can be made to "go together" and that successful color design drawing for presentation depends on the designer's skill at orchestrating all three dimensions of color within the illustration as a whole. The discussion that follows is an overview of the approach to color and drawing composition we frequently use at CommArts when developing color design illustrations and working with illustrators. You may find it helpful to think of this overview as a checklist to use when you develop your own color design drawings for presentation.

There are a number of illustrations in this chapter that have been created by professional illustrators. Although the media they use differ somewhat from those used in the rest of the book, it matters little, because the principles of color and pictorial composition these illustrations so exquisitely manifest can be created in many kinds of color media.

How Colors Relate to One Another: The Contrast of Colors

The relationships between colors are established by the similarities and differences that are created in their dimensions of hue, value, and chroma. These relationships can be described as degrees of *contrast*. As you know, when you experience contrast, you perceive differences in a quality of a thing. These differences can range from subtle variation to the maximum of opposites. For example, the temperature of an object may be hot in one area, cool in another. Its texture may be smooth, rough, or of several possible variations between the two extremes.

The same holds true for color. In Chapter 1, you saw that *each* of the three dimensions of color also had a range of possible expression. The chroma of an object's color can range from weak to strong; its value may be anything from very dark to very light—or its surface may gradate from one value to another. It may be of a single hue or made up of several hues that are similar—or are, perhaps, very different from one another.

The first systematic exploration of the differences in the qualities and dimensions of color expressed as contrast is credited to Johannes Itten. He was a master at the Bauhaus, where he conducted courses in color from 1919 to 1938. Itten formulated an approach to color study that expressed its qualities as seven kinds of color contrast: contrast of hue, light-dark contrast, cold-warm contrast, complementary contrast, simultaneous contrast, contrast of saturation, and contrast of extension (Itten 1973). Itten's book, *The Art of Color,* remains a classic in color instruction to this day.

The designers at CommArts also work with color in terms of its contrasts, but primarily as an expression of contrasts that occur within its three dimensions—contrast of hue, contrast of value, and contrast of chroma. *It is how these*

Fig. 6-1   This watercolor rendering of the San Diego Exposition was made for architect Bertram Goodhue by Birch Burdette Long sometime before 1915. It is an exquisite example of the classic approach to rendering exterior views of buildings. Long used a wide variety of hues, as well as a full range of values, for the colors in the illustration. The chromas of the colors, however, are limited to the very weak end of the chroma scale. (Illustration: Birch Burdette Long)

Fig. 6-1

contrasts are orchestrated that determine the expressive direction of not only the colors used for a project, but also the color illustrations used to communicate the project's various aspects.

Although these three color contrasts are discussed separately in the paragraphs that follow for the sake of clarity, you will generally experience these contrasts all at the same time when you look at a composition of colors. When a designer selects the colors for an interior color scheme, for example, he limits the range of contrasts of certain dimensions of the colors while allowing other dimensions a greater range of contrast. By judiciously selecting *which* dimensions are limited in contrast and to *where* in the range of possibility they are limited, he will determine the expressive direction of the color scheme. Further, it is the imposition of these limitations on the possible ranges of hue, value, and chroma contrast in a color scheme that helps to unify it by introducing a level of order. For example, an illustration of a building's exterior, including its site and context, may have a wide range of hue owing to the variety of building materials, plant materials, and sky. Its colors may range from very dark to very light in value, as certain parts are in shade while others are in sun. To introduce a level of visual order to the scheme of colors, the designer may choose to limit the contrast in chroma of the colors to within a narrow, relatively weak range. This allows the illustration to have interest and *punch,* but also imposes a degree of order resulting from the common level of chroma shared by the colors (6-1).

Hue Contrast

The contrast between hues can range from subtle to dramatic. Look at the color wheel in figure 6-2. You will notice a relationship between any hue you happen to select and the hues on either side of it. If you choose purple blue, for example, you see that it is related to both its neighbors, purple and blue. Green yellow and yellow red both contain a measure of yellow. Side-by-side hues on the color wheel contrast little with each other and are called *analogous hues* (6-3). The farther away hues are from each other on the color wheel, the more they contrast. The strongest contrast in hue, of course, occurs when hues are diametrically opposed on the color wheel—red and blue green, for example (6-4). Hues that occur opposite each other are called *complementary hues.*

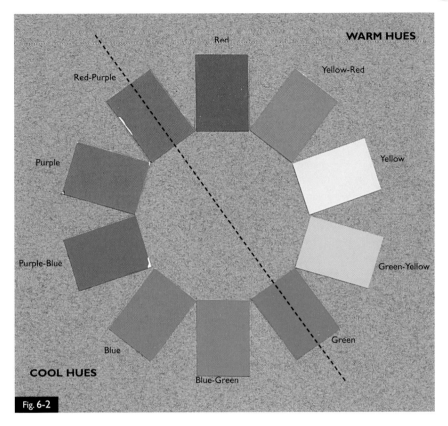

Fig. 6-2

Fig. 6-2 The color wheel. Every color wheel has a warm side and a cool side. On this particular wheel, the hues green and red purple form the dividing line between the warm and cool hues and can themselves be made either warm or cool.

Fig. 6-3

Fig. 6-3 Analogous hues red, yellow red, yellow, and green yellow are predominant in this illustration. Note that in the analogous color scheme for the building, the grays are actually very weak-chroma yellow. The hue yellow has been mixed, in varying amounts, into most of the colors used in the drawing.

Fig. 6-4 This simple cut-paper exercise shows what happens when a color composition has a wide range of hue contrast and the values and chromas of the colors are held consistent. In this example, the values of the colors are limited to the very high range, and their chromas are limited to a weak range. The color in the center is a neutral gray.

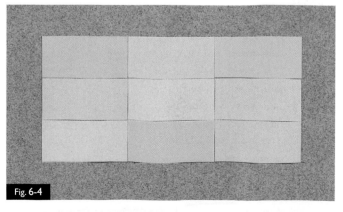

Fig. 6-4

Simultaneous Contrast

Complementary hues are so named because they enhance or "complement" each other. Red makes blue green look its "blue greenest," and vice versa. Green yellow most enhances the hue purple. In fact, the *Munsell System* hue arrangements are based on this phenomenon. Each hue is placed opposite its *visual* complement on the Munsell color wheel. When you see a color, your built-in perceptual faculties conjure up its complement. To experience this in its most obvious form, gaze at an intense color under good lighting for about a minute, then shift your gaze to a neutral surface of white or gray. You will experience an *afterimage* of the colored shape in its *complementary* color (6-5). For the same reason, if you look at a color and a neutral gray together, the gray will be tinged with the complement of the color with which it is seen (6-6). This effect is called *simultaneous contrast*. Likewise, when *any* two colors are placed together, each subtly influences the other by its presence. You can imagine, then, the variety of subtle color interactions that might occur when a viewer looks at an entire painting, illustration, or built composition. *Every arrangement of colors creates unique affiliations and tensions, depending on the amounts, qualities, and proximities of the colors in the arrangement.* This phenomenon has special meaning for designers of places, in that each intended arrangement of colors should be studied, first inexpensively on paper, then eventually mocked-up in its finished location as construction nears an end.

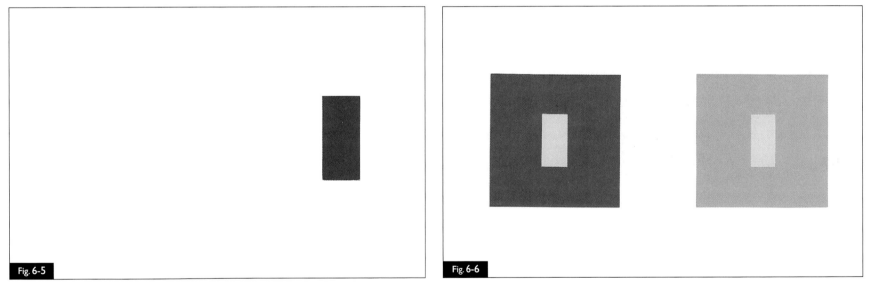

Fig. 6-5

Fig. 6-6

Fig. 6-5 Look at the red rectangle from about six inches away, under a fairly bright light, for about 30 seconds. As your eyes become accustomed to the red, they will begin to generate its complementary color, blue green. As you continue to look, the rectangle's edges will seem to fluoresce with an "aura" of blue green as your eyes make small movements. If you move your gaze about an inch to the side, you will see how the afterimage, still partially covering the red, begins to dull the red!

After about a minute, shift your gaze completely away from the red to the blank white area to the left. In a second or two, the afterimage, roughly in the rectangular shape, will fluoresce blue green for five to ten seconds before it fades away.

Fig. 6-6 The gray rectangles in the centers of the colored squares are exactly the same. Use a fairly bright light as you look from one square to the other from about six inches away for about a half minute. Each gray rectangle will become tinged with the complementary color of the square it is within.

Warm-Cool Contrast

A color wheel can be divided into halves, with warm colors on one side and cool colors on the other. On the Munsell color wheel, this division happens along a line formed between the complementary hues green and red purple (6-2). These two hues can be adjusted to become either warm or cool (6-7). *Warm colors* are so named because they are associated with the colors emitted from archetypal heat sources like fire or incandescent lamp filaments. They can also raise the perceived temperature of a place, subtly stimulate appetite, and increase a person's predisposition to outgoing behavior. *Cool colors* are associated with things cool, such as the color of north sky light seen on objects in the shade. Cool colors can lower the perceived temperature of a place and have a quieting effect as they subtly influence the occupants of a place to become more introverted. Warm-colored objects seem to advance toward the viewer and appear more figural in a composition (6-8), whereas cool colors are more passive and seem to recede. These principles are particularly important tools in the creation of spatial effects in an illustration (see figure 1-5).

Fig. 6-7 The hues red purple *(above)* and green *(below)* occur on the dividing line between warm and cool hues on the color wheel. The cool (slightly bluish) versions of both hues appear on the left, and the warm (slightly yellow-reddish) versions appear on the right.

Fig. 6-8 Note how the straightforward arrangement of the warm and cool hues in this illustration create not only a startling image of the building, but one with a very clear center of interest. The strength of this view is assisted by the arrangement of the major value groupings, whereby the subject building and the sky immediately beyond are the lightest values in the composition and everything else grades darker from there. In addition, the hue and value arrangements are believable in that they could be those encountered in an early morning sunrise. (Illustration: Douglas E. Jamieson)

Fig. 6-8

Value Contrast

Contrasting the values of colors is one of the most powerful ways to establish the impact of a color composition. Like the other dimensions of color, the values of the colors of a composition can range widely or can be limited to a particular location on the scale of light to dark. If the range of values of the colors is limited to light values, the composition is said to be done in a *high key* (6-9). Likewise, if the colors of a composition are mostly in the low range of values, it is a *low-key* composition.

The contrast of value is also the most powerful ally you have in making the idea in a design illustration easily legible. The skillful handling of this kind of contrast can make the illustration more compelling at first glance, as well as more easily readable from a distance. A typical color design drawing created for pre-sentation purposes should be *built primarily on value contrast* for its legibility and dramatic impact. The color dimensions of hue and chroma are used to further enhance legibility while adding character and richness. There are, of course, exceptions to this principle, especially when you attempt to create a particular quality in an illustration that calls for less value contrast, such as in the high-key illustration shown in figure 6-9. However, you will notice that in their strongest, most dramatic design illustrations, professional illustrators in most cases not only use a *full range of values,* from very dark to very light, they also arrange these values in a way that most advantageously and legibly guides the eye to the focal point of the design idea. At the same time, they use these arrangements to create the illusion of spatial depth in the illustration (6-10)! You will be introduced to an approach to creating these value arrangements in Chapter 7. A dramatic

Fig. 6-9 This illustration gives an example of restraint in the value and chroma dimensions of the colors used. Although the hues are analogous—red, yellow red, yellow, and green yellow—with complementary accents of purple blue in the shade and shadow, note how an overtone of the hue yellow informs all the other colors.

The values of the colors are limited to a very high range, and the chromas are restrained to the weak end of the scale.

Through the careful arrangement of its colors, the illustrator creates a powerful composition that allows the viewer to almost feel the bright sun, heat, and dust of Cairo, Egypt. (Illustration: Frank M. Costantino.)

Fig. 6-9

and thoughtful value arrangement not only gives a design illustration "punch," it provides for a more successful reproduction of the illustration in printed media, especially media with limited color or with only black-and-white reproductions, such as a newspaper.

Yet it is this very reason that certain kinds of computer-generated design illustration seem overbusy, to the point of appearing frenetic. When these illustrations are created by importing imagery from other sources, such as signing, figures, automobiles, skies, and backgrounds, they exhibit a wide variety of hues, values, and chromas. Such illustrations have a collagelike quality because that is the way they are composed.

6-10

Fig. 6-10 This illustration embodies many, if not most, of the color and composition ideas presented in this chapter. The vertical format, the repeated vertical forms, the location of the horizon line, and the use of color all work together to create a composition that is stunning in its impact.

The values of the colors range from almost black to touches of pure white. However, you need only to squint slightly to realize that the various areas of the illustration are carefully assigned groups of similar values, which not only help to frame the illustration, but also create a strong focus and sense of spatial depth within. To be sure, other contrasts of value occur within the illustration, but the illustrator took care to see that none of the minor contrasts were so strong or demanding that they compete with the impact of the major value groupings.

The hues used in the illustration come from all parts of the color wheel, and although the warm hues predominate, they are intermixed with each other *and* with the cool hues to produce many subtle and sophisticated colors.

The chromas of the colors are held to a relatively weak range throughout and act as a unifying agent for the composition. (Illustration: Thomas W. Schaller)

Chroma Contrast

The chromas of the colors in a composition can range from very weak—almost pure gray—to very strong and vibrant (6-11). The way chroma is orchestrated, as with hue and value, can help determine the emotional impact of the composition. Strong-chroma colors are stimulating to most people, connoting excitement and activity. In our culture, we often see a higher proportion of strong-chroma colors associated with places for children, retail establishments, and entertainment (6-12). Medium-to-weak-chroma colors are more frequently associated with places in which people spend longer periods of time, such as residences and offices. These kinds of color are also generally perceived as more relaxed, calm, serene, upscale, and sophisticated.

You will find that the colors of most exterior design drawings and illustrations are in the middle-to-weak chroma range, inasmuch as this is the chroma range of most natural materials. You have seen what happens to man-made materials left outdoors, as sun and weather conspire to bleach colors to their most grayed versions. Consequently, building designers often choose colors for the man-made materials and finishes on building exteriors that are sympathetic to these natural colors. Color drawings of many kinds of interior places are also in the middle to weak chroma range, particularly given our culture's propensities for colors in this range of chroma. However, accents of strong-chroma color are often found in illustrations of both interior and exterior views, not only because these accents tend to balance large areas of weaker-chroma colors, but because we enjoy strong-chroma colors in small doses (6-13). Such doses usually appear in our drawings in small, subordinate areas. They also often appear in our lives within small segments of time—in those things that are relatively short-lived, such as flower masses, clothing, walls, or pieces of furniture, whose colors can be easily changed as we tire of them.

Fig. 6-11

Fig. 6-11 This cut-paper exercise illustrates a color scheme with a limited range of hues (yellow through red purple) and strictly limited values, but the chromas of the colors are unrestricted and range from very weak to very strong.

Compare the impact of this color composition to that in figure 6-4.

Fig. 6-12

Fig. 6-12 This strong-chroma color design drawing perfectly captures the spirit of the casino entry it is intended to conceptually illustrate.

The designer created this illustration by first reproducing a line drawing on a color photocopier, using a setting that reverses the values—all black lines became white, and the white background became black. Because the resultant output image of a color photocopier is too slick to draw on, the image was photocopied onto bond paper on an ordinary black-and-white photocopier. Strong-chroma color pencil and white gouache were then applied to the bond copy. Once colored, the illustration was enlarged as it was color photocopied, then spliced together to create a large presentation-size image. See Chapter 8 for further discussion of color drawing enlargement. (Drawing: Bryan Gough)

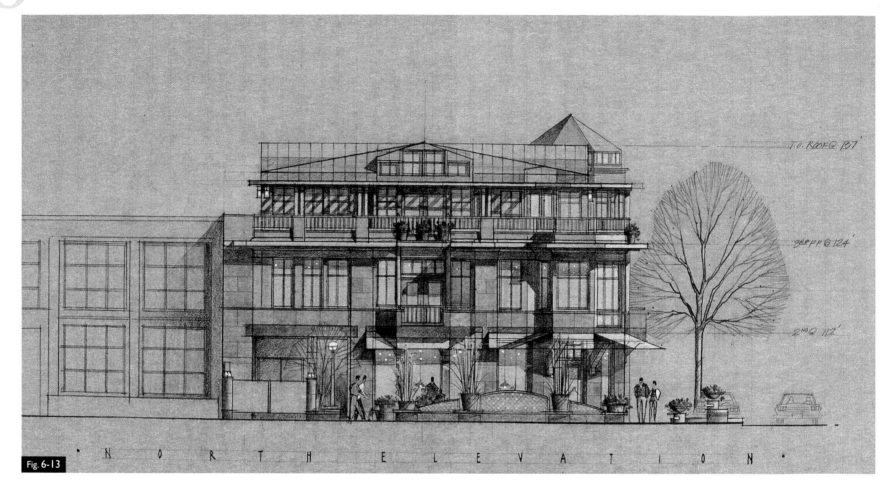

Fig. 6-13

Fig. 6-13 The colors of the roof and stucco on the third-level walls, column bases, and curb have a similar "weathered" look that is sympathetic, albeit in different hues, to that of the stone on the lower part of the building.

The warm gray stucco and gray-green roof were held to a similar value to that of the stone, and the chromas of the colors of the stucco and roof are even somewhat weaker than those of the stone, helping to feature it slightly.

Note the balancing effect the smaller accents of strong-chroma colors of the potted flowers, the figures' clothing, and the tiled fountain wall have on the overall composition.

COLOR CONTRAST AND IMAGE COMPOSITION

All illustrations that attempt to manifest a three-dimensional view on a two-dimensional surface—whether that surface is paper or a computer screen—are created with four basic visual elements. Line, shape, color, and texture must be arranged in the most effective way to create images of form, space, light, and materials.

Most color design drawings are created as vehicles to communicate design ideas. The viewer of a design drawing typically looks "into" the drawing to find the design information, whether it is a plan, elevation, axonometric, or perspective view. This information is usually made up of smaller, individuated ideas that have been assembled to form the illustration. A perspective view, for example, shows the designer's ideas about the floor plane—its variations in level, its finishes, the furnishings that might rest on it; the wall plane—its penetrations, its materials and finishes, shelving and cabinetry; and the ceiling plane—its fixtures, its penetrations, its variations in height, its colors and finishes, and so on. This view assembles these many ideas into a single drawing, often giving the designer her first view of how a multitude of ideas and decisions appear in concert. It also allows viewers to participate in the assessment of these ideas.

You will find, however, that during your career as a designer there will be many times when you want to create illustrations of your ideas that go beyond the simple delivery of design information. You will want to present this design information in the most effective way. This means you must shift your perception and begin to look "at" your drawings as graphic compositions, not only "into" them for the information they contain.

When you prepare a color drawing to present design information in this way, you must take into account the perceptual habits and needs of the viewer and understand the way in which he responds to various kinds of visual organization (Feldman 1987). However, each illustration is unique, so an approach that creates the most effective presentation in one situation may not be appropriate for another. Instead, it is more effective to begin each new presentation-level illustration by evaluating the opportunities and constraints that the subject matter presents to the designer. This part of the present chapter, as well as the first part of Chapter 7, introduces you to design principles that, when realized, can help you create more effective, dramatic, and satisfying design presentation drawings in color. These principles—unity, balance, proportion, and rhythm—reflect our innate perceptual needs and are common to all the representative graphic arts. Use them to evaluate your approach to color in your illustrations as you proceed. It is worth noting the degree to which these principles interrelate as each contributes to the visual order of the image.

A Unified Image

Unity is the design principle that is concerned with how an image will be seen *as a whole*. It is considered by some designers to be the only principle of pictorial composition, toward which all others work in support.

Effective color drawing for the purposes of presentation really begins upstream from the application of color. It starts with the initial compositional decisions the designer makes in regard to the underlying skeleton of the illustration, the line drawing. Many of these decisions are simple and easy, but only if the designer addresses them at the outset.

It is worth deciding, before you invest the time (and fee), whether a presentation drawing is needed or a quick sketch can serve the purpose. If a presentation drawing *is* justified, make sure you are clear about the purpose of the illustration and what exactly it must communicate. The line drawing that is generated initially is really the armature that shapes the image and determines its degree of impact. The time spent developing a well-composed line drawing will prove to have been worthwhile when you are ready to arrange its values, color, and effects of light.

For example, a simple and often overlooked consideration is the drawing format. Format is the orientation of the page: vertical, oblong, or square. A horizontal, or oblong, format can help a picture with a horizontal emphasis to appear more at home on the page. A vertical format can do the same for a vertically oriented subject, such as a high-rise building. Note the contribution of the picture's format to its impact in figures 6-8 and 6-18.

Another consideration is the location of the picture's horizon. The horizon is usually placed above or below the center of the picture, inasmuch as bisecting the picture with the horizon may give the composition a static quality. If you place the horizon high in the picture, more ground plane will show. This approach is particularly good if you have a large amount of information to communicate about the ground or floor plane, such as that found in an aerial or "bird's-eye" perspective view (6-14). However, a high horizon may burden the

Fig. 6-14 In this illustration the horizon line is above the picture and off the page by a significant distance, resulting in the aerial perspective, or "bird's-eye" view, shown. Views of this kind are particularly good for communicating forms, spaces, and plan relationships (such as circulation) simultaneously, especially to viewers unfamiliar with the conventions of plan views.

As a general rule of graphic design, diagonal lines introduced into a picture are more dynamic than those that run orthogonally. Note the degree to which this effect influences the view shown here.

It is also worth noting how the color is arranged in this illustration. The yellow-red roofs immediately dominate your attention. The larger roof in the upper center is balanced by the smaller roof in the lower left. Note, too, that although the cooler hues of green, blue green, blue, purple blue, and purple are dominant in terms of area, yellow has been repeatedly mingled with green to create many areas of green yellow. Moreover, the yellow red used on the roofs has been mingled into many of the other areas of the illustration, including the tree canopies. Likewise, the purple and purple blue of the shadows have also been mingled into many areas. As you can see in this and other illustrations in this chapter, mingling is another way to unify an illustration and create balance between the warm and cool hues.

Fig. 6-14

The picture gets darker toward its edges, particularly its bottom edge. This helps to keep the viewer's attention focused on the center of interest within the illustration. (Illustration: Douglas E. Jamieson)

unsuspecting illustrator of a single building exterior, for example, with having to illustrate more ground plane elements than she planned. A low horizon creates the opposite condition, with less ground plane and more sky or ceiling showing. It also provides the conditions for more dramatic perspective in drawing tall structures, such as those shown in figures 6-16 and 6-18.

Most designers and illustrators unify their drawings simply by making one feature dominate the viewer's attention, while other features are subordinate to the *dominant* feature. This is usually done by establishing a focus or center of interest in the picture—a dominant idea, form or group of forms, or space. This is the reason it is important to be very clear initially as to the purpose of the illustration, because without clarity of purpose, it is difficult to decide on its focus. The features of secondary or *subordinate* interest are arranged in visual support of the center of interest. For example, a view may be so arranged that the perspective lines of secondary elements lead the viewer's eye, usually gradually or indirectly, toward the center of interest.

Your arrangement of color contrasts can play a significant role in unifying the image. It may be that certain of the most vivid contrasts of the colors—for exam-ple, value contrast—occur within the center of interest and thereby help to hold the viewer's attention there (6-16). Ironically, the slight diminution of the contrasts of the colors throughout a composition can also help to unify a color design drawing. You can see this effect, called "mingling" of colors, in many works of fine art—particularly impressionist paintings—as well as in professional design illustrations (6-15). Stated simply, all colors used in the illustration are used in almost all parts of the illustration, but in differing amounts. For example, color pencil used in one part of a drawing may be used to flavor the colors of several other parts of the drawing. If this idea is repeated with many of the pencils used to color the drawing, the drawing begins to take on a more complex and interesting, as well as somewhat more muted, coloration. You can notice the unifying effects of this approach to color in many of the illustrations in this chapter and throughout the book.

The overall value arrangement plays a critical role in unifying the picture image of a presentation drawing. Many small, disparate patches of dark and light in a drawing or computer illustration can fragment its overall impression, unnecessarily distracting the viewer from seeing the ideas within as adding up to a whole or sum that is greater than its parts. Illustrations that have a pur-

Fig. 6-15

Fig. 6-15 This illustration is an excellent example of the intermixture or "mingling" of warm and cool colors to unify the illustration and produce subtle but lively colors as a result. The hues, taken from the yellow-red, green, and purple-blue regions of the color wheel, form an approximate *triad* that, when mixed with one another, create subtle, more neutral colors. However, the colors created by these mixtures are far more interesting and lively than any single colors that may have been used. (Illustration: Ronald J. Love)

poseful, overall arrangement of its *major* value groups are easier to understand and deliver a unified impression to the viewer (6-16). Developing your skill in arranging the major value groups of a presentation drawing is a critical part of successful presentation drawing; this subject is covered further in Chapter 7.

Although there are different kinds of color contrast in an illustration, some of the most vivid occurring within or on behalf of steering the viewer's attention to the center of interest, remember that these contrasts can occur only if they have a foil or background that allows them to be seen. Often, a consistent level in the chroma of the colors (usually on the weaker end of the scale of possibility) in an illustration not only helps to provide a foil against which accents of stronger chroma color can be perceived, but this consistent dimension is yet another means of unifying the illustration (6-17).

Fig. 6-16

Fig. 6-16 The illustrator of this image has marshaled a full range of values, from black to white, to create a very powerful image. The darkest range of values is utilized in the foreground, and a medium range is used for the background; the very lightest values are saved for the center of interest. Note, too, that the strongest value *contrasts* also occur here, between the focal point and its surroundings.

Even though, when squinting at this illustration, you see the values arranged in major groupings, there is still sufficient contrast within each grouping that its features and figures remain discernible.

Once again, as in many of the other illustrations in this chapter, the minglings and gradations of the colors help to unify the composition. (Illustration: Thomas W. Schaller)

Stainless steel tenant signing on polished stainless steel bar—uplit from lights mounted above curved "brow".
5th Street View of
GAS COMPANY TOWER
"brow" and pop-
indows for more
on the street
Beautiful polished metal identity plaque for tenants; top is internally illuminated

Fig. 6-17

Fig. 6-17 Although this study is composed mostly of weak-chroma colors, the strong-chroma accents are more noticeable because of them. This chroma contrast helps to keep the viewer's attention on the proposed display windows—the purpose of the illustration.

This drawing was created by applying marker and color pencil to a photocopy of a line drawing on Canson paper.

Introducing Balance

Each picture we see we perceive, whether consciously or not, on a visual scale somewhere between balanced and unbalanced. "Size, shape, color, 'temperature' and texture are experienced as if they are heavy or light, solid or transparent, floating or sinking. Also, there is no doubt that colors and textures can tip the optical scales we carry inside our heads. An artist who doesn't know about those scales is trying to walk with one leg" (Feldman 1987, 241).

Balance in pictures can be easily accomplished by using the device of *symmetry,* whereby the handling of the visual elements on one side of the picture is matched by that on the other side, whether horizontal or vertical. Symmetrical compositions lend an air of precision and order to an illustration and are useful for views of formal gardens, rooms, or building entries. Yet they can make a picture appear static if your intent is a greater degree of dynamism. For that reason, the majority of illustration compositions are *asymmetrical* and achieve balance through less obvious means. Asymmetrical balance is often approached through "leverage," whereby a substantial visual weight is counteracted by something much smaller, usually at some distance from the greater weight (6-18). The distance between the two acts as a "lever arm," balancing the weights much as objects are balanced in physics. "Although gravity does not actually operate on the objects in paintings, we perceive them *as if* it does" (Feldman 1987, 241).

Fig. 6-18 The illustrator says, "This particular image was designed expressly as a piece where pure color, rather than tonal value or representation of shape, was intended as the primary compositional device. Tangible elements of earth and man-made objects are expressed in warm tones of red and gold while atmospheric elements—sky and water—are treated in cooler shades of green and blue." Note how he has arranged the image so that the warm and cool colors are distributed in a way that balances the illustration.

You will also find that the value composition of the illustration is, nevertheless, in balance. The foreground cliff and the darkened water at the bottom of the illustration visually balance the larger mass of the structure sweeping to the upper left, grading darker as it does so. (Illustration: Thomas W. Schaller)

Fig. 6-18

Balance can be created by the way the artist stimulates and guides the interest of the viewer. Smaller areas that pique our curiosity can balance the larger areas in a composition. Color is often used to this end. Large areas of one color or a group of related colors are often balanced with a small, vivid "accent" of a similar color or one from the opposite side of the color wheel (6-19). For example, a composition made up of grayed blues and blue greens may be balanced by a touch of intense red in just the right location.

A Sense of Proportion

Proportion is the relationship of the *sizes* of the parts of a composition to one another and to the whole. Because there are no rules governing these relationships, they are largely dependent on the judgment of the artist or illustrator.

When you consider proportion, you are also considering the issue of balance. When the parts of an image seem to be in the right proportion to one

Fig. 6-19

Fig. 6-19 The small (in area) but vivid yellow red of the campfire helps to balance the weaker-chroma gray-green and green-yellow hues of the paper and applied color, respectively.

This study was made with color pencil and pastel (for the fire and smoke) applied to a photocopy of a line drawing on Canson paper.

another, you have a sense of balance. Symmetry, as mentioned in the discussion of balance, is based on equal proportions. When the subject of horizon line location was discussed, a composition having equal amounts of sky and ground was described as static. Better *proportions* of the picture might appear, for example, as one-third ground, two-thirds sky. When considering a vertical or horizontal format for an illustration, you must decide on the proportion of length to width of the picture. The Greeks derived what they considered the ideal proportions, called the *Golden Mean,* whereby the relationship of the smaller part to the larger part was the same as the larger part's relationship to the whole, or roughly 1:1.6. In whole numbers, this is 5:8. Throughout history, architects have used the Golden Mean to create height-to-width proportions for doorways, windows, and entire building facades. Artists have even used this proportion to format their pictures.

Proportion also applies to color. When is there too much of a certain color, not enough of another? What proportions seem balanced? Does the way the illustrator proportioned the colors in figure 6-14 give a sense of balance? When the issue of color is addressed in terms of proportion, you can think of it in terms of amount or *area.* In the previous discussion of unity, the terms *dominant* and *subordinate* were used to describe the degree to which parts of the illustration are intended to attract the viewer's attention. Here, these terms are used to describe the amount of area a particular color quality occupies in the composition. When a limited range of color dimensions are dominant (in terms of area) in a composition, it helps the picture to appear more coherent. For example, the preponderance (in area) of a particular hue in a picture—for instance, red, including the light reds and dark reds, the vivid reds and the grayed reds—will go a long way toward creating an image that appears unified (6-20). Likewise, the preponderance of other colors in the illustration whose dimensions are closely related will further help to unify the image. If most of the area of an illustration has colors that are mostly grayed, for example, a further level of unity is created. The same goes for the lightness/darkness of the colors in the illustration. Of course, the colors in this picture should contain areas of contrast in hue, lightness/darkness, and grayness/intensity as well (6-21). "When . . . similarities overpower contrasts, the result is boredom. When contrasts overpower similarities, the result is chaos. A successful design must avoid both these extremes" (Goldstein 1977, 216).

Fig. 6-20 This marker and color pencil drawing on a blackline print shows a preponderance of a yellow-red hue in the composition. Although the dominance of a particular hue helps to unify the image, closer inspection shows that the yellow red is more red in some places and more yellow in others. Such variation adds interest to the drawing and does not detract from the ability of this hue—or, more accurately, this close-knit group of hues—to unify the composition. Other hues, the green in particular, play a subordinate, balancing role. (Drawing: Henry Beer)

Fig. 6-20

Fig. 6-21

Fig. 6-21 Another way to unify an illustration with hue is to give it a certain hue "cast." This watercolor illustration uses a variety of hues—yellow red, green, purple blue, and purple. However, all colors have been infused with a yellow-reddish cast—even the green trees and the purple-blue sky. The effect not only gives this illustration the glow of a sunrise (or sunset), it also implies the relaxed and magical atmosphere of an oceanside retreat.

A similar effect can be created in illustrations that use the media covered in this book, by flavoring each color with pencils appropriate to the hue you wish to cast. (Illustration: Curtis James Woodhouse)

These are all questions of judgment not answered by a simple rule. Rather, the answers come from a consideration of the purpose of your illustration and your artistic and design intent. A landscape scene at dusk will, for example, be more likely to have a predominance of blue and blue-green hues than an illustration of an interior finished with natural wood (6-22).

Proportion is often confused with *scale*. Whereas proportion is concerned with the relationship of the sizes of things to one another, scale is the relationship of the sizes of things to *people*. Compositions meant to communicate ideas about places for people should include illustrated people, or at least human-scaled elements such as cars or furniture, so that the viewer can evaluate the ideas about a place, focused on those who must use it and live with it.

Fig. 6-22 This rendering from the 1920s shows a winter dusk scene created for the purpose of illustrating a residence. The predominant hue is purple blue—even the seemingly white snow is actually a very high-value, weak-chroma purple blue for the most part.

Notice how color has been used by the illustrator to push beyond mere illustration of a house. By arranging the house as a winter dusk scene, with cool and weak-chroma colors on the exterior and touches of warm, strong-chroma colors to imply the interior glow, the illustrator communicates the very essence of shelter—warm, protected, and secure against the elements. (Illustration: Edward Dixon McDonald)

Fig. 6-22

The Beat of the Rhythm

Rhythm helps to unify a pictorial composition by introducing flow and various kinds of repetition, whether of line, shapes, colors, or textures. Such repetition can be regular, irregular, or progressively changing. The gradations of value and color shown throughout this book, for example, introduce rhythm into the compositions by consistently repeating change of color or value—or both—across a surface.

Discrete areas of color can be used to introduce rhythm in a composition by positioning them in various parts of the picture repeatedly (6-23). Or a color can be woven more subtly through the composition by mingling it with the other colors, as mentioned earlier and illustrated in such examples as figures 6-15 and 6-21.

Repetition of limited ranges of the dimensions of the colors in an illustration, so that these limited ranges occupy a dominant portion of the illustration area, is another way of introducing rhythm. This is implicit in various other parts of this chapter, such as in the discussion of high-key and low-key illustrations. In figure 6-9, for example, the repeated quality of the various colors is their lightness of value. Note, too, the other qualities of the colors in this illustration that have been repeated. A yellow hue, for example, has been used in almost every area of the illustration, along with the other hues employed. Through the repeated use of certain color qualities, the illustration is quite successful in creating a clear and unified image.

If you are new to the idea of color and pictorial composition, the contents of this chapter may seem a bit overwhelming. If you have had previous experience with these ideas, you may find this chapter a good refresher. Whatever your level of experience in composition, one thing is certain: The more you work with these ideas when composing your own presentation drawings, the more familiar they will become. Before long, you will find that they are an integral part of your abilities as a designer and are applicable not only to design illustration, but to a wide range of design circumstances.

Fig. 6-23

Fig. 6-23 The same colors—yellow red, yellow, green yellow, and purple blue— occur repeatedly throughout this study drawing. By limiting your palette of colors, the rhythms created by repeated colors become unavoidable.

APPROACHES TO CREATING COLOR DESIGN DRAWINGS

This chapter discusses and illustrates a step-by-step process for creating various types of color design drawings. Some of the examples are simple illustrations of design ideas and were made quickly, and others were somewhat more carefully prepared for presentation purposes.

First, you will review some of the basic considerations useful for beginning a drawing, including how to prepare a line drawing, the creation of a value strategy, and how to transfer the line drawing to the paper you choose in order to make your final color illustration. The rest of the chapter shows the approaches we use at CommArts for creating color design drawings on the variety of useful papers first introduced in Chapter 2, how to include written information in these drawings, and how to revise and repair them.

THE FIRST CONSIDERATION: MAKE THE LINE DRAWING

Line is the most basic graphic convention used for creating images in the design professions. Whether a designer works by hand or on a computer, he is responsible for apprehending three-dimensional ideas on a two-dimensional surface, whether a sheet of paper or a computer screen. Line drawings also form the basis for the approach to color design drawing covered in this book.

At CommArts, we use both hand-generated perspective drawings and computer *setup* drawings. A quick, hand-drawn perspective sketch is often sufficient to communicate an early idea to a client and is frequently the most cost-effective approach in terms of fee. If orthographic drawings—plan, elevation, section—are being developed by computer and a perspective view is needed, a perspective line drawing, a setup, can be instantly generated by most computer programs, providing an adequate skeleton for a color design drawing, such as that in figure 7-17. However, scale elements, figures, furniture, and accessories are usually most easily added by hand. Quite often a perspective view of a design idea is also the most effective communication tool, as it is one of the few devices that can instantly show the *relationships* between the boundary planes of the space and its contents. An interior perspective study sketch, for example, may include walls, ceiling, floor, furnishings, and a first attempt at choosing materials and colors.

If an existing building or space is being remodeled, it is usually most effective to simply trace a photograph of the desired view after it has been adequately enlarged on a black-and-white or color photocopier. While tracing the photograph, the designer can add the design changes by hand, using the vanishing points and horizon line established by the photograph.

Sometimes it is most efficient to build a quick and simple scale study model of a particularly difficult view, either by computer or by hand. If the model is created by hand, remember to keep it simple, building only the necessary elements (7-10). A Polaroid picture can be taken of the model, which can then be enlarged on a black-and-white photocopier (or a color photocopier if better tonal resolution is needed) and traced to make a line drawing that includes the necessary additional detail (7-11).

Keep your line drawings small. Since the advent of high-quality color reproduction techniques, it is no longer necessary to create design drawings the size of a bed sheet. We typically create line drawings ranging from 8½" x 11" (letter size) to 11" x 17" (ledger size) and enlarge them during the photocopying process. Working at this size, the designer can create design drawings much faster and remain at a greater "distance" from the image, allowing her to keep an eye on the "big picture" and not get lost in the details. When line drawings are conceived at a small scale, it is important to keep your linework correspondingly *thin,* because photocopy enlargements enlarge *everything,* including line thickness. It is not necessary to use a hierarchy of line weights when making line drawings destined for color, inasmuch as the color—especially the value arrangements—will make the finished image legible.

We typically use a Micron 005 pen or a 4x0 technical pen for very small line drawings (7-18). The Micron works best on tracing paper, and the technical pen works best on drawing *vellum.* A *Black* Prismacolor pencil is another excellent line medium for these drawings; its line can be kept quite thin if the pencil is applied with the use of a straightedge (see figure 7-56). Although a *Black* Prismacolor can generate a rich, dark line similar to that of a felt-tipped pen, it has the advantage of being easily erasable. Use an electric eraser with the soft, white erasing strip intended for use on mylar. These line media can, of course, be mixed in a single drawing as necessary. Their common advantage is that they all reproduce well

when photocopied on a black-and-white copier. Graphite pencil can also be used when necessary and can be combined with other line media. However, graphite pencil does not photocopy as well as the line media mentioned earlier, unless it is soft or is applied with sufficiently firm hand pressure.

Color Sketch or Presentation Drawing?

Most situations in the earlier parts of the design process do not require the designer to plan the perspective views he uses to communicate his design ideas, beyond making sure that the image includes the information he intends to convey. The edges of this view may simply fade away or may be delineated by a rectangular boundary that defines the edges of the picture more uniformly.

However, you have found that there are occasions during the design process—most frequently in the latter parts of concept development through the design development phase of a project—when you want your illustration, whether created by hand or computer, to convey your ideas with more visual impact.

When you intend to create greater impact with your color design drawings, it does not mean you have to spend significantly more time making the drawing in an attempt to attain the perfection of a rendering. Instead, you must look at your drawing in a different way. Rather than only looking *into* the drawing for design information, you must also begin to look *at* the drawing as a graphic composition in its own right.

The ideas introduced in Chapter 6—unity, balance, proportion, and rhythm—can be brought to bear as you create your line drawing, in deciding on issues such as format, horizon location, symmetry, and scale. These ideas will continue to inform your drawing in various other ways as you apply the color media, as illustrated by the examples in Chapter 6 and later in this chapter. However, there is another important compositional issue worth considering when creating a line drawing for presentation purposes.

Layers of Space

When you look at the work of professional design illustrators, you may notice that there are objects and elements that appear quite close to the viewer and, depending on whether the view is an interior or exterior, objects and elements in the distance as well. The focus of the illustration is usually found between these close and distant components. In other words, the illustration has a foreground, a middle ground, and a background. This layering of space creates, in the words of William Kirby Lockard, FAIA, considerably more "spatial interest," because the various objects and elements between the foreground and distance successively and partially obscure one another.

This spatial situation differs from typical design drawings that have little or nothing behind or in front of the subject of the drawing. To be sure, there is nothing wrong with the typical design drawing, as it can be created quickly and efficiently communicates the essentials of the design idea. Drawings with foreground and background take slightly longer to create, but tend to have more impact inasmuch as that is how we see the world, more contextual information is communicated, and more opportunities are provided for a strategic arrangement of the major value groups of the drawing.

The first step in creating layers of space in an illustration is to select your view. Walk your plan in your imagination, as a photographer might, mentally composing views of the part or parts you intend to illustrate. You can turn from side to side, zoom in or pull back for a wider, more inclusive shot. Usually, by including some foreground feature or element in your view, you may ensure more opportunities for creating visual impact when you begin the value studies (7-1, 7-2). The feature or element may be an architectural element, furnishings, plant materials, or figures—or a combination. Except for figures, the elements shown in the illustration should either exist or be proposed, because to add gratuitous elements to a design drawing solely for the purposes of picture composition can be misleading.

Fig. 7-1a

Fig. 7-1b

Fig. 7-1 Line drawings of a conceptual view for a restaurant. Figure 7-1(a) shows how the view may have looked had the issue of spatial interest not been considered. The foreground, in particular, is even and uneventful. The view shown in figure 7-1(b) resulted after the plan was consulted and the view broadened to include the proposed stands of bamboo and the potted bonsai tree. Standing figures were also introduced to help punctuate the rather even field of seated figures.

Fig. 7-2a

Fig. 7-2b

Fig. 7-2 These line drawings show the exterior view of a proposed building for office and retail uses. In figure 7-2(a), the building is shown as an isolated entity, mostly devoid of context. Figure 7-2(b) shows the building viewed from across the intersection, on the entry patio of a neighboring building. The architectural elements, plant materials, and figures introduce a foreground to the drawing.

THE SECOND CONSIDERATION: CREATE A VALUE STRATEGY

Once the line drawing has been created and its major parts have been arranged in a spatial hierarchy, it is important to consider the arrangement of its *major groups* of value, particularly if your intent is to use your drawing for presentation purposes. Value is particularly important and the most influential of the three dimensions of color in a design drawing, not only because it is the most pivotal in creating the effects of light, but because it is the only one of the three dimensions of color that produces a visual impact on its own, independent of the remaining dimensions.

Rather than allowing unlimited variations in the arrangement of the major values, as fine art and graphic design illustrations may, most color design drawings lend themselves to a more limited number of possible value arrangements. This is because those values will be influenced by the general level of the values of the colors selected for the project *and* by the lighting possibilities for the project, both natural and artificial.

When you look at an illustration whose *major values* are arranged in a way that give it impact, you will notice that the areas of dark, medium, and light values tend to be contiguous—that is, linked together in zones of like value—rather than scattered in many independent spots of lights, mediums, and darks. You can see these major value groups, either in an illustration or in a real-life view, by simply squinting your eyes almost closed as you look at the composition. What at first appears to be a wide range of values now migrates toward the lighter, medium, and darker parts of the value spectrum, making it easier for you to distinguish the larger arrangements of these value groupings. It is these major value groupings that, if arranged for maximum visual impact *before* the color application is begun, will make a dramatic color design drawing far more probable.

Creative arrangement of the major value groups will give your color design drawings more impact—but why? First, they help to hold the illustration together and focus the viewer's eye in the direction of the center of interest. If the illustration has no major groupings of value, it will appear unnecessarily fragmented or "busy." Second, the contrasts of major value groupings can give the view an appearance of depth or distance. Stronger contrasts are a general characteristic of the value relationships between things that are closer to a viewer. As distance increases, this contrast lessens. When this phenomenon is used in a drawing, the appearance of depth is increased dramatically.

Perhaps the most graphic benefit of the effective arrangement of major value groups, however, is how these arrangements can create a luminous drawing. When you see a lighter area against or through a darker area, the lighter area appears even lighter. The darker the surrounding dark area, the brighter the lighter area appears. This phenomenon is particularly effective in creating dramatic illumination in a drawing.

The Value Study

A *value study* may appear to be of little consequence, even somewhat of a bother, as compared with the power of a dramatic color drawing. However, the value study is your ticket to that compelling color illustration. Once you have completed your line drawing, but before you attempt to apply color, you will need a road map that tells you, in general terms, how dark or light to make your colors as you apply them to the drawing. By arriving at a satisfying and dramatic arrangement of values before you begin color application, you complete a critical series of decisions which then allows you to focus on color application techniques.

Value studies are quick and easy to make. Begin by using a black-and-white photocopier to reduce your line drawing to a small size, about 5" x 7". Make a few copies, as you may do more than one study. The smallness of the paper allows you to keep your illustration at "arm's length" for this important step and to stay focused on the major groups of value instead of getting caught up in the details of the drawing (7-3).

Restrict yourself to the use of black and white media, so you can focus on value *only*. Black and gray markers (your choice of warm, cool, or French gray makes little difference), *Black* Prismacolor pencil, and white gouache or correction fluid can all be useful in making these studies. You can work directly on the photocopies on bond paper, or you can place white roll tracing paper over the small images and quickly scroll through a series of possible value arrangements (7-4).

These studies should be accomplished fairly quickly. It will probably take between 20 and 40 minutes to make each study. You may have some initial difficulty in arriving at a satisfactory value arrangement, in part, perhaps, because of the novelty of planning a drawing in this fashion. You may create two or three studies before you arrive at an arrangement of values that is most appropriate for the view you have selected for your design ideas. The hardest part is settling on an arrangement of large value patterns that feels right for the drawing. Once you hit this "aha!" point in your exploration, finishing the study becomes easy.

You may find it helpful to somewhat exaggerate the values in your studies so you can easily perceive their impact. In the finished color drawing there will, of course, be smaller areas of value contrast within the major areas of value you have established, but these contrasts should not be so large or emphatic that they overwhelm or fragment the major value groups within which they lie.

It is a good idea, after you create a value study, to do something else for a while and then come back to it. This allows you to look at the study with a fresh eye and usually results in the addition of refinements to the study or ideas for a better value arrangement in a new study. Once you arrive at a value arrangement that suits your goals for the drawing, keep it in view and use it as a frequent reference as you apply color to the finished drawing. It will prove to be an invaluable guide as you create a strong and dramatic color design drawing, regardless of the hues you use.

Your ability to arrange the major values of color design drawings will become stronger as you increasingly take notice of the most interesting and dramatic major value groupings in your surroundings, as you think more frequently in strategic terms about the value arrangements of your drawings, and as you generate more of these studies.

Fig. 7-3a

Fig. 7-3b

Fig. 7-3c

Fig. 7-3 These quick, rough studies—4" x 5" each—were created to explore some of the possible major value arrangements for the interior shown in figure 7-1(b). In figure 7-3(a), *Black Prismacolor* pencil was used to create the light conditions for an overcast day, when no direct sunlight enters the space. Parts of the soffits and spandrel panels were darkened with graded values so that the exterior appears sufficiently bright. Note also how the foreground was made very dark, allowing the lower

central part of the drawing to appear quite bright by contrast.

In figure 7-3(b), the value study was drawn on white tracing paper placed over the small line drawing. Direct sunlight is coming from the right, creating a dark mass on the right side of the drawing. However, this mass would not be uniformly dark in the finished drawing, but would be a series of contrasts within this dark mass. Notice how the darks on the left side of the drawing help to balance the dark mass on the right.

Figure 7-3(c) shows a value study as a night scene, where gray markers were used to quickly add dark, even values to the sky and building beyond the glass plane. Because of the dark exterior, as well as the darkened foreground, the main part of the interior appears quite bright by contrast.

Each of these studies holds the kernel of a value arrangement idea for the finished drawing. Figure 7-3(a) was selected to guide the value arrangement for the drawing shown in figure 7-47.

Fig. 7-4 Three different lighting conditions were studied for the line drawing shown in figure 7-2(b). In figure 7-4(a), the light comes from behind the viewer and toward the building. This creates a situation in which the foreground is quite dark, the building is generally a medium value (owing to the values created by local tone as well as shade and shadow), and the background is light in value.

In figure 7-4(b), a dusk scene was created in which, although the sky is brighter toward the left side, the brightest area remains at the center of interest—the main corner of the building. This area is brightest because the highest value contrasts were deliberately created there. The sky was darkened with a series of *Cool Grey* markers ranging from 20% on the left to 70% on the right. The foreground was also created with *Black* marker, keeping it in silhouette to help the building and sky appear brighter. The values of the building walls and street surface were created with *Black* Prismacolor pencil, and the windows remain the white of the paper.

Figure 7-4(c) shows the building illuminated by morning sun. In this situation the entire left side of the building is in shade. In response, the sky and building against the brighter facade were darkened. This not only forces the sunlit facade to appear brighter, but helps to balance the distribution of values in the drawing. Note how these two dark masses are also balanced by a third set of dark values at the ceiling, column, and planter wall on the left side of the drawing. White gouache was applied to the upper windows on the shaded side of the building to create reflections of brighter sky, adding interest and "sparkle" to the darker face of the building, but not in such amounts as to fragment the dark mass.

Figure 7-4(a) was the study used as a value guide for the completed drawing shown in figure 7-60.

Fig. 7-4a

Fig. 7-4b

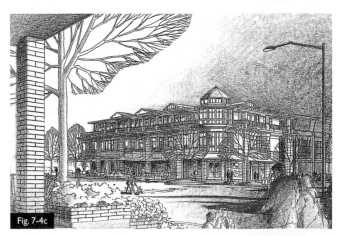
Fig. 7-4c

THE THIRD CONSIDERATION: THE TRANSFER

Once your line drawing has been made and you have arrived at a value strategy, you must consider whether to use the paper on which you have created your line drawing for your color application, or whether you want to use another kind of paper for that purpose. Line drawings or computer-generated tonal images can be transferred easily to the paper of your choice—including white roll tracing paper—by means of a black-and-white photocopier. The only exception is a diazo print, which must be accomplished with the use of a diazo print machine. Photocopiers can, of course, also be used to reduce, enlarge, and edit your design drawings as you transfer them to the drawing paper of your choice. This enables you to enlarge small sketches or parts of drawings, allowing them to become design communication tools for use with a larger audience.

Most photocopiers have a side feed that will accept individual sheets of paper intended to receive the photocopy image, preempting the paper in the paper tray. An office-quality photocopier will, of course, accept bond paper, but Canson paper can usually be sent through the side feed with no problem. How-

ever, because of the texture of Canson paper, you may sometimes find that the black toner does not completely fuse to its surface. You can determine whether the toner has fused to the Canson by simply rubbing lightly a line in a corner of the photocopy. If the line smudges, spray the photocopy with Krylon Crystal Clear acrylic coating and allow a few minutes for it to dry. This will fix the lines and reduce or eliminate smudging but will not interfere with your color media.

Bristol paper accepts photocopy toner quite well and does not usually require a fixative. If two-ply Bristol is too stiff to pass easily through your copier, switch to the thinner single-ply version.

Because roll tracing paper works so well with the color media and techniques described in this book, it was important to find a way for it to accept photocopied images. In fact, it accepts these images quite successfully and requires only a "carrier" for it to be sent through a photocopier. This carrier keeps the thin paper from being crumpled and distorted as it proceeds through the machine. Follow the steps in figures 7-5 through 7-9 to photocopy onto roll tracing paper. Note, however, that certain copiers will provide only a blurry or par-

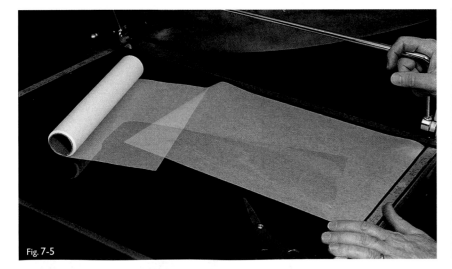

Fig. 7-5

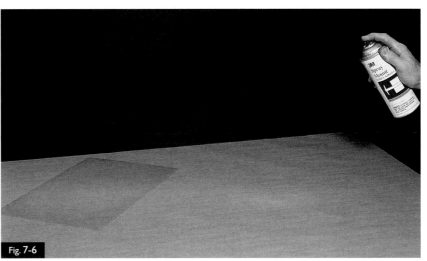

Fig. 7-6

Fig. 7-5 A sheet of 5 mil (.005" thick) acetate and a sheet of white roll tracing paper are cut to the same size. This size can be letter, legal, or ledger—whatever the photocopy machine can accom- modate and depending on the size you wish to make your copy. Here, 11" x 17" sheets of acetate and tracing paper are being prepared. Scissors can be used, but a paper cutter is usually faster.

Fig. 7-6 The acetate carrier sheet is sprayed with an _extremely light_ coat of spray mount. It is sprayed at a distance to ensure a light coat. The surface of the acetate should be only _very slightly_ tacky to the touch. If the acetate becomes too sticky by mistake, roll a sheet of scrap paper onto the acetate and peel it off, several times. Each time this is done, the acetate should become progressively less sticky.

tial image on the tracing paper that is introduced into the machine in this way. This usually happens because the trace tends to pull away from the carrier due to a convoluted paper path within the copier. If your copies turn out poorly, you can hand-trace your line drawing onto the tracing paper or you can photocopy your drawing onto drawing mylar by introducing the mylar into the copier's side-feed. Although mylar is slightly more difficult to work on and does not provide results as vivid as those on trace, it is a good second choice for retrocolor drawings when trace cannot be used.

There may be times when you want to produce a black-and-white photocopy that is larger than 11" x 17". Many copy shops have large-format black-and-white photocopiers, such as the Xerox 2080 or the OCE Bruning 9400. If you attempt to add color to a drawing of this size, you may want to consider using pastel as a color medium, as it can cover large areas very quickly.

Diazo printing is a direct copy process with no enlargement or reduction capabilities. However, once transferred to diazo paper and colored, the finished image can be enlarged or reduced with a color photocopier or a bubble-jet copier. Diazo prints can have a background as light or dark as you wish, depending on where you set the machine's speed; *the faster the speed setting, the darker the resultant print.* A major advantage with the diazo printing process is that you can create a *graded* background across your print by gradually increasing or decreasing the machine speed as your original drawing and accompanying print paper proceed through the machine.

Remember to use alcohol-based markers when working on photocopies; xylene-based markers will smear the photocopy lines. Either alcohol- or xylene-based markers can be used on diazo prints, although xylene-based markers appear to work slightly better in that the color is smoother and richer than that of alcohol-based markers.

Fig. 7-7

Fig. 7-8

Fig. 7-7 The sheet of trace is aligned with the acetate and pressed into place. A roller is used to remove air bubbles and ensure complete adherence. The best roller to use is one that is slightly spongy, such as that made by Speedball.

Fig. 7-8 The original drawing is placed facedown in the copier. Once the top is closed, the acetate carrier and tracing paper are fed into the machine, using the side feed. Most copiers require that the surface on which the copied image is to appear be placed *faceup* in the side feed.

Fig. 7-9

Fig. 7-9 When the copy is completed, the tracing paper is slowly peeled from the acetate. The back of the tracing paper should have little or no glue residue on it and be ready to accept color media. If there is too much glue residue on the back, place the back of the copy on a sheet of bond paper and roll and peel it several times to remove the residue. **A very slight residue will not hinder the application of color media, including pastel.**

The acetate can be set aside for future use. It need only be sprayed as necessary and can usually carry several more copies without having to be resprayed.

THE FOURTH CONSIDERATION: PAPER AND COLOR

If you choose to transfer your line drawing to a kind of paper other than that on which you created the drawing, as discussed earlier, you are already thinking about paper. The kinds of paper that work best with the color media discussed in this book were introduced in Chapter 2 and are shown in the step-by-step examples in this chapter.

Your selection of specific colors for your design drawings will depend on a number of factors: the scheme of colors you have chosen for the place you are designing, the colors of the natural materials you intend to include in your project—stone, brick, wood—as well as the colors that are available in the natural and man-made materials that you *have* chosen. The specifics of color scheme development are beyond the scope of this book and will be discussed in a separate book.

However, there are some general color ideas you may wish to keep in mind as you develop your color design drawings. First, when the expression of your color scheme is an important part of your purpose in creating a drawing, accompany the drawing with a color and materials board that shows actual paint samples, material swatches, and pieces of the natural and man-made materials you intend to use. By doing so, you can minimize misunderstandings about color that result from the effects of illumination or mismatches that occur within your drawing.

Second, you will notice that the color media used for the illustrations in this chapter tend to fall into four groups: warm colors—reds, yellow reds, and yellows; cool colors—purples, purple blues, and blues; transitional colors—greens or red purples (usually greens in these drawings) that can be made either warm or cool (see figure 6-7); and the neutrals and near-neutrals, including white, black, cool gray, warm gray, and French gray markers and pencils.

Third, almost *any* combination of colors can be made to work together to create a design drawing that appears unified. This can be done by intermixing the various color media used to create the drawing, much the way artists—particularly painters—work with color, as discussed in Chapter 6. Even though an object in the drawing may be predominantly of one hue, other color media used elsewhere in the drawing can be used to flavor that hue. In figure 7-38, for example, the *Terra Cotta* pencil was also used on parts of the green grass; the *Copenhagen Blue* pencil was used on the darker parts of the green grass as well as the trees; *Jasmine* pencil was used to flavor the sunlit surfaces of most of the objects, regardless of their predominant hue. This intermixture of colors is a key to rich and interesting color design drawings.

White-Paper Drawings

Color media appear at their lightest value and strongest chroma when applied to white paper. For this reason, white paper is excellent for illustrating design ideas that have "high-key" (light-value) or strong-chroma color schemes. White papers useful for color design drawing range from the lower-quality bond paper to the high-quality Bristol paper.

Bond Paper

Bond paper, the type found in most photocopiers and laser printers, lends itself to quick sketches in which color quality is not paramount but some color is desirable. Duplication is rapid, the original is preserved, and there is no need to seek out special paper. Color design drawings on bond paper are adequate for many kinds of design illustration task (7-12). You may want to stock your photocopier with 24 lb. or heavier paper which will give your drawing surface a more substantive feel.

Fig. 7-10

Fig. 7-11

Fig. 7-10 A photocopy of a Polaroid photograph of a cardboard and foam-core study model. The photo was taken as close as possible to the eye level of the scale figures. Certain light lines were darkened so that the image was easier to trace. (Model: Taku Shimizu)

Fig. 7-11 A perspective line drawing generated by tracing the study model. Additional design information was easy to add once the larger elements were in place.

Fig. 7-12

Fig. 7-12 The finished color design drawing on bond paper. This study was quickly enhanced with alcohol-based markers, color pencil, and white gouache, particularly because its actual size is only 8½" x 11".

Bond paper is also a good surface for generating conceptual design ideas over enlarged photographs of existing conditions (7-13, 7-14, 7-15). In much the same way, images (both line and tone) printed on bond paper by laser jet printers make excellent base drawings over which color media may be used to quickly develop and enhance design ideas expressed as rudimentary computer images (7-16).

Fig. 7-13

Fig. 7-14

Fig. 7-13   An enlargement of a 3" x 5" color photograph of an existing condition to roughly 6" x 10", reproduced on bond paper by a black-and-white photocopier.

Fig. 7-14   A sketch study in color, using Pilot Razor Point, alcohol-based marker, and color pencil, drawn directly on the photocopy shown in figure 7-13.

"TERMINUS" PLANTING HELPS TO DEFINE REAR OF STREET-INFLUENCED SPACES.

LOW SHRUBS with POTS of FLOWERS MITIGATES "SEA OF PARKING" WITHOUT BLOCKING SIGNING

FOREGROUND COLOR (ANNUALS, PERENNIALS, ETC.) INFLUENCE PERCEPTION OF BACKGROUND VIEW...

FOREGROUND CANOPY TREES AWAY FROM STREET. (PALMS ON STREET) BUT STILL SHADES SIDEWALK — ALSO FRAMES DISTANT BUILDINGS.

Fig. 7-15

Fig. 7-15 Another study in the series, created in the same fashion as figure 7-14.

Fig. 7-16

Fig. 7-16 This 8½" x 11" study was drawn using alcohol-based marker, pastel, and color pencil over a tonal image produced by a laser jet printer on bond paper. The tonal image was generated by computer using Form-Z. (Drawing: Jim Babinchak)

Bristol Paper

The development of a color design drawing on Bristol paper is shown in figures 7-17 through 7-23. Bristol paper was chosen for this drawing because its approximately triadic hue scheme—yellow/blue green/purple blue—is mostly light in value. Note that in the value arrangement for the drawing (7-19), a darker-value foreground also forces the main part of the drawing to appear lighter. Another level of luminosity is established by placing the row of dark-value figures in front of the brightly illuminated food-service tenants in the distance.

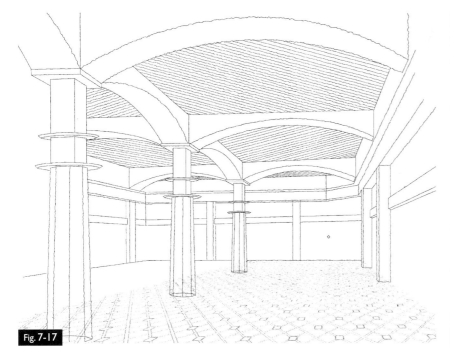

Fig. 7-17

Fig. 7-18

Fig. 7-17 This computer image began as a typical straight-line wire-frame with the hidden lines removed. It was imported into Adobe Illustrator, all the lines were "selected," and the "roughen" filter was applied so that the drawing appeared more hand-drawn. The "size" setting was .20, and the frequency was 20/inch.

The illustration was then imported into Adobe Photoshop to add the floor pattern. Diagonally oriented floor patterns can be more quickly and successfully added to a drawing by computer than by hand. The pattern was first developed as an orthographic image, then made to conform to the perspective view by using the "perspective" command within the "transform" menu.

Once the floor pattern was added, the image was photocopied onto a sheet of 11" x 17" translucent drawing *vellum* (Clearprint 1000H). Note that drawing vellum does *not* need a special carrier when introduced into the photocopier's side feed. (Computer illustration: Nat Poomviset)

Fig. 7-18 A sheet of ordinary roll tracing paper was placed over the vellum image shown in figure 7-17, and the additional elements of the view—furniture, people, accessories, and details—were roughed out. This rough was then placed *behind* the vellum image, and the rest of the view was traced onto the vellum with a Micron 005 and a 4x0 technical pen. Newly hidden or unwanted lines were easily erased, using a pink erasing strip in an electric eraser. Correction fluid can also be used, because the finished line drawing will be photocopied onto the Bristol.

Once the gray marker was applied to create the basic value arrangement, pastel was applied to the major expanses of color in the illustration (7-21). The pastel not only smooths the appearance of the marker strokes and has a luminous quality in its own right, but it is a color application over which further refinements of color can be added with color pencil.

It is informative to look closely at the line illustration shown in figure 7-18, in that it is a hybrid of computer and hand drawing. However, it is hardly recognizable as such, as it appears hand drawn in its entirety. You may find that in many drawing situations, a computer can quickly and conveniently supply the basics of the larger architectural forms and spaces, as shown here, whereas hand drawing is often faster and more appealing in illustrating figures, furnishings, accessories, and detail. To unify the look of the hand-detailed computer drawing *and* avoid retracing the computer portion of drawing, the computer-generated portion was first "filtered" on the computer to make its lines appear hand drawn (7-17). This resulted in a line illustration in which the hand-drawn and computer-generated portions are indistinguishable.

Fig. 7-19

Fig. 7-19 The value study shown at the top is a 5" x 6" photocopy reduction of the line drawing. Note how the main part of the view appears brighter because of the darkened foreground.

The color media used for this approximately triadic hue scheme are as follows. In this example, the near-neutrals happen to be all markers: (1) *French Grey 10%*, (2) *French Grey 20%*, (3) *French Grey 30%*, (4) *French Grey 50%*, (5) *Cool Grey 10%*, (6) *Cool Grey 20%*, (7) *Cool Grey 30%*, (8) *Cool Grey 40%*. The greens are (9) *Permanent Green Deep 619.9* stick pastel, (10) *Deco Aqua* pencil, (11) *Celadon Green* pencil. The purple blues and purple are (12) *Ultramarine Deep 506.9* stick pastel, (13) *Blue Slate* pencil, (14) Derwent *Blue Violet Lake #27* pencil. The reds are (15) *Light Oxide Red 339.9* stick pastel, (16) *Poppy Red*, (17) *Tuscan Red* pencils, (18) *310* pencil pastel. The yellows and yellow reds are (19) *Raw Sienna 234.9* stick pastel, (20) *Gold Ochre 231.8* stick pastel, (21) *#690* pencil pastel, (22) *Cream*, (23) *Light Peach*, (24) *Jasmine*, (25) *Burnt Ochre*, (26) *Raw Umber*, (27) *Dark Umber* pencils.

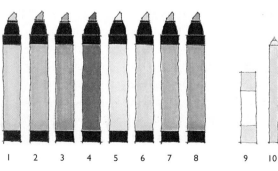
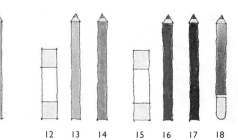
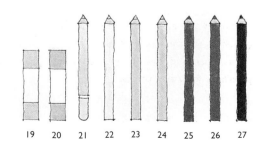

1 2 3 4 5 6 7 8   9 10 11   12 13 14   15 16 17 18   19 20 21 22 23 24 25 26 27

Fig. 7-20

Fig. 7-21

Fig. 7-20 Once the line drawing was photocopied onto Bristol paper, the major values were applied with gray markers, with the value study used as a guide. The use of gray marker is an easy way to establish the value arrangement while still allowing subsequent layers of pastel and pencil. The cool grays make a good base for cool colors, and the French grays and warm grays make a good base for warm colors.

All the French gray markers *(10%, 20%, 30%,* and *50%)* shown in figure 7-19 were used to establish the value gradations in the lower part of the foreground; all the cool gray markers shown were used on the upper part. However, the contrast was intentionally diminished as the drawing recedes, and only the *10%* and *20%* grays were used in the distance.

Fig. 7-21 To keep the drawing light, pastel was used to tint its major elements and surfaces. On the smaller of these surfaces, the pastel was drawn directly on the surface; on the larger surfaces, the pastel was scraped onto the drawing surface from the pastel stick with an **X**-acto knife. This avoided the possiblility of the pastel application showing streaks. Once the pastel was applied, it was smoothed with a finger, then by a facial tissue.

Raw Sienna 234.9 stick pastel was applied to both the floor and ceiling. *Gold Ochre 231.8* stick pastel was used on the foreground floor and blended into the lighter pastel in the distance.

The illuminated undersides of the arches near the columns were colored with a blend of *Raw Sienna 234.9* and *Light Oxide Red 339.9* stick pastels to express the color of the incandescent uplighting.

The columns, as well as the sign panels in the distance, were colored with a blend of *Permanent Green Deep 619.9* and *Ultramarine Deep 506.9* stick pastels. Note the gradation of the column color, created by adding *Raw Sienna 234.9* stick pastel to the lower parts of the columns.

Once the pastel was applied, unwanted coverage was easily erased with an electric eraser with a soft white erasing strip and an erasing shield.

Fig. 7-22 Color pencil and pastel were used to bring up the color of the details of all parts of the drawing except for the figures. *Raw Umber* pencil and a flavoring of *Burnt Ochre* pencil were applied to the corners of the ceiling where the illumination drops off. *Blue Slate* and Derwent *Blue Violet Lake #27* pencils were used to darken the the corners where the arches meet.

    Cream and *Light Peach* pencils were combined to color the banding on the sign panels and the banquette seating. *Jasmine* and *Dark Umber* pencils were used to create a cross-hatch pattern over a light wash of *Burnt Ochre* pencil on the foreground banquette seat back to simulate the pattern created by cane backing. The corresponding seat backs in the distance received only a light wash of *Burnt Ochre* pencil.

    Celadon Green and Derwent *Blue Violet Lake #27* pencils were used to color the tabletops, chair backs, and legs. The table edges and chair seats were colored with a mix of *Burnt Ochre* and *Jasmine* pencils.

    Tuscan Red pencil was applied to the dried flowers on the tables, the dried wreaths, and the wine bottles. The bluish floor tiles were colored with *Blue Slate* and Derwent *Blue Violet Lake #27* pencils, and the dark tiles were colored with a *Dark Umber* pencil.

    A mixture of *Gold Ochre 231.8* stick pastel and *#692* pencil pastel was applied lightly across most of the food-service tenant openings, figures included, to approximate the glow of colored light.

Fig. 7-22

Fig. 7-23

Fig. 7-23 The only exception to the use of lighter markers in the more distant parts of the drawing is the application of *French Grey 50*% marker to the line of figures in front of the food-service tenants. This play of value was used to allow the food-service tenants to appear more luminous.

Once color was applied to the various parts of this design idea, the same color pencils were recombined and applied to the figures. First, *French Grey 30*% and *50*% markers and *Cool Grey 30*% and *40*% markers were applied randomly to the hair and clothing, followed by the pencils. One exception is some discrete touches of *Poppy Red* pencil.

White gouache was mixed with yellow opaque watercolor to create an opaque color to apply to the letters of the food-service tenant signs with a very thin brush. This color was intended to approximate a gold leaf finish on the letters. Note that these letters were applied slightly above and to the right of the existing letters, resulting in what appears to be a drop shadow beneath each letter. Touches of white gouache were also applied to the recessed light in the ceiling.

Toned-Paper Drawings

When you make a white-paper drawing, the illusion of illumination must be created by surrounding lighter values with darker values. Toned papers provide an opportunity to easily and quickly create dramatic color design drawings, because the designer can apply both dark *and* light values to the drawing.

One of the major advantages in working on a toned drawing surface is that partial color application on a line drawing not only can have a dramatic impact by itself, but often precludes having to add color to the rest of the drawing. This makes toned-paper drawings both effective and efficient as design communication devices.

Design drawings on toned paper are particularly effective in communicating lighting concepts. Interior illumination, dusk scenes, and night views are easy to create with the use of toned papers.

Canson Paper

Canson paper comes in a wide variety of subtle light-, middle-, and dark-value colors. It has a distinct texture that imparts a pleasing, diffuse quality to applications of color pencil. This not only adds a consistency to a drawing, but also helps to mask streaky applications of pencil.

Figures 7-24 through 7-30 show the development of a color design drawing of an interior seating area on Canson paper. The paper color was selected because it was sympathetic to the preponderance of warm analogous colors in the scheme. These colors were emphasized by the addition of purple-blue complementary accents.

The foreground was darkened to emphasize the skylight illumination of the more distant part of the drawing. Note, too, that color media were applied to only about two-thirds of the drawing, helping to define its center of interest.

Fig. 7-24 This line drawing was drawn on tracing paper with a Micron 005 pen.

Fig. 7-25 The line drawing was photocopied onto "Sand" Canson paper and sprayed with Krylon Crystal Clear acrylic coating.

Fig. 7-26

Fig. 7-26 A small value study was done first with *Black* Prismacolor pencil on a photocopy reduction of the original line drawing. The foreground was darkened, because it was under the curved balcony and because such treatment would emphasize the skylighted fireplace area beyond. The darkened foreground also provides a good "frame" through which to view the seating area.

The color media used in this analogous-with-complementary-accent scheme are the neutrals and near-neutrals of (1) *White*, (2) *Black* pencils; (3) *French Grey 30%*, (4) *French Grey 50%*, (5) *French Grey 70%*, (6) *French Grey 90%*, (7) *Black* markers; the reds, yellow reds, and yellows of (8) *Terra Cotta*, (9) *Light Peach*, (10) *Peach*, (11) *Mineral Orange*, (12) *Burnt Ochre*, (13) *Spanish Orange*, (14) *Yellow Ochre*, (15) *Jasmine* pencils; (16) *310*, (17) *680*, (18) *685* pencil pastels; (19) *Eggshell*, (20) *Blush Pink*, (21) *Sienna Brown* markers; the green yellows of (22) *Olive Green*, (23) *Dark Green* pencils; (24) *Olive Green* marker; the purple-blue complementary accents of (25) *Blue Slate*, (26) *Light Cerulean Blue*, (27) *Indigo Blue* pencils; (28) *Peacock Blue* marker.

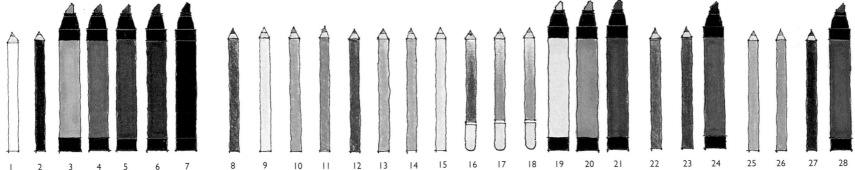

1   2   3   4   5   6   7   8   9   10   11   12   13   14   15   16   17   18   19   20   21   22   23   24   25   26   27   28

Fig. 7-27

Fig. 7-28

Fig. 7-27 The near-neutral marker base was added to the foreground first, with the value study used as a guide. *Black* marker was used along the edges of the ottoman, the vase, and the table and on the darkest parts of the armchair on the left. *French Grey 90%, 70%, 50%,* and *30%* markers were applied, becoming progressively lighter as they moved away from the *Black.*

Fig. 7-28 The marker base colors were applied to the remaining elements in the center of interest of the drawing. *Olive Green* marker was added to the chair on the right and the rug. *Peacock Blue* marker was applied to the upholstery of the sofa on the left; *Sienna Brown* marker was used to color all the woodwork as well as some of the carpet pattern.

The ceiling that forms the underside of the curved balcony was darkened in places with gradations of *French Grey 50%, 30%,* and *10%* markers to effect a contrast with the more brightly illuminated space beyond *and* between the pendant light fixture and the ceiling itself.

The areas directly beneath the fireplace mantle, the hearth, and the upper cornice (above the painting) were treated with gradations of *French Grey 50%, 30%,* and *10%* markers. The sandstone was colored with *Blush Pink*

and *Eggshell* markers. Note how the toned paper mutes the marker colors. Gradations of *French Grey 90%, 70%,* and *50%* markers were applied to the interior of the fireplace to provide adequate contrast and make the flames appear more luminous.

The value contrasts in the distance were deliberately made weaker than those in the foreground of the drawing.

Fig. 7-29

Fig. 7-29 Detail was added to the foreground elements with color pencil. A zigzag pattern was applied to the green armchair with *Dark Green* pencil, followed by *Terra Cotta* pencil for the reddish dots within the pattern. A wash of *Peach* pencil was applied to the illuminated surfaces of the chair, slightly more heavily closer to the table lamp. Note how the *Peach* pencil not only adds highlights but also mutes the green hue. *Indigo Blue* pencil was used on the surfaces in shade. *Blue Slate* pencil was added as a natural-light highlight on the edges of the chair that face the skylight above.

The sofa on the left was first washed lightly with *Olive Green* pencil. *Blue Slate* pencil highlights were added, followed by *Indigo Blue* pencil for shading. The highlights on the cushions of the armchair to the left were applied with *Mineral Orange, Yellow Ochre,* and *Jasmine* pencils. The rug was detailed with *Burnt Ochre, Yellow Ochre,* and *Indigo Blue* pencils. A graded wash of *Peach* and *Spanish Orange* pencil was applied lightly to the rug to create the effect of illumination from the table lamp.

Because the table lamp was intended to be a replica of a Dirk Van Erp lamp, it was colored with *Mineral Orange, Spanish Orange,* and *Jasmine* pencils. *Mineral Orange* and *Jasmine* pencils were also used to wash the top of the end table. The ottoman in the right foreground was very lightly washed with *Terra Cotta* pencil. A highlight from the table lamp was added to the seat cushion with a blend of *Mineral Orange, Spanish Orange,* and *Jasmine* pencils.

The foreground ceiling was quickly colored with *#680* pencil pastel, followed by *Yellow Ochre* and *Jasmine* pencils. The pendant light fixture shade was colored with *Light Peach* pencil, grading into *Blush Pink* pencil near the top. Once the shades were colored with the light pencils, the silhouetted cutout patterns were darkened with a Pilot Razor Point. The ceiling highlights were also added with *Light Peach* pencil.

The vase with the flowers was colored with a *Blue Slate* pencil; the leaves were colored with *Celadon Green* and *Olive Green* pencils. The flowers were colored with *#310* and *#680* pencil pastels to give them added brilliance.

Fig. 7-30

Fig. 7-30 Once the foreground seating area was completed, it was easier to determine how light the surface of the fireplace should appear. First, the fire was drawn in the fireplace according to the illustrated steps in figures 4-84 and 4-85. After the fire was drawn, the wrought-iron screen was drawn directly over it with a *Black* pencil.

Because a skylight was destined to go directly above the fireplace, beyond the top edge of the drawing, a wash of *Light Peach* pencil was applied to the tops of the stone ledges, the mantle, and the floor. The same pencil was used to apply a light wash across the face of the fireplace, with care taken not to extend this wash up into the marker shadows cast by the stone ledges. As these washes were worked progressively higher, toward the source of light, more pressure was applied to the pencil. The upper ledge and the stones above it were also washed with *White* pencil to make them even brighter. These washes were applied directly over the details of the fireplace, such as the candles on the mantle and the hanging utensils, which

allowed these washes to remain smooth and consistent. Highlights were also added with *Light Peach* pencil to the tops of some of the stones on the face of the fireplace. Note, too, the addition of a flavoring of *Light Cerulean Blue* pencil to the shaded wall on the upper right side.

After the stone colors and highlights had been applied, the candles were colored with *Cream* and *White* pencils. The wrought-iron candlesticks and fireplace utensils were retraced with a *Black* pencil. The remaining ceiling pendant lights were colored in the same way as the foreground fixture; the ceiling directly above them was highlighted with *Jasmine* and *Mineral Orange* pencils.

Final touches were added. The column beside the fireplace was tinted with *#680* and *#685* pencil pastels. White gouache highlights were added to the candle flames and light fixtures. The foreground vase at the top of the ottoman was highlighted with *Light Cerulean Blue* pencil to introduce a balancing touch of blue to the composition.

Diazo Print Paper

Diazo prints have a superior surface for developing color design drawings. They have excellent "tooth" and accept marker, pastel, and color pencil equally well. Because the lines of a diazo reproduction are the result of a subtractive process, they cannot be easily removed, although color pencil can be erased from a print without affecting its lines. The "background" or tone of the print surface can be of any uniform value, ranging from white to black, or a graded value, depending on how the speed control is manipulated. The faster the speed setting, the darker the background of the resultant print.

It is important to remember that diazo prints are sensitive to light even after the paper is exposed to light during the printing process. Over time, particularly if the print is on display, the paper will fade. Make a color photocopy, a bubble-jet copy, or a transparency of your diazo print illustrations once they are completed.

Diazo print machines have fewer size limitations than office photocopiers and can typically generate prints ranging from 8½" x 11" to 36" x 48." If roll-stock print paper is used, the size of the print is limited only by the width of the machine and can be of any length. However, because color design drawings are typically generated as small as possible in the interest of efficiency, the diazo prints on which these drawings are executed should also be as small as workable.

Diazo print machines are fairly ubiquitous and can be found in most professional design offices. However, diazo print paper colors are limited. Most offices stock blueline and blackline paper, and some may stock brownline paper as well.

Figures 7-31 through 7-39 show the development of a color design drawing on a *blackline print* with a graded background. The line drawing and unexposed print paper were sent through the diazo machine at a diagonal orientation, upper left first. As the combination progressed through the machine, the

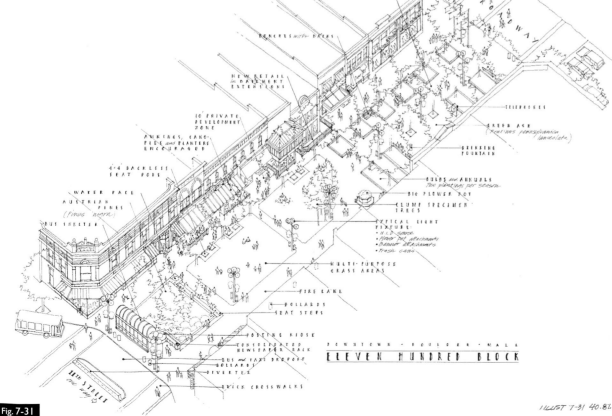

Fig. 7-31 This paraline drawing was done on an 11" x 17" sheet of **Clearprint 1000H** drawing vellum with a 4x0 technical pen. It was created with the use of a paraline image from a computerized data base that contained the rough proportions of the buildings and the street. Infill information was derived from photographs of the existing building fronts and a design plan showing the proposed street elements. This information was combined and added by "eyeballing" it into place on a rough copy of the data-base image, then tracing it with the technical pen, creating the fairly accurate final image shown here. Notes were added, but they were kept clear of the relevant parts of the design images.

If you look closely, you can see that the outlines of the tree canopies are drawn, but that all design information still remains visible through them.

Fig. 7-31

speed was gradually increased to full, creating the graded print shown in figure 7-33. This particular gradation adds visual weight to the lower part of the drawing. A darker graded print was used for the night scene shown in figure 7-40.

Diazo papers and prints are not intended to be of artistic quality. You will notice small flaws, such as spots, streaks, or fingerprints on the prints, but they are usually of insufficient magnitude to distract the viewer's attention from the design-communication purposes of the drawing. In figure 7-33, for example, you may notice faint, pale streaks that run in the direction of the print progression. Although visible, these streaks are of little consequence in the finished illustration.

The general value composition of this illustration, as the value study in figure 7-32 shows, is intended to make the subject of the illustration—the design of the street—more luminous by surrounding it with darker values. Note how this effect was enhanced by flavoring the darker rooftops with cool colors and by lightly washing most parts of the street scene (an analogous color scheme of yellow red, yellow, and green yellow) with a complementary yellow hue. The application of this common color also helped to tie together visually the various colors of the elements on the street—trees, walkways, grass, and building fronts.

Aerial views such as this, whether paraline or perspective drawings, are quite useful in communicating larger-scale landscape and urban design information. They are less abstract than plan views and are easier to understand for those less familiar with the conventions of plans and elevations.

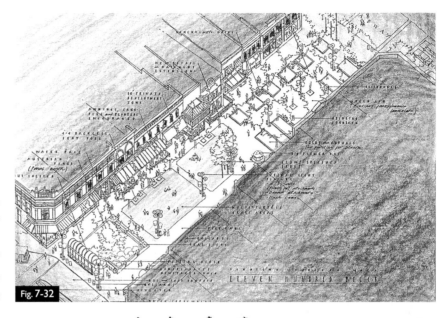

Fig. 7-32

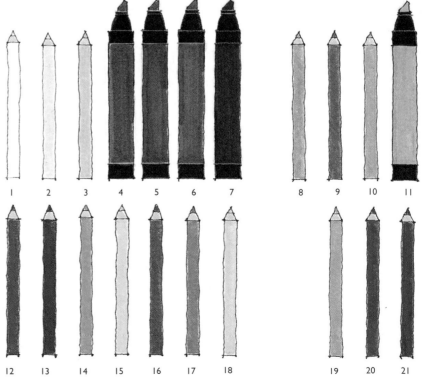

Fig. 7-32 In this value study, the subject of the drawing—the street and its context—was surrounded by darker values to make it appear more luminous and thus stronger in its presentation.

The color media used for this illustration are as follows: The neutrals and near-neutrals are (1) *White*, (2) *French Grey 10%*, (3) *French Grey 20%* pencils; (4) *Warm Grey #5 (Warm Grey 50%)*, (5) *Warm Grey #7 (Warm Grey 70%)*, (6) *Cool Grey #5 (Cool Grey 50%)*, (7) *Cool Grey #7 (Cool Grey 70%)* markers. The green-yellows are (8) *Limepeel*, (9) *Olive Green*, (10) *Celadon* pencils (which is actually a green, but is washed with yellow in the drawing); (11) *Limepeel* marker. The reds, yellow reds, and yellows are (12) *Poppy Red*, (13) *Terra Cotta*, (14) *Peach*, (15) *Light Peach*, (16) *Burnt Ochre*, (17) *Mineral Orange*, (18) *Jasmine* pencils. The purple blues and purple are (19) *Blue Slate*, (20) *Copenhagen Blue*, (21) *Violet* pencils.

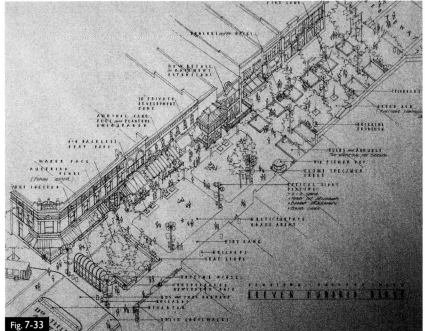

Fig. 7-33

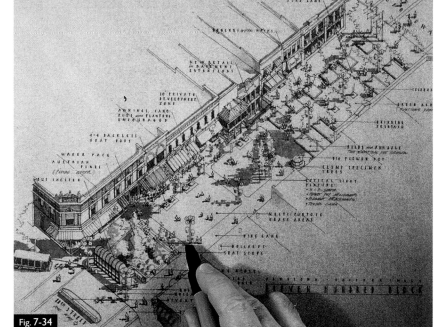

Fig. 7-34

Fig. 7-33 The graded blackline diazo print. The original drawing and the unexposed print paper were fed into the machine together, diagonally, upper left first. As the combination progressed through the machine, the speed of the machine was gradually increased, ultimately to full, with the results shown here. The best results in attempting this kind of print are achieved by trial and error.

Fig. 7-34 Shade and shadow were applied with *Warm Grey #5 (Warm Grey 50%)* and *Warm Grey #7 (Warm Grey 70%)* markers, as the finished drawing was to have a warm-hued cast. The *Warm Grey #5 (Warm Grey 50%)* marker was used for the larger patches of shadow, and the *Warm Grey #7 (Warm Grey 70%)* marker was used to give the shadows of the smaller elements more punch. Marker was used for the shadows so that color pencil could be more easily applied over the shadows.

It is important to note—particularly in the upper parts of the drawing—that although the shadows of the smaller elements (awnings, people, light fixtures) are shown, the shadows of the tree canopies *that fall behind other tree canopies* are *not* shown. These shadows were eliminated so the smaller elements and detail information would remain visible through the mass of canopies once the drawing is complete.

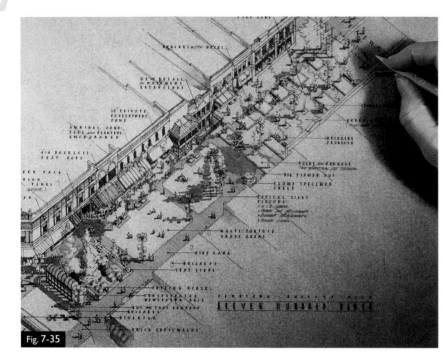

Fig. 7-35

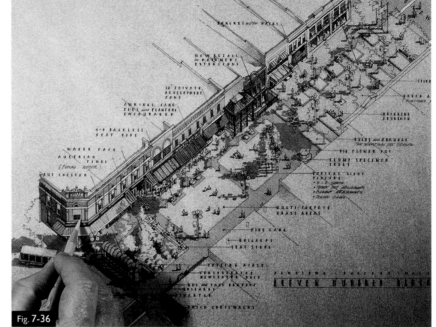

Fig. 7-36

Fig. 7-35 The sunlit parts of the brick paving surface were added with a light wash of *Peach* pencil, and the shadows were washed lightly with *Violet* pencil followed by *Peach* pencil. The brick surfaces beyond the tree canopies were lightly flavored with *Peach* pencil only.

A line texture was added to the sunlit brick surface with *Terra Cotta* pencil and a straightedge. The same texture was carried into the major shadow areas with a *Light Peach* pencil.

Fig. 7-36 Next, *Cool Grey #5 (Cool Grey 50%)* and *Cool Grey #7 (Cool Grey 70%)* markers were used as a base value for the windows of the building fronts, as well as for some of the awnings and canopies. Because of their small size, pencil was used to add color to the building fronts. Although touches of a variety of pencils were used, most of the color was applied with *Peach, Light Peach, Terra Cotta, French Grey 10%, French Grey 20%, White, Burnt Ochre, Mineral Orange, Jasmine, Celadon Green,* and *Blue Slate* pencils.

Celadon Green pencil was used as a wash on some of the larger windows and glass canopies, giving this glass a slight greenish tint before the mullions were drawn in. A Pilot Razor Point and a Micron 005 pen were used to trim the edges of the windows and canopies and to add dark mullions to many of the windows.

Jasmine pencil was used to lightly wash most of the opaque parts of the building fronts to give them a warm, sunlit appearance and to tie the various colors together.

Fig. 7-37 Color was then applied to all the remaining elements on the ground plane, with the exception of the trees and figures.

The top of the bus shelter was colored with *White* pencil; *Jasmine* pencil was used to flavor the sunlit side, and *Blue Slate* was used to flavor the side in shade. The black metalwork was retraced with a Pilot Razor Point.

The globes on the light fixtures were colored with *White* pencil; *Poppy Red* pencil was used for the flowers, *Mineral Orange* for the pots, and Pilot Razor Point was used on the poles and arms.

A *Yellow Green (Limepeel)* marker was applied to the grass areas, followed by *Olive Green* pencil on the darker parts of the color gradation, and *Jasmine* pencil was applied to the lighter part. *Copenhagen Blue* pencil was added to the darker parts of the grass, followed by a wash of *Terra Cotta* pencil over the entire grass area to mute the green slightly and to distribute the colors that make up the drawing. The designer applied these pencil colors lightly and built them up gradually, using the sides of the pencil points. The shadows on the grass were colored with *Olive Green* pencil, followed by *Copenhagen Blue* pencil.

The red flowers in the planters in the upper part of the drawing were colored with *Poppy Red* pencil. It was applied with full pressure where the flowers are seen directly. Where the tree canopies "block" a direct view of these flowers, the pencil was applied much more lightly.

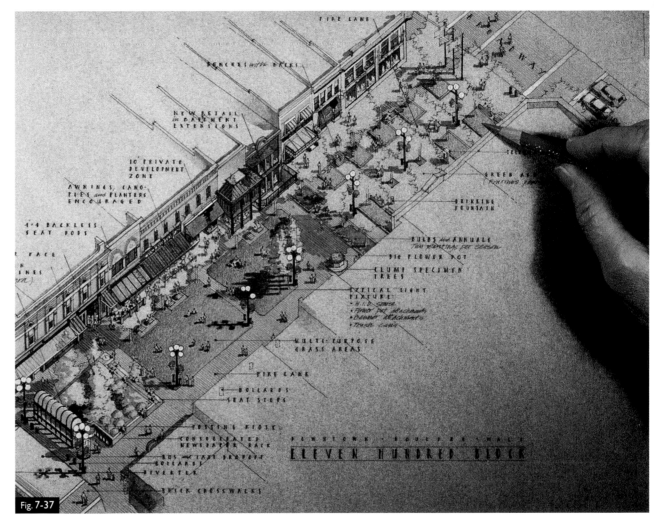

Fig. 7-37

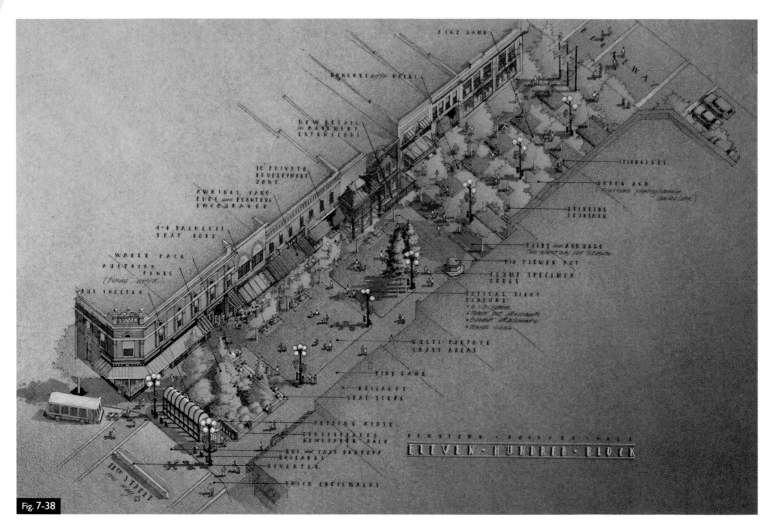

Fig. 7-38

Fig. 7-38 Touches of color pencils that were used elsewhere in the drawing were used to add color to the figures, including *Poppy Red, Olive Green, Copenhagen Blue, White,* and *Blue Slate.* Pencil colors were selected that provided maximum contrast with the figures' immediate backgrounds.

Color was added last to the tree canopies. *Jasmine* pencil was applied to the sunlit sides of the canopies, *Limepeel* pencil to the middle, and *Olive Green* pencil to the shaded sides. *Copenhagen Blue* pencil was used to flavor the *Olive Green* pencil. The designer applied these pencils carefully, with a delicate touch, using the sides of the pencil points and a gentle, circular motion. Particular care was taken not to obscure the information imparted by the elements seen through the canopies.

Accents were added, with the use of white gouache, to the light fixtures, bus shelter, big flower pot, and certain signs on the storefronts to provide highlights and touches of sparkle. The locator lines for the notes were darkened with a Pilot Razor Point, inasmuch as the color application had somewhat obscured them.

A graded wash, with a combination of *Copenhagen Blue* and *Violet* pencils, was applied to the roofs to increase the contrast between the roofs and the sunlit surfaces.

A *White* pencil was used to highlight the title of the drawing. The white was offset to the upper right slightly, allowing the original dark letters to serve as a drop shadow that helps to emphasize the title.

Fig. 7-39

Fig. 7-39 A close-up of the lower part of the drawing in figure 7-38.

Fig. 7-40

Fig. 7-40 This night scene was begun as a graded diazo print, lighter at the bottom and darkest at the top. This helped to instantly make the scene appear as if light were reflecting from the ground onto the fronts of the buildings.

The uplighted ivy on the walls was colored with *Jasmine* and *Olive Green* pencils. The lower windows were flavored with *Deco Orange* pencil, and the upper windows and background behind the figures were colored with *Pink* pencil to approximate the glow of neon. The rich color cast by the neon lighting on the undersides of the awnings on the right was applied with gradations of *Cobalt Blue 512.5* stick pastel and *#310* and *#690* pencil pastels.

The neon and other colored lighting were created by first applying a diffuse "halo" of pastel around it (color pencil can also be used). Then white gouache mixed with opaque watercolor (to tint it the color of the proposed light) was applied with a thin brush to the light fixture or neon letter. Once the colored gouache dried, a touch or line of pure white gouache was added to the center of the light or neon letter. This white gouache was thinned slightly with water so that it would flow easily from the brush, but not to the extent that it reduced its opacity. The white lights, the highlights on the vertical elements, and the highlights on the space frame above were also added with white gouache.

The foreground figures and those on the escalator and balconies were darkened with *Black* marker.

Tracing Paper

Ordinary white roll tracing paper is perhaps the most versatile of all the papers used in the design profession. Its translucency facilitates the iterative process of design. It easily accepts the color media used in this book and is capable of allowing color to show through the paper, a distinct advantage. It can be used as a white paper or a toned paper of any color. It can be used for quick sketches or more finished design drawings, for interiors as well as exteriors, for daytime scenes or dusk views.

Its major advantage for color design drawing is the *quality* of its translucency. Color applied to the back of a drawing on white roll tracing paper shows through the paper more brilliantly and less muted or tinted than through either of its thicker cousins, drawing vellum and drawing mylar. In addition, color applications to the back of a drawing on this kind of tracing paper appear more *evenly* applied than they actually are. This means that a designer can apply color media to the back of a drawing more quickly and less carefully than when applying color in the usual fashion to the front of a drawing.

When a drawing of this kind is placed over a sheet of muted-color or gray paper, a more subtle version of that color also shows through the translucent tracing paper and forms a background color for the drawing. In addition, the backing paper can also subtly influence the colors and, especially, the values of the color media. If marker has been applied to the drawing, its colors will shift toward the backing paper color in both hue and value, because the marker is transparent. Darker-value color pencil on the drawing tends to appear slightly darker; lighter color pencils appear more luminous because of their semiopacity and their contrast with the darker-value backing paper. In other words, if a paper color other than white is placed behind a color design drawing on trace, it becomes a toned-paper drawing instantly (see figure 3-25). When this kind of drawing, together with its background, is reproduced by color photocopier or bubble-jet copier, the result is a toned-paper image.

Retrocolor

The process of applying color to the back of a drawing on tracing paper can be called *retrocolor*, a term passed along to this author by architect, teacher, and professional illustrator Paul Stevenson Oles, FAIA.

The complexities of color application can be separated into simpler, more discrete tasks by using the retrocolor technique. Figures 7-41 through 7-66 show the various steps involved in using retrocolor for four different kinds of illustrations. In all four, the value arrangements—including shade and shadow—were applied first, to the *front* of the line drawing, using *Black* Prismacolor pencil. The color media, usually color pencil (although marker and pastel can also be used), are subsequently applied to the *back* of the tracing paper drawing. Of course, color can also be applied to the front of the drawing as well when the need arises.

The retrocolor approach to color design drawing has a number of advantages. The first concerns the value arrangements of the drawings. As mentioned before, value is one of the three dimensions of color and, where illustration is concerned, is the most important. In retrocolor, it is considered and applied separately, not only simplifying the color design drawing process, but also greatly increasing the chances that the drawing will have a stronger value composition.

Second, this approach can be more efficient than others. At any stage during the development of a retrocolor drawing, its useful life as a design communication tool can begin. In a professional design office, a designer must be prepared to present her ideas at any point during the design process, not only upon its completion. If necessary, a retrocolor drawing can be shown as a line drawing. It can also be shown as a tone drawing if it must be pressed into service before the application of color to the back or if the color and materials decisions are delayed.

A third advantage is a component of efficiency, speed. After the values are applied to the front of the drawing, the color can be added to the back very quickly. This is because a rough, quick application of color on the back will neither disturb nor diminish the crisp, dark quality of the linework on the front of the drawing. Moreover, loose applications of color on the back do not appear so from the front, because the undisturbed linework maintains the ordered look of the drawing.

Fourth, the retrocolor technique is forgiving. Colors can be quickly altered or erased and changed without disturbing the lines or value applications on the front of the drawing.

Fifth, color design drawings made with the use of the retrocolor technique lend themselves to dramatic, high-quality reproductions even before the color is applied. The line drawings by themselves can be reproduced by office photo-copier or diazo print machine (line drawings can also be enlarged considerably during photocopy reproduction by means of a large-format photocopier, such as the Xerox 2080 or the OCE Bruning 9400, at a copy shop). After the values are applied to the front of the drawing, but before color is added to the back, excellent black-and-white copies can be made of the drawing by employing the black-and-white function of a *color* photocopier or by using a digital black-and-white photocopier. These copies possess a far greater range of grays than those made by an ordinary black-and-white office photocopier. Once the color *is* applied to the back of the drawing, color photocopiers and bubble-jet copiers will yield excellent results, whether the drawing is backed with white or toned paper. You will find that the mood and dramatic qualities of your drawing can be altered simply by changing the color of the backing paper.

The four retrocolor drawings discussed in the following paragraphs are examples of types of color design drawing that find widespread use at Comm-Arts.

The Pastel "Quickie"   Pastel can be a very useful color medium for designers. The extent of the color capability of pastel ranges from brilliant to subtle, and perhaps its most useful attribute is that it can be applied very quickly and easily, making it an ideal medium for use in concept studies (7-41 through 7-47).

Yet pastel is also, to some degree, uncontrollable. This is especially true of pastel as compared with color pencil in attempting to apply color to the edges of shapes. However, rather than trying to control the medium precisely, most designers tend to relax and apply pastel more loosely than other color media. The results can be less uncontrolled than the designer may fear at first, because the undisturbed network of lines on the front of the drawing orders the color application more concisely than it appears from the back.

This medium also blends beautifully and easily, particularly on tracing paper, often giving the colors of the finished drawing a mingled quality similar to that of watercolor.

Fig. 7-41

Fig. 7-41   The basic forms for this line drawing were created by computer as a wire-frame drawing. It was used as an underlay, over which the furnishings, figures, and design details were added. The combination was traced onto an 11" x 17" sheet of drawing vellum with a Micron 005 pen and a 4x0 technical pen.

Fig. 7-42

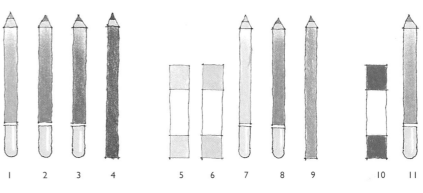

1 2 3 4   5 6   7 8 9   10 11

Fig. 7-43

Fig. 7-42 The line drawing was reduced to a small size, about 6" x 8", so that value studies could be made quickly. The study shown here took about 20 minutes to make and was drawn on bond paper with a *Black* Prismacolor pencil.

Because the illustration this study was prepared for was intended as a quick concept study, it was decided that the light should be diffuse rather than direct sunlight. This saves the time of illustrating extensive shade and shadow. Moreover, because this place is a story below grade, it was decided that the colors should be light in value. Ironically, to make this appear so, the foreground elements were darkened and linked together by the darkened floor. Thus, the rest of the space appears lighter by contrast.

Note, too, that contrasts still occur within the major areas of value. Although the main part of the space is generally of much lighter value, contrasts still occur even though they are smaller and weaker than those between foreground and middle ground. It was still possible to take advantage of value-contrast opportunities to make things "read"—figures were darkened against lighter backgrounds, and window frames were both lightened and darkened against contrasting backgrounds.

Fig. 7-43 The pastels and pencils used for the illustration. The simple color arrangement of the finished illustration is a warm-cool relationship, a complementary scheme mostly between the hues of yellow and purple blue, with some secondary use of green yellow and yellow red. The green yellows are (1) *#599,* (2) *#600,* (3) *#575* pencil pastels and (4) *Olive Green* pencil. The warm hues used were (5) *Raw Sienna 234.9* stick pastel, (6) *Indian Red 347.9* stick pastel, (7) *#692,* (8) *#680* pencil pastels, and (9) *Peach* pencil. The cool purple blues used were (10) *Cobalt Blue 512.5* stick pastel and (11) *#430* pencil pastel.

Fig. 7-44

Fig. 7-45

Fig. 7-44 This quick color study took about 15 minutes. A sheet of white roll tracing paper was placed over the value study shown in figure 7-42. Pastels were loosely applied and blended in order to experiment with colors being considered for the final application.

Fig. 7-45 The line drawing was photocopied onto white roll tracing paper, using the process shown in figures 7-5 through 7-9. *Black* Prismacolor was applied to the front of the drawing, with the value study being used as a guide. Notice the other, more subtle, contrasts established to help create the effects of light, such as the spandrels and soffits darkened against the window edges and diffuse shadows radiating from probable sources of light.

Even though the foreground is much darker than the middle ground of the illustration, it is worth noticing that value contrasts, weak as they are, still *do* occur within this darker part of the drawing. This is particularly noticeable on the paving, as it keeps the foreground from appearing two-dimensional and diorama-like.

Fig. 7-46

Fig. 7-46 Here the color media are being applied to the back of the tracing paper, which took about an hour. The pastels must be applied slightly more heavily on the back of the tracing paper to have them appear sufficiently dense on the front of the drawing.

The pastel was roughly scribbled on the back, staying approximately "within the lines." Once it was applied, it was lightly blended with a fingertip. The result as seen from the front of the drawing is similar to the minglings of color seen in watercolor illustrations. Of course, the heavier the black pencil application on the front of the drawing, the more heavily the pastel had to be applied to the back so that it would show through the pencil—hence the heavy application of *Cobalt Blue 512.5* stick pastel to the foreground

area of the drawing. Errors in color application were quickly erased with an electric eraser with a soft, white erasing strip.

The color was generally applied from the top of the drawing, working downward, to avoid unnecessary smearing or lifting of the pastel. The only color pencil used was *Peach* for skin tones and *Olive Green* for the foreground bamboo plants. The *Olive Green* pencil was applied to the

front of the drawing because the bamboo was sufficiently dark as to be opaque.

The pastel was *not* sprayed with fixative upon completion of the color application, inasmuch as fixative can deaden the color. Rather, the finished drawing was handled very carefully. The back of the illustration was protected with another layer of tracing paper and stored in an individual folder.

Fig. 7-47

Fig. 7-47 The finished illustration, shown with a white paper backing. White gouache highlights were added to the elements in the store window and to the water in the pool on the left. To minimize handling of this mostly pastel drawing, a color bubble-jet enlargement of the drawing was used for presentation purposes and smaller color photocopies were used for distribution.

Retrocolor Hybrids A *retrocolor hybrid* is a retrocolor drawing whose front-side images are created by both computer and hand. These drawings capitalize on the advantages that both the computer and hand drawing bring to the design process.

A designer is often called upon, during the earlier stages of the design process, to provide a preview of what a project or its parts may look like upon completion. These preview drawings are partly design ideas that exist thus far in the process and partly wishful thinking—the design team's intention for the feel of the completed project, even before its specifics are designed. These drawings often provide a kind of visual goal as well, images that can guide the design team as it develops the project.

Computer-generated illustrations are usually inadequate for this task. In most cases, only a rudimentary data base is established early in the design process, capable of producing only generalized, unrefined images. Requiring any more of the data base early in the process means, of course, that more information must be provided to it. Therefore, many more design decisions must be provided, often far too prematurely, and more support imagery such as figures, plant materials, building materials, color, and lighting must be sought out and imported. This is often a time-consuming and, thereby, in terms of design fees, expensive proposition.

On the other hand, the brain/hand combination of the designer not only has a vast capability for imagining what a proposed place may look and feel like by relying on a lifetime of visual experience, it can also quickly produce useful impressions of these imaginings with few additional inputs and with the simplest of drawing materials. The slowest and most inefficient part of the brain/hand process is "setting up" the rudiments of the view—determining the best angle, locating the horizon line and vanishing points, and developing the basic forms.

A retrocolor hybrid brings together the best of both human and computer, offering capabilities appropriate to the early stages of the design process. The crude computer information available early is often adequate to quickly provide a setup view for the designer to work over by hand. The designer can then conceptually design and execute the parts of the illustration much more quickly than he could beginning from scratch, in a far more fluid undertaking than attempting this kind of illustration solely by computer.

Figures 7-48 through 7-53 illustrate the development of just such a study as a retrocolor hybrid drawing, beginning with a Form-Z tonal image.

Fig. 7-48

Fig. 7-48 This simple Form-Z image, produced by a laser printer on bond paper, was used as the starting point for the retrocolor drawing to follow. These tonal images can be printed slightly faster, because a hidden-line-removal step is not required, and serve well as early "block outs" of a design idea. (Illustration: Grady Huff)

Fig. 7-49

Fig. 7-50

Fig. 7-49 The Form-Z image shown in figure 7-48 was photocopied onto a sheet of white roll tracing paper. Make sure the dark-light setting on the photocopier is set light enough that the darker values will allow the color media to show through from the back of the tracing paper. To make the copy shown here, the photocopier was set to its lightest setting.

Once the photocopy was completed, the design idea was explored in more detail. Scale elements, figures, landscape materials, architectural details, and refinements were added directly over the photocopied Form-Z image by hand with a *Black* Prismacolor pencil.

Fig. 7-50 *Black* Prismacolor pencil was used to add shadows and create a simple value arrangement that surrounds the center of interest—the entry to the trains and its reader board above—with darker values. Note how the figures, trees, foreground, and sky on the upper right are darkened to help give the drawing focus.

Fig. 7-51

Fig. 7-52

Fig. 7-51 Color was quickly applied to the back of the illustration with color pencil. A sheet of the same dark blue paper that was used as a backing paper when the drawing was color photocopied was used as an underlay as the color was applied. Thus, as the drawing was turned right-side-up to check the color progress, it could also be checked against the proper background.

The sky is a gradation, beginning in the upper left with *Indigo Blue* pencil, grading to *Light Cerulean Blue* and, finally, to Derwent *Blue Violet Lake #27* pencil.

Celadon Green pencil was applied to the dark upper windows of the building. Its lower windows were "illuminated" by the application of *Jasmine* and *Deco Orange* pencils.

The paving colors were added with *Terra Cotta* and *Peach* pencils. The darker of the two paving colors was further darkened in the foreground with *Dark Umber* pencil, and the illuminated paving beneath the arching canopy was washed with *White* and *Jasmine* pencils. The flowers in the pots were colored with *Poppy Red* pencil, and *Olive Green* pencil was used for the leaves. The pots themselves were colored with *Terra Cotta* pencil, and *Peach* pencil was used to help model the distant pots.

The street and the plain concrete in the foreground were colored with Derwent *Blue Violet Lake #27* and *Light Cerulean Blue* pencils.

Fig. 7-52 The front of the drawing after the color media were applied to the back, but before the finishing touches, with white paper used as a backing.

Fig. 7-53 To show an image on the large reader board, a printed image was simply cut out and applied to its surface. Another way of approaching this problem is to scan the completed drawing and import it into a computer program such as Adobe Photoshop. Likewise, a photographic image can be imported into the same program and made to conform to the reader board's shape by using the "perspective" command within the "transform" menu.

Touches of white gouache were applied to the underside of the canopy arches, the signing elements, letters, and the stars in the sky with the small, thin brush shown. Some gouache was mixed with yellow-red opaque watercolor and applied to the underside of the threshold arch above the stairway, the large lanterns, and between the figures on the far wall of the stairwell.

A small amount of color pencil was added to the *front* of the drawing in a few places where the original Form-Z image conflicted with design information that was added later with *Black* pencil. For example, a light wash of *Terra Cotta* pencil was added to the threshold arch over the stairs to make it appear as a coherent element.

The completed drawing is shown here with a dark blue **Canson** paper backing. (Reader board image part of an illustration created by Dave Tweed.)

Fig. 7-53

An Exterior Daytime View   Figures 7-54 through 7-60 illustrate an approach to creating a more finished exterior view of a proposed building within its context, using the retrocolor technique. Discussions of how the line drawing was made, the shade and shadow approached, the color applied, and foreground drawn are included in the captions to the illustrations.

The line drawing of this building (7-54) was done on white roll tracing paper with a *Black* Prismacolor pencil and a straightedge. A straightedge was used for two reasons: First, the lines can be made finer (appropriate to the small size of the drawing and the detail involved). Second, such lines can be drawn more quickly with a straightedge, particularly when they must be aligned with distant vanishing points.

A value study was developed (7-55) that used the darker foreground and surrounding contextual elements as a darker frame that sets off the subject building. The middle ground (the building itself) is a medium value; the background is the lightest value, although it too darkens near the top, completing the effect of a darker "aperture" through which the subject building is viewed.

A rather unrestricted palette of colors was used for the drawing, with the lightest and warmest colors reserved for the subject building. Although the foreground also has warm colors, these colors have been both darkened and "cooled" by the application of blue pencil. Many of the colors in the composition were determined either by existing colors, such as those in the foreground, or by the range of colors available for local natural materials, such as the sandstone shown on the building.

Fig. 7-54

Fig. 7-54 Because the original drawing was used for the color application, a black-and-white photocopy of the drawing (shown here) was made both to keep as a record and in case the original was ruined and another line image had to be made. (Hand shown for scale.)

The original drawing is 12" x 17½".

Fig. 7-55

Fig. 7-55 The value study and color media used for the drawing are the neutrals and near-neutrals of (1) *White 100.5* stick pastel; (2) *White* pencil; (3) *French Grey 10%*, (4) *French Grey 30%*, (5) *Cool Grey 30%*, and (6) *Black* pencils; as well as (7) *French Grey 20%*, (8) *French Grey 30%*, (9) *French Grey 50%*, (10) *French Grey 70%*, (11) *French Grey 90%*, (12) *Cool Grey #3 (Cool Grey 30%)*, (13) *Cool Grey #5 (Cool Grey 50%)*, (14) *Cool Grey #7 (Cool Grey 70%)*, (15) *Cool Grey #9 (Cool Grey 90%)*, and (16) *Black* markers.

The cool colors are (17) *Ultramarine Deep 506.9* and (18) *Cobalt Blue 512.5* stick pastels; as well as (19) *Blue Slate*, (20) *Copenhagen Blue* and (21) *Derwent Blue Violet Lake #27* pencils. The warm colors—reds, yellow reds and yellows—are (22) *Jasmine*, (23) *Light Peach*, (24) *Peach*, (25) *Yellow Ochre*, (26) *Terra Cotta*, (27) *Burnt Ochre*, and (28) *Tuscan Red* pencils; as well as (29) *Redwood (Sienna Brown)*, (30) *Burnt Umber (Dark Umber)*, and (31) *Delta Brown (Black)* markers.

The greens and green yellows are (32) *Yellow Chartreuse*, (33) *Limepeel*, (34) *Deco Aqua*, (35) *Celadon Green*, and (36) *Olive Green* pencils; as well as (37) *Olive (Olive Green)*, (38) *Dark Olive (French Grey 80%)*, (39) *Deep Evergreen (Peacock Blue + Dark Green)* markers.

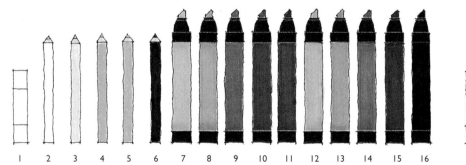

1 2 3 4 5 6 7 8 9 10 11 12 13 14 15 16   17 18 19 20 21

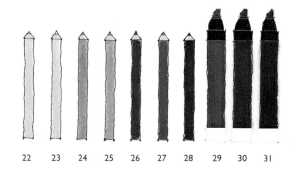

22 23 24 25 26 27 28 29 30 31

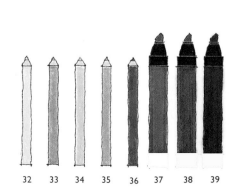

32 33 34 35 36 37 38 39

Fig. 7-56 Once the line drawing on tracing paper was made, the shade and shadow were applied to the *front* of the line drawing with *Black* Prismacolor pencil. The shade and shadow were first "roughed in" with red pencil on a photocopy of the original, then placed behind the tracing paper to use as a template for the drawing shown enlarged here. Thus, the primary focus could be on the quality of the pencil application instead of layout issues.

Note that the shadows are drawn more lightly on the glass. Although shadows do not actually fall *on* glass (unless it is dirty), but *through* it, the shadows in this drawing were lightly drawn on the glass to avoid confusion and to allow the forms of the building to be more completely revealed in this particular case. Note, too, that the shadows are graded darker toward their edges, "forcing" the sunlit surfaces to appear slightly brighter.

Fig. 7-56

Fig. 7-57 Once the shade and shadow application was completed on the front of the drawing, it was turned over to begin the color application on the back. The color was begun on the left (tentatively at first, to determine how much hand pressure was needed) and progressed toward the right.

The color application could have begun at any point on the building, but it is best not to have your hand resting on a finished color application as you work, because you can smear and lift the color, as well as buckle the paper with hand oils and moisture. If you must rest your hand on completed color, rest it on a folded piece of bond paper placed over the color.

The drawing was placed over a sheet of brown kraft paper as the color was applied and evaluated, as that was the paper intended for use as a backer sheet when the finished color photocopies were made.

French Grey 10% pencil was applied nearest the shadow edges on the upper part of the building, then graded to a *French Grey 30%* farther away, helping to force the shadow with a lighter value. The lighter parts of the shadows were flavored with *Peach* pencil, grading into the Derwent *Blue Violet Lake #27* pencil that covers the rest of the shadow. Notice how roughly (and, thus, quickly) the color can be applied and still achieve the subtle and refined results visible from the front of the drawing, seen in figure 7-58.

The lighter parts of the glass were colored with *Deco Aqua* pencil, which grades into the darker *Celadon Green*

Fig. 7-57

pencil. The parts of the glass in shadow were flavored with *Jasmine* pencil to imply an illuminated interior. The designer used this approach to the glazing color, instead of drawing reflections, to ensure that the finished illustration did not appear too busy.

The darker-value stone, as well as the stone in shadow, was colored with a blend of *Burnt Ochre* and *Terra Cotta* pencils. The lighter, sunlit stone was colored with a loose mixture of *Light Peach, Peach,* and *Yellow Ochre* pencils. Note

how the *Light Peach* pencil is used to force the shadow.

The designer took time to add touches of color to the elements displayed in the storefront windows. This ensures that the windows will appear both interesting and transparent; when there is nothing to see through an important window, it can appear unnecessarily opaque. A blend of *Celadon Green* and *Jasmine* pencils was used to color the awnings directly above the storefronts.

Fig. 7-58 This stage shows the completed color on the building and the sky.

Before color pencil was added to the roof, the sky was quickly applied, with pastel, to the back of the drawing. A blend of *White 100.5* and *Ultramarine Deep 506.9* stick pastels was applied to the lower part of the sky, just above the roof. This mixture was graded into *Cobalt Blue 512.5* stick pastel, applied to the upper part of the sky. A small amount of the *White 100.5* stick pastel was also applied to the *front* of the drawing to create the faint, streaked clouds.

Once the pastel colors were blended, the overcolor on the roof area on the back of the drawing was erased with an electric eraser using a soft, white erasing strip. The roof color was applied with a *Cool Grey 30%* pencil. *White* pencil was used over the roof color to highlight the center roof panel on the turret.

A blend of *Olive Green, Limepeel,* and *Yellow Chartreuse* pencils was applied to the planters. To ensure adequate brightness for the polychrome terra-cotta capitals at the top of each stone pilaster, white gouache was mixed with various opaque watercolors and applied to the capitals on the *front* of the drawing.

Fig. 7-58

Fig. 7-59 After the color was applied to the subject building in the middle ground, it became clear how dark the foreground must be to provide adequate value contrast. Owing to the size of the drawing, dark markers, instead of pencils, were first applied to create base foreground colors of appropriate value. Once the marker was applied, the designer used color pencil to "tune" the marker color by applying it both on the back and the front of the drawing.

Black marker was applied to the ceiling supported by the brick column; *Burnt Umber (Dark Umber)* marker was used on the lighter sides of the column and brick planters, and *Delta Brown (Black)* marker was added to their darker sides.

The low plant materials were darkened with a mixture of *Dark Olive (French Grey 80%)* and *Deep Evergreen (Peacock Blue + Dark Green)* markers. Note that the mixture of these markers, although looking rough and blotchy on the back side of the tracing paper, appears much smoother on the front and looks rather like watercolor. The concrete sidewalk and planter bases were colored with *French Grey 70%* and 90% markers; the grass was colored with *Olive (Olive Green)* marker and graded into *Dark Olive (French Grey 80%)* marker. Color was added to the flowers with *Burnt Umber (Dark Umber)* and *Redwood (Sienna Brown)* markers.

The figures were colored with *Black* and *Burnt Umber (Dark Umber)* markers, and *Redwood (Sienna Brown)* marker was

Fig. 7-59

used to add color to the skin, sweater, and handbag. The shirt on the center figure, as well as the curb behind him, was toned with a *Cool Grey #5 (Cool Grey 50%)* marker.

The shadow in the street was colored with a series of cool gray markers to create a gradation. Beginning at the outer edge, *Cool Grey #9, #7, #5, and #3 (Cool Grey 90%, 70%, 50%, and 30%)* markers were applied across the shadow. The same markers were also used to create

the strong contrast against both ends of the subject building by darkening the neighboring and background buildings. Note that the sunlit portion of the street is also progressively darkened toward the right with *French Grey 20%, 30%, 50%, 70%, and 90%* markers.

Color pencil was used to flavor many of the dark foreground elements by applying it to the *front* of the drawing. *Copenhagen Blue* pencil, used to imply reflected sky color, was lightly applied to

the lower left of the foreground column, planter, and concrete, as well as to the building shadow in the street. *Olive Green* pencil was used to flavor the shrubs and grass. *Tuscan Red* pencil was added to bring up the colors of the flowers.

Fig. 7-60

Fig. 7-60 An image of a bubble-jet copy of the finished drawing. This copy was made with brown kraft paper placed behind the tracing paper original.

Before this copy was made, touches of white gouache were added to the potted flowers, as well as to upper parts of the storefront windows and some of the office windows, to imply the sparkle of light sources. *White* pencil was added to the sidewalks and crosswalks and was used to highlight bare tree branches in front of dark backgrounds.

A Dusk View A dusk view of a project can convey the drama of its illumination while its exterior forms, materials, and colors remain visible. Dusk views are often more useful than night views from a design communication standpoint, in that they convey more design information.

Figures 7-61 through 7-66 show the development of a dusk view of the same building illustrated in the preceding daytime view. A dusk view of a project has some similarities to the way its daytime counterpart is developed, although the shade and shadow and the window treatment are handled differently.

Fig. 7-61

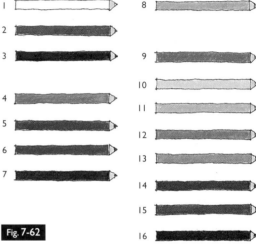

Fig. 7-62

Fig. 7-61 The line drawing used for the daytime view of this building was photocopied onto tracing paper.

This close-up shows shade and shadow being applied with a *Black* Prismacolor on the front of the drawing, in much the same way it was applied in the daytime view. You can see, however, that the shadows do not have distinct edges, because the only light sources— the windows and the ambient sky—are diffuse. The surfaces facing away from

(or hidden from) the sky and the windows are the darkest, such as the soffits and the tops of the stone pilasters. Note that the values applied to the building are still light enough to allow color to show through them from the back of the drawing.

Fig. 7-62 The color pencil palette used to create the dusk scene. The neutrals and near-neutrals are (1) *White*, (2) *Cool Grey 70%*, (3) *Black*. The cool colors are (4) Derwent *Blue Violet Lake #27*, (5) *Violet*, (6) *Copenhagen Blue*, (7) *Indigo Blue*. The green pencil is (8) *Celadon Green*. The warm colors are (9) *Pink*, (10) *Jasmine*, (11) *Deco Orange*, (12) *Mineral Orange*, (13) *Peach*, (14) *Terra Cotta*, (15) *Burnt Ochre*, (16) *Dark Umber*.

Fig. 7-63 Once the values were applied to the front side of the drawing, the window illumination and its effects were added to the back side of the drawing. *Deco Orange, Jasmine,* and *White* pencils were applied as graded washes of color to the windows, right over the smallest mullions. These gradations span several windows at a time, resulting in some areas of the windows being lighter in value and others darker. This creates a less even lighting effect and imparts a less institutional, more intimate feel to the building.

The designer approached the retail windows at the first level by first coloring the items in the windows with small, intense touches, using a variety of color pencils. Because the downward-oriented halogen lighting is often used as retail display lighting, the remaining uncolored areas at the bottom of the window were colored with *White* pencil. This pencil was graded into *Jasmine* pencil farther up the window, which in turn was graded into *Deco Orange* pencil.

The surfaces perpendicular to the window plane that would logically recieve spill light from the windows (soffits, sides of pilasters, sidewalks, etc.) were colored with *Deco Orange* and *Jasmine* pencils. Note how these surfaces were kept lighter in value when the the front of the drawing was shaded in the previous step.

This stage of the drawing is shown backed with a sheet of dark blue paper to make it more visible.

Fig. 7-63

Fig. 7-64 The pilasters and lower stone-clad portions of the building were the next areas to receive color. *Terra Cotta* pencil was used to add color to the foundation and header band that appears at the top of the first-story windows and the bottoms of the projecting balconies. The spandrels just above the header band were colored with *Burnt Ochre* pencil.

A gradation of *Mineral Orange, Burnt Ochre,* and *Dark Umber* pencils was applied to the pilasters. The illuminated edges of the columns were colored with *Peach* pencil.

Celadon Green pencil was added to the awnings and the metal roof. *Cool Grey 70%* pencil was applied over the green pencil on the roof to shift its color to a cooler hue and to increase its contrast with the sky beyond.

The near-neutral surfaces on the upper part of the building—columns, fascias, and stucco walls—were washed with a Derwent *Blue Violet Lake #27* pencil. This step shifted these neutral colors from a dull gray to a more probable color that implies a reflection of the sky.

This stage of the drawing is shown backed with white paper.

Fig. 7-64

Fig. 7-65 In this step, color pencil was used to make the sky, although pastel could have been used as well. *Indigo Blue, Copenhagen Blue, Violet, Pink,* and *Mineral Orange* pencils were rapidly applied and graded one into another, in that order, from left to right. The hand pressure on the pencils was gradually decreased as the sky became brighter in the lower right.

Fig. 7-65

Fig. 7-66

Fig. 7-66 Final touches were added to the *front* of the drawing. *Poppy Red, Yellow Chartreuse, Pink, Blue Slate*, and *White* pencils were added to enhance the colors in the store windows.

Touches of white gouache were added to the upper parts of the retail windows to imply display lighting. White gouache was also used to apply the sliver of moon and the stars.

The finished drawing was backed with brown kraft paper because of the warm color it imparts to the scene.

ADDITIONAL LAYERS OF INFORMATION

Color design drawings must do more than communicate a beautiful (it is hoped) image. They differ from strictly artistic drawings in that they must communicate information about design ideas, usually for places—buildings, interiors, landscapes, urban districts, and regions.

These drawings frequently act as the "working drawings" for the early stages of the design process and, as in working drawings, their communicative power can be greatly magnified by additional layers of information. One such layer of information is notation.

Notes

Notes work well with design drawings as long as they do not block critical graphic information. They usually work best by occupying a secondary, rather than dominant, role in the overall image. Notes can range from a more formal arrangement, such as those in figure 7-69, to one less formal, as in figure 7-38, or the casual annotations in figures 7-14 and 7-15. Generally, the more "finished" the drawing or presentation of the graphic material, the more formal the arrangement of the accompanying notes. Thoughtfully sized and placed notes can enhance a color design drawing just as words, beautifully designed and applied, can enhance the architecture of a building.

Notes can be as helpful to the designer as they are informative to the drawing's intended audience. Because design drawings are a synthesis of an often surprisingly large amount of disparate information, the detailed thought that goes into forming them is sometimes forgotten. Adding notes directly to the design drawing is a good and easy way to document such thinking.

Notes are also frequently added to design drawings as a way to ensure that specific points about the design are clearly evident. They can even help guide the designer through a presentation of the drawings, particularly if the notes are numbered. The audience will find notes helpful when they review copies of the drawings at a later time, especially once memory of the presentation has faded.

Hand Notations

Handwritten notes are quite adequate for design drawings. There is no need to use "architectural" lettering unless you prefer it. Script, or a hybrid of script and lettering, can often be faster and yet still attractive (7-67).

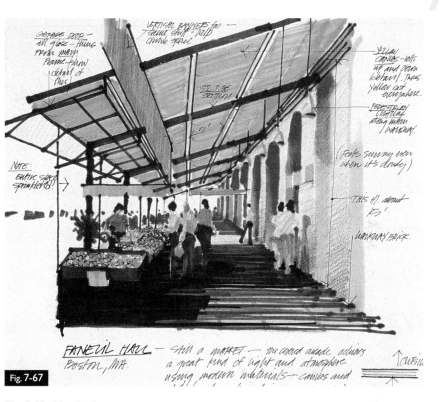

Fig. 7-67

Fig. 7-67 Handwritten notes accompany an on-site sketch. When each note is given a title, the information is easier to take in at a glance.

Computer-Generated Notes

The introduction of a typeface into a color design drawing can be an attractive way to present notes while ensuring legibility (7-68). These notes are usually produced on a sheet with the use of a computer, printed on a laser printer, then cut out and applied. They can be adhered directly to the surface of a drawing or applied to a transparent acetate cover sheet before a color photocopy of the combination is made. The latter approach allows the designer to easily change or replace the notes—or to eliminate them altogether when it becomes necessary to use the drawing for certain applications, such as a cover sheet, title page, or project site sign.

The Computer-Composed Page

Color design drawings can also be annotated as part of a larger composition. This is easily accomplished with the use of a computer page-composition program in which the graphic information is scanned, imported into the program, and composed in concert with notes and headings (7-69).

There are both advantages and drawbacks to this approach. It can result in a very handsome and refined presentation that can be easily output in any size, from small to large. However, it is important first to make sure that the time and expense involved in such an approach is justified. A designer can easily be seduced into spending far too much time (and, consequently, fee) composing sheets such as these when a stand-alone, hand-annotated drawing would do the job, particularly during the early and fluid stages of the design process.

Fig. 7-68 Computer-generated notes accompany this concept study and provide a level of formality that helps to balance its informality. (Drawing: Doug Stelling)

monitors, interactive computer network, and lights.

Paving patterns and landscaping should reinforce the urban quality of this intersection.

Associate seating areas with heavy landscaped zones for maximum comfort.

Fig. 7-68

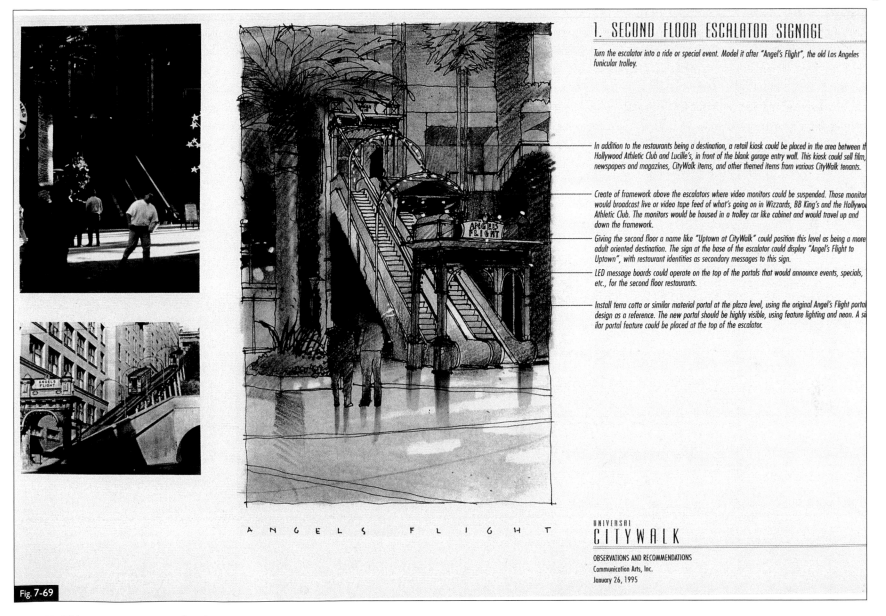

1. SECOND FLOOR ESCALATOR SIGNAGE

Turn the escalator into a ride or special event. Model it after "Angel's Flight", the old Los Angeles funicular trolley.

In addition to the restaurants being a destination, a retail kiosk could be placed in the area between the Hollywood Athletic Club and Lucille's, in front of the blank garage entry wall. This kiosk could sell film, newspapers and magazines, CityWalk items, and other themed items from various CityWalk tenants.

Create of framework above the escalators where video monitors could be suspended. Those monitors would broadcast live or video tape feed of what's going on in Wizzards, BB King's and the Hollywood Athletic Club. The monitors would be housed in a trolley car like cabinet and would travel up and down the framework.

Giving the second floor a name like "Uptown at CityWalk" could position this level as being a more adult oriented destination. The sign at the base of the escalator could display "Angel's Flight to Uptown", with restaurant identities as secondary messages to this sign.

LED message boards could operate on the top of the portals that would announce events, specials, etc., for the second floor restaurants.

Install terra cotta or similar material portal at the plaza level, using the original Angel's Flight portal design as a reference. The new portal should be highly visible, using feature lighting and neon. A similar portal feature could be placed at the top of the escalator.

ANGELS FLIGHT

UNIVERSAL CITYWALK

OBSERVATIONS AND RECOMMENDATIONS
Communication Arts, Inc.
January 26, 1995

Fig. 7-69

Fig. 7-69 This page was composed and annotated using Adobe Pagemaker. (Drawing: Henry Beer)

Photographs

The advent of inexpensive, high-quality color and black-and-white photocopy capabilities has enabled designers to communicate design ideas in new and easier ways by including photographs with—and within—color design drawings.

Drawings can be accompanied by photographs that show existing conditions of renovation projects, as well as by color photocopies from books and magazines that convey a character similar to that intended a project before it is designed. This approach can help the designer work with the client to confirm a direction for the character of the project without investing inappropriate amounts of time in drawing ideas that may be rejected.

Photographs can also be used in a collage within design drawings whenever such use enhances the ability of the drawing to communicate, introduces a necessary level of quality difficult to obtain by hand, or saves a significant amount of time (7-70). Signs and type are often added to drawings either as a color photocopy simply cut out and glued in place, as in figure 7-53, or by computer, whereby the drawing and the signing imagery are scanned and put together (7-71). Either way is preferable to replication by hand, which is often too time-consuming to be efficient.

Fig. 7-70 An early concept sketch that employs photocopied images. These images are simply adhered to the bond paper surface of the sketch. (Drawing: Max Steele)

'Tailight' decorative light fixtures mounted to kiok structure. (3)

'IMAX' anchor neon sign

Directional signs identifying other Mills projects

Entertainment District directory. (3) one at each corner.

Freestanding bank ATM machines: refer to plan for quantity and locations.

Neon ring

Anchor identity billboard sign w/ neon outline. (2)

Anchor identity 'traffic' signs. (2) per anchor

Video monitors for entertainment anch trailers and 'Mills TV': refer to plan for quantity and locations.

Theater ticket ATM machines: refer to plan for quantity and locations.

Painted metal bench seat

Fig. 7-71

Fig. 7-71 Although this directory kiosk study was illustrated entirely by computer, its signing and type were added by importing the illustration and signing imagery into a separate program, the same way this imagery would be added to a hand-drawn image.

This particular illustration was modeled in Point Line (by Point Line USA, Inc.), then imported into Studio Pro (by Strata, Inc.) for rendering. The signing, color, and lighting were added after the image was imported into Adobe Photoshop, and the neon and the figure were added with Adobe Illustrator. (Illustration: Taku Shimizu)

REVISIONS AND REPAIRS

Color design drawings are in extensive service during the early parts of the design process. The ideas the drawings communicate will almost certainly evolve and change as the design effort proceeds, requiring, of course, updates of the drawings themselves. Design drawings are often created very quickly in the busy and exciting environment of the studio. Mistakes will be made. Because of these universal conditions, the design process is necessarily iterative. You may frequently be inclined to make new drawings to incorporate new design ideas or to repair mistakes. However, there are ways that existing drawings—and their color photocopies—can be revised and repaired that can often help you avoid having to start over.

Most of the color design drawing media, papers, and techniques shown in this book are quite forgiving, in that small revisions and repairs can be made by simply erasing the linework and color, usually with an electric eraser and erasing shield, and redrawing. Given the nature and life span of these drawings, it is good not to lose sight of the fact that such repairs need not be perfect, only good enough to allow the drawing to hold together visually.

You may find, less frequently, that larger parts of an illustration may have to be revised or repaired. These parts may be too large to erase efficiently, yet too small to necessitate redrawing the entire illustration. There are three general approaches we use at CommArts when faced with this situation, and the techniques can be combined or altered to suit the needs of the situation. The goal is to make the most effective revision or repair using the least amount of time and effort.

The Patch

A *patch* is a revised section of a drawing that, once applied, blends into the rest of the image. Patches work well on drawings made or reproduced on *opaque* papers, including bond, Bristol, diazo prints, color photocopies, and bubble-jet copies (7-72 through 7-78).

Fig. 7-72 This image is a bubble-jet enlargement of a retrocolor drawing and was made with brown kraft paper placed behind the original.

Although the client liked the design direction for this part of the building's interior, he wanted to reduce the amount of glass in the skylight and substitute flowering plants for the kentia palms shown in the large pots.

Fig. 7-72

The area to be patched will, of course, be slightly larger than the area of the revision so that the lines at the edges of the patch can match the lines of the existing illustration. The coloration of the patch, particularly at its edges, should match the existing illustration as closely as possible.

It is advisable always to make an extra copy of your line drawing on the same paper on which you intend to initially create the color drawing, be it a photocopy or a diazo print. In addition, if you intend to work on diazo paper and design revisions are possible later, you may want to make a *blank* print at the same machine speed setting. Thus, you will have an adequate amount of blank paper, for revision patches, that is of the same color and value as your original.

If a revision must be made, the original line drawing can act as an underlay over which the revised line drawing can be created. If necessary, use a light table to make the tracing easier.

In most cases you will find it easier to color the patch *before* you cut it out and apply it to the drawing. You can then color it freely, without having to take additional care at the edges of the patch. This will also allow for a smoother-looking patch.

Fig. 7-73

Fig. 7-73 White roll tracing paper was placed over the *original drawing*, and the revised images were drawn with the use of the same media.

Fig. 7-74

Fig. 7-74 The revised line images are shown here with white paper placed behind the tracing paper. Notice how the proposed cut lines are included in the image and that these cut lines follow the lines of the drawing wherever possible. Cuts that run alongside existing lines help to camouflage the edges of the patch.

Fig. 7-75 The revised images are shown here after color pencil was applied to the back of the sheet. Note how the color is taken *past* the cut lines.

Fig. 7-75

Fig. 7-76 The patch sheet was enlarged by bubble-jet to the same size as the "original" bubble-jet copy shown in figure 7-72. This sheet is far smaller and, thus, much less expensive than the copy shown in figure 7-72.

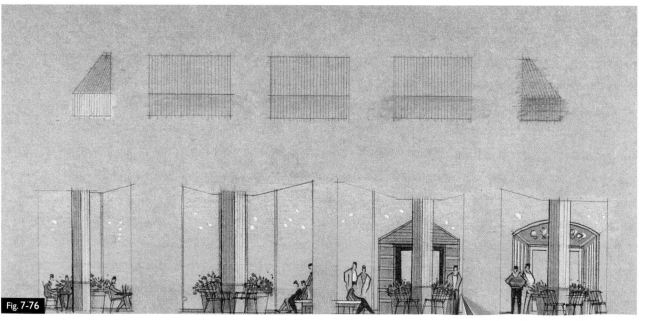

Fig. 7-76

Fig. 7-77 The patches were cut out, and spray adhesive was applied to the back of each. The patches were applied directly to the "original" bubble-jet copy.

Fig. 7-78 The completed revised image.

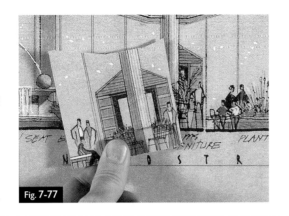

Fig. 7-77

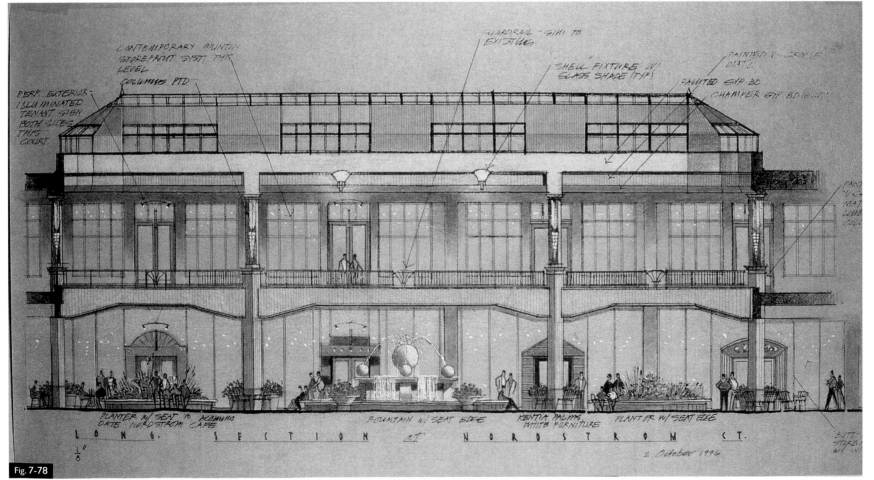

Fig. 7-78

The Splice

There are situations in which patches are inappropriate for revising or repairing a color drawing. These situations arise, in most cases, in working on paper that is *translucent* instead of opaque, because patching a translucent surface simply results in an area of increased density when the drawing is reproduced. Line drawings on vellum (that will be made into diazo prints) and retrocolor drawings on white roll tracing paper are two frequently used drawing types that should be spliced instead of patched.

Splices differ from patches in that patches are applied *over* the original or copy of the drawing, whereas a splice results in the revised and existing portions of a drawing being butted together in a precise manner, with no overlap, and taped together on the back with translucent "frosted" tape (7-79 through 7-83).

Fig. 7-79 The existing image was a retrocolor drawing on white tracing paper.

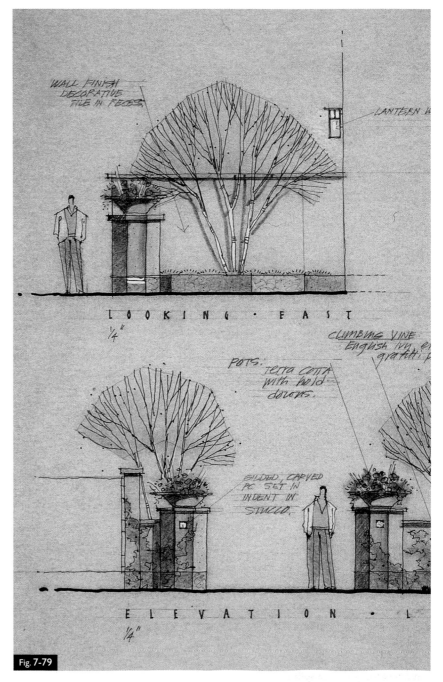

Fig. 7-79

Fig. 7-80

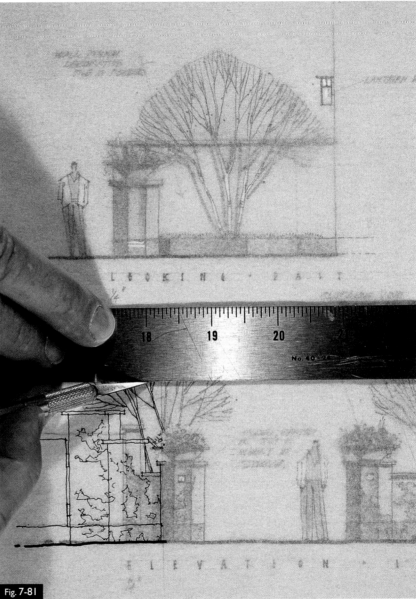

Fig. 7-81

Fig. 7-80 The revision was drawn on a new sheet of white roll tracing paper placed over the original drawing. Note that a boundary for the splice was drawn lightly with pencil so the designer would know how far to draw the revision and where to cut it.

Fig. 7-81 The original drawing and the revision were both taped to the drawing surface. An **X-acto** knife and steel ruler were used to cut along the boundary of the splice. The cut was carefully made through both the revision and the original sheets.

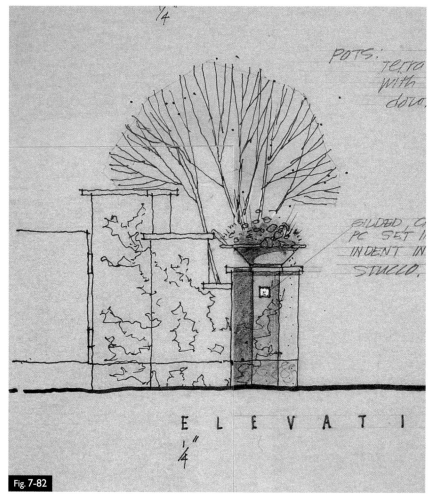

Fig. 7-82

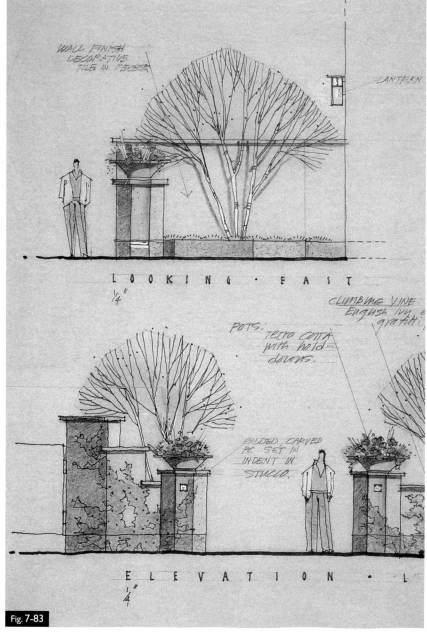

Fig. 7-83

Fig. 7-82 The unwanted portion of the original was removed and replaced with the revision. The edges of the revision and the remaining portion of the original match perfectly. Frosted tape was applied to the back, joining the two. Note that the tape should be continuous along the splice.

Fig. 7-83 The completed revision. Pastel and color pencil were applied to the back of the revision, including over the frosted tape, matching the colors on the original part of the drawing. Although the frosted tape has a different finish than the tracing paper, it has sufficient "tooth" that it takes color media and allows a color match with the original part of the drawing.

Computer Revisions

Sometimes drawings are most easily revised by computer. Hand drawings can be scanned and digitized, imported into such programs as Adobe Photoshop or Fractal Design's Painter for revision, then printed by color printer, through a color photocopier, or by a large-format bubble-jet printer/copier.

However, at this point, computer revisions of existing hand drawings are most effective in *removals of unwanted elements from fairly uniform backgrounds.*

Once an unwanted element is removed, the blank shape that remains must be filled in with something else (7-84, 7-85, 7-86). You can achieve a more visually seamless result if you fill this shape by replicating a surrounding uniform background color rather than creating a computer-generated patch. A computer-generated patch, even one that attempts to replicate hand drawing, will usually appear too obvious to blend unobtrusively into the surrounding drawing.

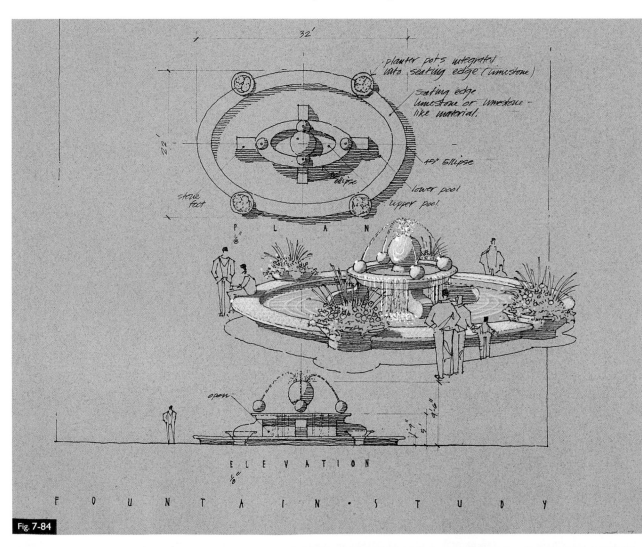

Fig. 7-84

Fig. 7-84 This original of a fountain study was created as a line drawing on tracing paper, then photocopied onto "Moonstone" colored Canson paper. The color was kept simple—only *White* and Derwent *Blue Violet Lake #27* pencils were used.

The client requested the sphere in the center of the fountain to be removed, because there was concern that it would obstruct certain important views within the project.

Fig. 7-85 The drawing was scanned and imported into Adobe Photoshop for revision. The drawing was enlarged on the computer screen, allowing the designer to remove unwanted lines easily and completely. An advantage to working at a magnified scale on a digital image is that small errors in line removal subsequent to repair of the image are not noticeable when the drawing is returned to its normal size.

The "cloning tool" (also called the "rubber stamp" tool) was used extensively to replace lines with the background color and texture, as well as to extend lines.

The "graphic pen" tool was used to reconstruct and complete missing lines, such as where the ball had occluded the far edge of the upper bowl. Once the graphic pen tool located the places where the missing lines were to be drawn, the graphic pen path was stroked with a "paintbrush tool" to draw them. The paintbrush tool and the "airbrush tool" were also used to draw in the falling and splashing water that results from the four arching jets meeting in the center.

Fig. 7-86 The revision took about 40 minutes and resulted in the printout you see here. Although the color of the printout will rarely match either the original or the image shown on the computer monitor, the result is usually worthwhile when a drawing cannot be easily altered any other way. (Revision: Jason Howard)

Fig. 7-85

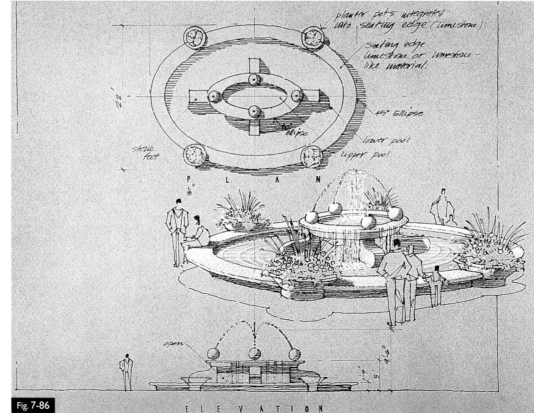

Fig. 7-86

PRESENTATION AND DISTRIBUTION OF COLOR DESIGN DRAWINGS

It was not long ago that when a designer wanted to show a color design drawing to a classroom or conference room group of 5 to 20 people, he had to create an illustration that was at least 18" x 24" or, more likely, 24" x 36" in size. Needless to say, color drawings of that size can take many hours, if not days, longer than one of similar quality created on an 8½" x 11" sheet of paper. In addition to the enormous amount of time invested, the additional detail a large-format drawing involves usually does little to enhance the concept the drawing is intended to communicate.

The evolution of high-quality color photocopy processes has allowed designers to create much smaller illustrations. As you know, small-format (8½" x 11" to 11" x 17") color design drawings have been advocated throughout this book. They can be created much more quickly than large drawings and can keep the designer at a greater "distance" from the image. This distance not only allows her to more easily keep her eye on the conceptual overview, the "big picture," but also keeps her from being drawn prematurely into the details of the project.

Creating color design drawings as small as workable, then enlarging them for presentation, is an efficient way to work during the early phases of the design process. Although enlarged color reproductions can be expensive, their cost is far less than the difference in fee cost for creating a small drawing versus a large one. If you are a practitioner, the cost of color reproductions is usually passed on the client. If you are a student, you must typically absorb such costs. In any case, it is important to become familiar with the capabilities of these reproduction processes. Although every color drawing created for every project need not be expensively reproduced, you will find it informative to at least occasionally reproduce and present your color drawings using the color photocopy and bubble-jet processes.

Generally speaking, presentation usually requires that design information be *enlarged,* whereas distribution of that information usually requires that it be *reduced* in size. This chapter shows some of the ways we present and distribute color design drawings at CommArts. We present to both small and large groups, so the presentation format is an issue we must consider as we make our final preparations for a presentation. We frequently compile the design information we present to clients into a reduced "sketchpack," which is distributed to them after each appropriate milestone in the progress of the project's design phase.

PRESENTATION

Designers must frequently prepare for both small- and large-scale presentations. Your familiarity with both formats will enable you to plan your efforts accordingly, so that your preparations can proceed smoothly.

Small-Scale Presentations

You will most often find yourself involved in small-scale design presentations, typically in a conference room or classroom with about 5 to 20 people in attendance. These presentations have varying degrees of formality, ranging from a less formal "pin-up" session to more highly organized and orchestrated presentations. Most of the time our clients prefer to dispense a with formal presentation and have a pin-up work session instead.

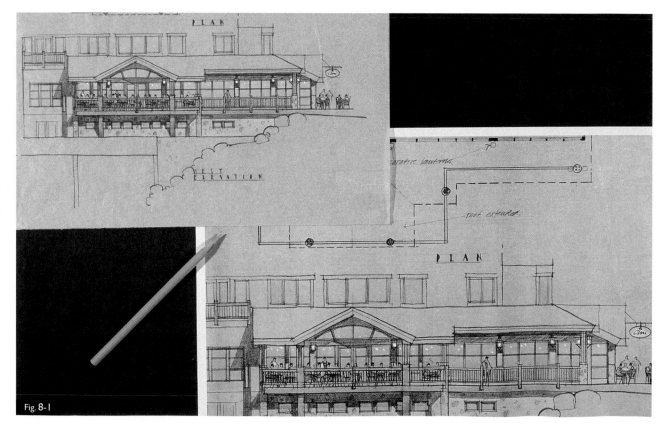

Fig. 8-1 This modest 150% enlargement helped the original drawing *(upper left)* become more visible for a presentation. A sheet of brown kraft paper was placed behind the original before it was color photocopied, which, along with adjusted photocopier settings, helped the image become richer and somewhat more pronounced. The photocopy size is 11" x 17".

The original line drawing was created with a *Black* Prismacolor pencil on white tracing paper. Color was added to the back with color pencil.

Fig. 8-1

In small-scale presentations, the images you show should be large enough for all participants to see comfortably. This size ranges from sheets that are 11" x 17" to 24" x 36" and sometimes larger, depending on the content of the drawings. Most ordinary color photocopiers can enlarge an image up to 400%, and an 11" x 17" color photocopy is typically the largest output image size they can manage (8-1). An 11" x 17" image is often satisfactory in a group this size. If a larger image is required, however, the original drawing can be enlarged one part at a time, then spliced together (8-2). Many color photocopiers have a "tile" or "poster" function, so that if the enlargement requires multiple sheets, the copier can be programmed to provide them automatically. The enlarged image is output on a series of 8½" x 11" or 11" x 17" sheets, ready to be spliced together (8-3).

When you need a larger, contiguous high-quality color image of an original color design drawing, you may wish to use a bubble-jet color photocopier (8-4). At this writing, this kind of copier produces the best color reproductions of original art of all the widely available color photocopy technologies (8-5). It can enlarge up to 1200% and reduce to 35% of original size and can produce an image up to 24" wide and of any length, as the paper is dispensed from a 24" wide roll.

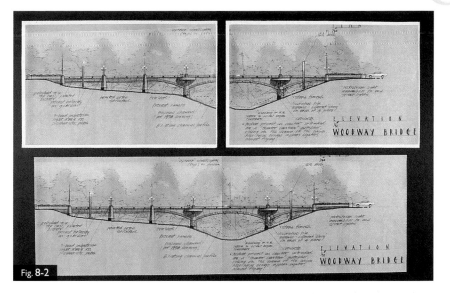

Fig. 8-2

Fig. 8-2 The design study shown here was enlarged 200%, requiring two 11" x 17" sheets *(top)*. The sheets were spliced together, with the use of a light table to align the overlapping parts of the images on the sheets. The two images were then cut with an X-acto knife and a straightedge, through the overlap, then taped together with a continuous strip of tape on the back to join the sheets *(bottom)*.

The original line drawing was made with a Micron 005 pen on white tracing paper. Color was applied to the back of the drawing. Color pencil was used on the bridge, and pastel was applied to the background trees and sky. The white highlights were added with touches of white gouache to the front of the drawing.

Fig. 8-3 The four-page enlargement shown here is the result of using the "poster" function on a Xerox color photocopier. The 11" x 17" sheets are ready to be spliced together.

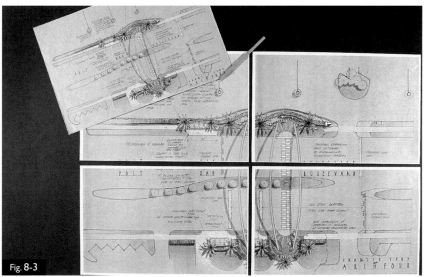

Fig. 8-3

Fig. 8-4 The Canon 2436 bubble-jet photocopier. It produces excellent color copies on a matte-finish paper stock that takes marker and color pencil quite well when premeeting touch-ups are required.

Although this copier is about the same height as a typical photocopier, it is wider—about 5' wide—and deeper—about 4' deep. (©1995 Canon Inc. / Canon U.S.A., Inc. Reproduced with permission.)

Fig. 8-5 This hotel garden study is a 400% single-sheet bubble-jet enlargement of the 4" x 10" drawing shown at the top.

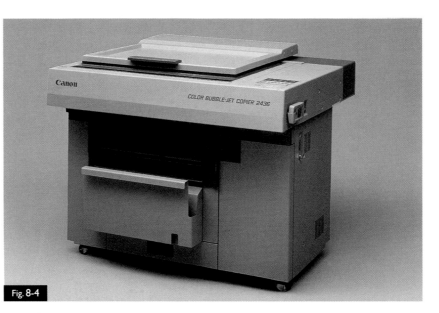

Fig. 8-4

Fig. 8-5

There will be occasions when you are required to arrange your design ideas in a more highly organized way, even early in the design process. One way we do this quickly and easily is to adhere all the various and disparately sized drawings to large (usually 24" x 36"), blank uniformly sized "carrier sheets." To one side, the title block, project name and logo, and other relevant information is printed (8-6). These sheets are usually diazo prints or large-format black-and-white photocopies. Various kinds of design information, including sketches, notes, photocopies, photographs, and color chips are neatly affixed to the carrier sheets with spray adhesive and transparent tape. Although the component parts vary in size, the uniformity of the carrier sheets lends a well-organized appearance to the variety of design information.

Another effective way to organize a presentation is to format the graphic and written information with a computer. Color design drawings can be scanned and imported into such programs as Adobe Illustrator or Macromedia Freehand, then sized, cropped, arranged, and overwritten with typeset headings and notes. Although usually more time-consuming than the carrier-sheet approach, the use of the computer can yield a highly polished result. A hard copy of this kind of presentation can be generated at any size up to 60" wide and of any length on an ink-jet printer or as small as 8½" x 11" on a standard color printer (8-7).

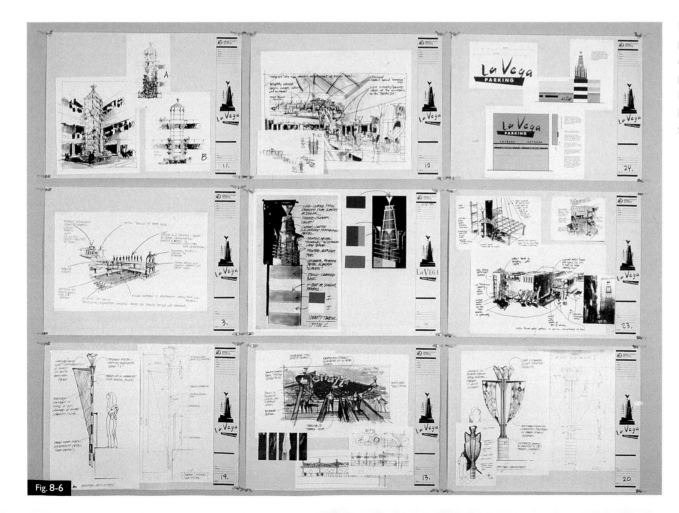

Fig. 8-6

Fig. 8-6 These various-sized drawings, photocopies, and color chips were applied to uniform carrier sheets for a presentation. (Drawings by Jim Babinchak and Doug Stelling; digital images by Patty Van Hook, Margaret Sewell, and Keith Harley.)

Fig. 8-7 This is part of a 5' x 10' digital image, produced by a large-format ink-jet printer, used as part of a more polished presentation. Note how the hand-drawn design studies are incorporated into the digital image. This image was composed using Macromedia Freehand. (Drawings by Bryan Gough; digital image by Patty Van Hook.)

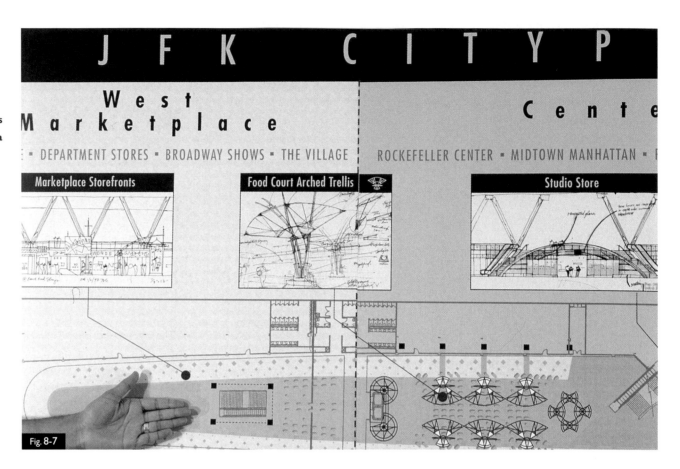

Large-Scale Presentations

There will be occasions during your career as a designer when you will be called upon to give a presentation to a large group. In most cases you will need a projection system with which you can create high quality images large enough to be seen comfortably in a large meeting room or auditorium. Two readily available ways of presenting these images are by means of color transparencies and by use of a digital LCD projector.

Color Transparencies

Color *transparencies,* usually called "slides," offer a way to show large, high-quality color images to a large audience. They also offer an excellent way to archive your design work.

You can make your own high-quality slides of your color design drawings—or of entire carrier sheet arrangements—by following the steps shown in figures 8-8 through 8-16.

Slides have a number of advantages as a large-format presentation system. They are relatively inexpensive to make, inasmuch as you are likely to already own or have access to most of the equipment required through your office or school. The photography of original art for the purpose of making slides can be accomplished fairly quickly after the equipment is set up; once the lighting and camera settings are established for the first picture, the same lighting arrangement and settings are used for each of the subsequent exposures. The film can also be developed quickly. Kodak Ektachrome, a film commonly used for slides, can be developed in a day, in most locations, at normal prices and as quickly as in one hour for an additional rush fee.

How to Make Perfect Slides of Your Color Drawings

Perfect color slides, called "transparencies" in photographic parlance, are easy to make with the proper equipment and a little patience. You will need controlled lighting conditions, whereby your drawings are *evenly* illuminated with light sources that match the film you intend to use. In addition, you will need a way to accurately measure that light at the surface of your drawing, so that you know at what f-stop and shutter speed to set your camera. Once you know these settings, take *three* pictures (this is known as "bracketing"): one at the recommended settings and one each at a half stop *above* and a half stop *below* the recommended f-stop setting. Leave the shutter speed at the same setting for all three shots.

This section will show you the steps to making these slides. When photographing drawings that are about 8½" x 11" and larger, the setup shown in the following steps works well. A wide-angle/telephoto zoom lens that can operate in the 28 mm to 105 mm range will serve you best, allowing you to zoom in or out, depending on your drawing sizes. You can also use a standard 50 mm lens, but you will find you have to move the camera and tripod more often as you photograph various-sized drawings. If you wish to photograph smaller drawings, use a close-up "macro" lens and a copy stand. A copy stand is a tabletop setup in which the camera is mounted on an adjustable riser and the attached lights illuminate the drawing from both sides. The principle is exactly the same as in the setup that follows, except that the camera tripod and light stands are dispensed with, allowing the camera to get closer to the small drawings.

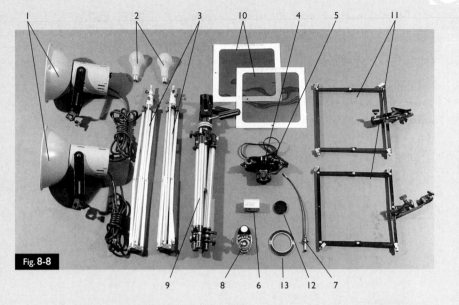

Fig. 8-8

Fig. 8-8 The equipment you will need is shown here. Although not particularly sophisticated, it will provide excellent results: (1) two photoflood reflectors, (2) two 250 watt, 3200° K "tungsten" photoflood lamps, (3) two stands for the photoflood reflectors, (4) 35 mm SLR camera with manual adjustments, (5) zoom lens (although a regular 50 mm lens will work), (6) slide film for use with tungsten lamps; Kodak Ektachrome 64T slide film will give very good results, (7) cable release; this allows you to take your shots without jiggling the camera, as you will be using slow shutter speeds, (8) light meter, (9) camera tripod.

The remaining equipment is optional. Certain kinds of drawing— those on which a large amount of graphite or marker has been used, those on wrinkled tracing paper, and those

with very dark or black backgrounds— often do not photograph well because they show reflections no matter how you adjust your lights. By using (10) polarizing filters, held in front of your lights with (11) filter holders and a (12) polarizing filter over the camera lens, you can adjust the filter on the lens and "dial out" the reflections from these kinds of drawing. A word of caution: Polarizing filters are made with a kind of plastic that can char and melt from the heat of the photoflood lamps. Make sure you arrange your filter holders to hold the filters as far in front of the lights as possible. Cropping tape (13) is a heat-reflective mylar tape you can use to crop out unwanted edges on your finished slides.

Fig. 8-9 This is the arrangement of lights, camera, and wall-mounted drawing used to create slides. The lights and camera are roughly in line, *horizontally,* with one another. The lights should point in at the drawing at about 45°, as shown. The distance of the camera and lights from the drawing can vary widely, depending on how close you must get to the drawing to fill the camera's viewfinder adequately with the image. Here, the lights and camera are arranged to photograph a drawing that is 24" x 36" in size.

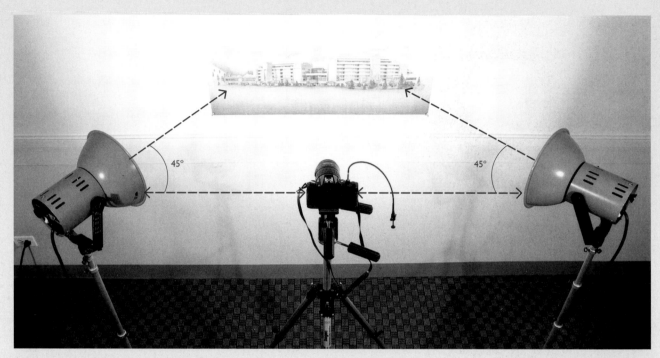

Fig. 8-10 Note also that the lights and camera are approximately aligned *vertically* with each other.

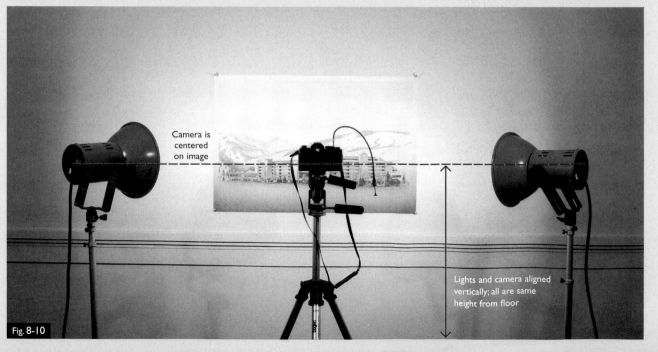

Camera is centered on image

Lights and camera aligned vertically; all are same height from floor

Fig. 8-10

Fig. 8-11

Fig. 8-12

Fig. 8-11 Once your lights and camera are arranged, use a light meter to determine the camera f-stop and the shutter speed settings you should use. The meter will give you a wide variety of corresponding f-stop and shutter-speed settings to choose from. *Do not use the camera's through-the-lens metering system,* as you may get erroneous readings. The light meter can be used to take *reflected* readings from a standardized "gray card," or it can be used to take *incident* (incoming) light readings, as shown in figure 8-12.

Fig. 8-12 You can measure the level of incident light reaching the drawing's surface by holding the meter, sensor outward, against the drawing's surface as shown here. Note that the photographer has ducked low to avoid casting a shadow on the drawing.

You should take light readings in more than one location on the drawing's surface to make sure that the light is even across the drawing. It is good to take additional readings at the drawing's edges, in the vicinities shown by the crosses. *If your light meter indicates that the light levels vary by more than a half stop between the center and the edges of your drawing,* adjust your lighting to avoid "hot spots" on your finished slides. You may need to move your lights farther away from the drawing, so they illuminate the drawing's surface more evenly, then remeasure the light levels. Even lighting is the most important part of creating perfect slides.

Fig. 8-13

Fig. 8-13 Choose an f-stop setting at about 8 or slightly higher to achieve a good depth of field. You will find, given the lamp wattages and the distance of the lights from the surface of the drawing, that your light meter will recommend a corresponding shutter speed in the vicinity of ¼ second to ⅛ second.

Once all is ready and you have set the f-stop and shutter speed on your camera, use the cable release to take the picture. Then *bracket* your shot by taking two more pictures, one at ½ stop *below* the setting recommended by the light meter and one at ½ stop *above* that recommended by the light meter. The camera pictured here shows the f-stop set at f8 and the shutter speed set at ⅛ second. To bracket below, move the f-stop ring on the lens to *between* 8 and 5.6, then take your second shot. To bracket above, move the f-stop ring to *between* 8 and 11, then take your third shot. The shutter-speed setting stays where it is throughout the three shots. When you receive your finished slides, arrange them on a light table and select the best of the three shots.

You can photograph any remaining drawings using the *same* camera settings, as long as the lights stay in the same place. You can move the camera closer or farther away from the wall as you wish. However, *once you move the lights, new camera settings may be necessary.* Take new measurements with the light meter whenever you move the lights.

Fig. 8-14 This is a typical image taken during a slide-shooting session. Although it is a good idea to fill the frame with the image to the degree possible, you will still probably see some wall surface, pushpins, or tape in the corners of your image.

Fig. 8-14

Fig. 8-15

Fig. 8-15 You can apply cropping tape to block unwanted edge conditions seen in your finished slides.

Fig. 8-16 The finished image, after cropping tape has been applied. The color version of this image can be seen in figure 6-3.

Fig. 8-16

The Digital LCD Projector

The *digital LCD projector* offers another way to present your color design drawings as large-scale images. This system can project the images from a laptop computer onto the same kind of screen used for slides (8-17). Your drawings can be scanned and formatted into the same programs mentioned earlier in preparation for projection and subsequent distribution. Although the clarity of the images shown by a digital LCD projector depends on their resolution, they are typically not as clear and vibrant as a good-quality color transparency. However, given the purpose of the images, as well as the ease with which presentations can be created, the disparity in clarity is of little consequence.

Fig. 8-17

Fig. 8-17 A digital LCD projector is another convenient means of making large-scale presentations of color drawings and design information. (Courtesy: Sony Electronics, Inc.)

DISTRIBUTION OF COLOR DESIGN DRAWINGS: THE SKETCHPACK

There will be situations in which you want to provide a small, portable compilation of the design ideas you present during a meeting, something at CommArts we call a *sketchpack,* to your client and other members of your design team. The sketchpack is an invaluable coordination tool during the early parts of the design process because it is a record of that process. It is also a clear indication to your client that her participation in the process is welcome and, as such, acts as a small but effective way to strengthen that relationship.

A sketchpack is just that—a pack of sketches. It is not intended to be a belabored book, nor should it appear too "finished." It is simply a set of ideas, progressing from those generated early in the design process to those distributed at the meeting. You can distribute sketchpacks before a meeting to make it easier for everyone in attendance to follow the presentation and to provide an opportunity for each person to make notes on her or his own set of drawings. Or you may wish to distribute the sketchpack upon completion of the presentation to provide participants with a record of the ideas and images on which they can further reflect at their convenience.

Reduced Wall Presentation

Sketchpacks are prepared in two basic ways. They can be prepared by hand or with the help of a computer—or, when appropriate, by a combination of the two approaches.

The most direct way to prepare a sketchpack is to simply reproduce the original drawings (which were enlarged for a wall-mounted presentation) or adhere them to a small, formatted carrier sheet, usually 11" x 17", then reproduce the assembled sheets with a color photocopier, making as many copies as necessary. To save space, black-and-white line drawings that were a part of the original presentation can be further reduced before they are adhered to the sketchpack carrier sheet. It is helpful to include a graphic scale with reduced orthographic drawings so that the sketchpack user can make at least rough measurements.

Another way of quickly creating a sketchpack is to reduce larger-scale wall presentations that use carrier sheets, like those shown in figure 8-6, using a bubble-jet copier, this time reducing the sheets to fit within an 11" x 17" format.

Once these reduced 11" x 17" bubble-jet copies are created, they are used as the new, small-size "originals" from which multiple copies can be made. This is possible because the bubble-jet "original" possesses a kind of screen pattern, as well as excellent color quality, that allows it, in turn, to generate good color copies. The subsequent multiple copies can be made less expensively with a regular color photocopier. Although the resultant multiple copies are second- (and in some cases, third-) generation color copies, they are usually adequate as a record of the presentation (8-18). If truer colors must be communicated in a sketchpack, first-generation color copies or actual color chips can be inserted into each sketchpack.

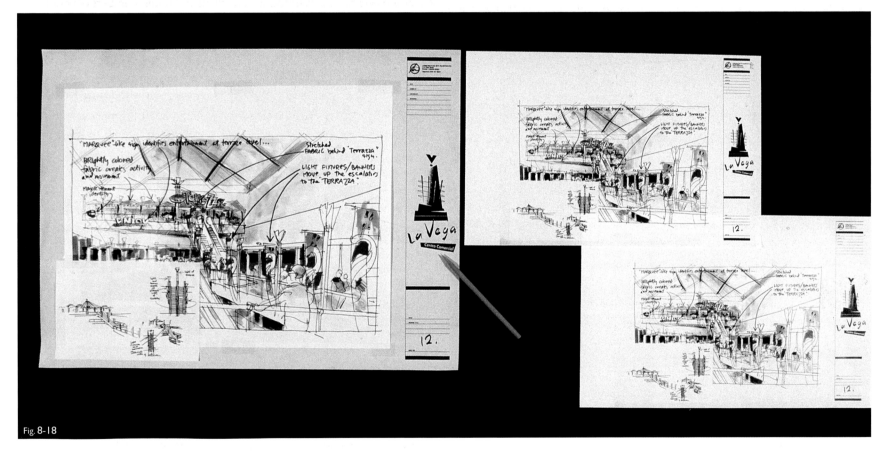

Fig. 8-18

Fig. 8-18 An 18" x 24" carrier sheet and its images (left) have been reduced to 11" x 17" with a bubble-jet copier (upper right). A color photocopier was used to make subsequent copies (lower right) for distribution, using the bubble-jet copy as the "original." (Drawings: Doug Stelling)

The Computer-Generated Sketchpack

If your wall presentation was originated on a computer, as in figure 8-7, or if your original color drawings and other design materials are small enough to fit on a flatbed scanner, they can be scanned and imported into a page-making program to be sized and arranged in a sketchpack format. Although digitally generated sketchpacks usually take slightly longer to prepare, one of their advantages is that once the materials are scanned, it is easier to size, manipulate, arrange, and format them than to work with hard copies of various images. Moreover, the output images are usually somewhat better, because they are first-generation rather than second- or third-generation images. These images can also be output directly through a color printer (8-19).

A word of caution is in order concerning computer-generated sketchpacks. Page-making programs give designers many wonderful tools with which to create professional-looking publications. However, if you use these programs, you will likely be tempted by the "snazz factor." The snazz factor manifests itself when a designer spends too much time making a sketchpack look *too* good. The result is twofold: First, it wastes design fee on something that is meant to be a simple record of the *real* design ideas—the ideas you were hired to generate. Second, sketchpacks that are very polished also have the effect, often subliminal, of communicating to the viewer—especially the client—that the design process is closed and the decisions have been made. See how "finished" it is? Exercise judgment when preparing sketchpacks and presentations. Think twice about how finished you want your sketchpacks to look and, if they *do* appear finished, that this is your intent.

Fig. 8-19 The large digital ink-jet image shown in figure 8-7 was subsequently produced at an 11" x 17" size for distribution as part of a sketchpack. For the small version, the designer revised the color of the center background panel.

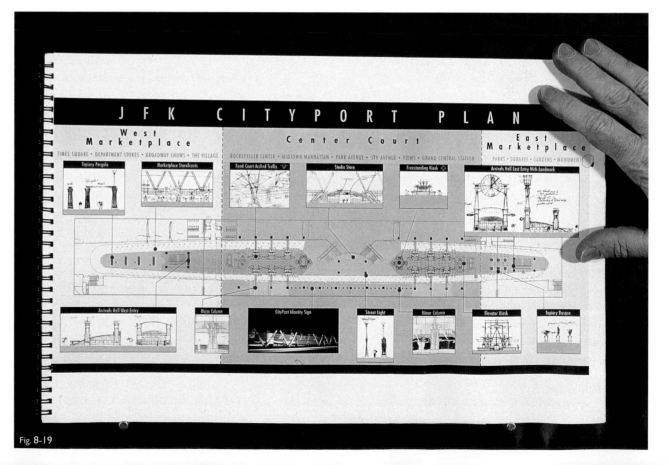

Fig. 8-19

Binding Your Sketchpack

Sketchpacks can be packaged simply, by placing a staple in the upper left-hand corner or three staples in the left-hand side with a binding strip, similar to the way architectural drawings are packaged (8-20). Arrangements of this kind may require the use of a heavy-duty stapler if the sketchpack is too thick for an office stapler.

A somewhat more finished booklet can be created (when this level of finish is appropriate) if you have access to a binding machine (8-21). With a spiral binding, a stiff cardboard back, and a clear acetate cover sheet, the sketchpack can become a more permanent record of your design process.

Fig. 8-21

Fig. 8-20

Fig. 8-21 You may wish to provide your more finished sketchpacks with a spiral binding. A spiral-binding machine can punch multiple holes through a group of pages and hold the spiral wire binding open while the operator assembles the booklet.

Fig. 8-20 Sketchpack bindings can range from a staple in the upper left corner (above) to a stapled binding strip (below). Thick sketchpacks may require the use of a heavy-duty stapler like that shown on the left. (Drawings: Taku Shimizu)

GLOSSARY

aerial perspective A view from above, created by making a drawing below its horizon line. This kind of perspective is also known as a "bird's-eye perspective" (see also *atmospheric perspective*).

afterimage The imagery seen floating before one's eyes after the stimulus has been withdrawn.

analogous hues Hues related to one another owing to their side-by side relationship on the color wheel.

aniline dye The dye used as the colorant in markers. Aniline dye is sensitive to ultraviolet light, and drawings using markers should be archived by color slides. If such a drawing is to be displayed, make a color bubble-jet photocopy for display purposes and store the original in a dark place.

atmospheric perspective The pronounced illusion of distance caused by the progressive changes in colors as they recede in space. Generally, colors become weaker in chroma, higher in value, and shift in hue toward the purple and purple-blue range. Artists sometimes call this effect "aerial perspective."

background (of a diazo print) The general value of exposed diazo print paper. The more the diazo machine speed is increased, the darker the background becomes.

background (of a drawing) The part of a drawing that occurs behind the center of interest.

balance The quality of a drawing whereby its various parts appear to be in proper proportion to one another.

base, marker base The initial application of color to a drawing, often made with marker.

blackline print A diazo reproduction of a drawing made on blackline paper. It has a gray background, and its lines range from gray to black.

blueline print A diazo reproduction of a drawing made on blueline paper. It has a bluish background and blue lines.

bond paper An inexpensive white paper used in most black-and-white photocopiers. Use 24 lb. or heavier bond paper for color drawings if possible.

brilliance Another word for the chroma of a color, also called "intensity," "saturation," or "purity."

Bristol paper A high-quality white paper often used for presentation-quality color drawings. This paper has excellent tooth and shows marker, color pencil, and pastel very well. The two-ply "vellum" finish is the best to use for the types of drawing shown in this book and easily takes a black-and-white photocopy image.

bubble-jet photocopier A color photocopier that, at this writing, creates the best color photocopies of original color drawings.

Canson paper A high-quality textured drawing paper that shows marker, color pencil, and pastel well. It can also receive images from a photocopier, although it may need to be sprayed with a fixative such as Krylon Crystal Clear spray acrylic, as the toner from the photocopier may not completely fuse to the paper because of its texture. Canson is part of the Mi-Tienes line of paper made by Canson-Talens.

chiaroscuro The light-to-dark shading of an illustrated form, used to make it appear three-dimensional.

chroma The strength of a color, which can range from weak (almost gray) to strong (pure). Other names for chroma include "saturation," "purity," "brilliance," and "intensity."

color wheel A circular arrangement of hues based on the side-by-side relationship of colors seen in visible light when it is refracted. The circular arrangement is useful to designers and artists because it makes the relationships between the hues more readily visible.

complementary hues Hues that are diametrically opposite each other on the color wheel. When these hues are placed side by side, each makes the other appear its most intense.

composition An arrangement of elements intended to be seen together, as a whole.

contrast A perceivable difference between two parts of the same color dimension. This difference can range from subtle to strong.

cool gray A gray that is very slightly bluish.

cool hue, cool color A hue or color that is associated with cool temperatures. Blue green, blue, purple blue, and purple are the cool hues on the Munsell color wheel (see figure 6-2). Green and red purple form the border between the warm and cool colors on the color wheel and can be made to be either warm or cool.

design drawing Exploratory drawing used to manifest early design ideas for oneself and to communicate those ideas to others.

diazo print A reproduction of a drawing made with use of the diazo printing process. The print is produced by exposing the drawing, together with photosensitive paper, to a special light and subsequent developer, usually ammonia. Diazo prints are commonly made on blue-, black-, or brownline paper, but other colors are available.

diffuse shadow edge A shadow edge that gradually changes from shadow to light and forms no distinct boundary.

digital LCD projector A projector that can project an image from a computer, usually a laptop, similar to that of a slide projector.

dimension of color A perceivable, measurable quality of a color. A color has three dimensions—hue, value, and chroma—and each may be theoretically altered without affecting the others.

distinct shadow edge A shadow edge that forms a distinct boundary between shadow and light.

dominant, dominance Relates to that which perceptibly occupies most of the area in a drawing; usually used in reference to the presence of a particular dimension of color in a composition.

entourage Elements that are added to a design drawing, such as figures and automobiles, that help give the drawing scale and context.

even wash A coating of color, usually by color pencil, that does not vary over the area to which it is applied.

fixative A sprayed coating that helps to keep powdery color media, such as pastel, from smearing. Fixatives should be used with care, as they can somewhat deaden the brilliance of pastels.

flavoring A wash that imparts only a subtle hint of color, usually with color pencil.

forcing the shadow The act of grading a shadow darker toward its boundary, so the illuminated surface next to it appears brighter by contrast. This term also includes the converse, whereby an illuminated surface is made lighter next to a shadow.

foreground That part of a drawing that lies in front of the center of interest. Foreground elements are often used compositionally to make the middle ground appear more luminous and to help "frame" the center of interest.

French gray Grays that are very slightly yellowish or yellow reddish.

Golden Mean A guide to proportional relationships between two parts of a thing, developed by the Greeks, whereby the relationship of the smaller part to the larger part is the same as the larger part's relationship to the whole.

gouache An opaque watercolor paint.

gradation A gradual change in the dimensions of color over a given surface. A gradation can occur in one, two, or all three dimensions of a surface's color simultaneously.

graded wash A wash of color, applied with marker, pencil, or pastel, whose dimensions are made to change over a given surface.

grain The texture of a paper, also known as its "tooth." A fine-grain paper, such as Bristol, has less apparent "tooth" than a coarse-grain paper, such as Canson.

highlight The lightest spot or area of a surface, usually created by a light source or specular reflection.

hue The name of a color and one of its three dimensions.

hue chart A chart of orderly samplings of a hue that displays its range of value and chroma. The extent of the ranges depends on the color medium used.

hue scheme A set of hues intended for a composition that are chosen for their particular relationship on the color wheel.

indistinct shadow edge See *diffuse shadow edge.*

key A closely related group of values that dominate the colors of a composition. Light values dominate a "high-key" composition, and dark values dominate a "low-key" composition.

lightness The degree to which the value of a color approaches white.

local tone The inherent value of an object, regardless of its illumination.

lowlights Small areas of shade, shadow, or very dark reflection on an object that usually also contain highlights.

luminosity The appearance of giving off light.

marker A color application device that has a chisel-shaped tip made of an absorbent proprietary plastic. The coloring medium is composed of a carrier and a dye. The carrier is either alcohol or xylene, and the colorant is aniline dye. The colors are transparent and dry very quickly upon application.

medial mixture The color created as the result of a visual averaging or mixing of several separate colors.

mingling Creating a mixture of different colors in which each color retains some of its original identity. Mingling is often used in watercolor illustrations, and similar effects can be achieved with markers, with color pencils, and with pastels.

monochromatic Having or consisting of a single hue. In a monochromatic hue scheme, the dimensions of value and chroma may vary, but only one hue is used.

Munsell Student Charts A series of 10 hue charts and a chart containing the Munsell color wheel, a value scale, and a sample chroma scale. These charts are useful references for color composition work and can be obtained from Fairchild Books, 7 West 34th Street, New York, NY 10001; 800-247-6622.

Munsell System of Color A system in which color is organized visually rather than according to the mixture of pigments or dyes. It was originated by Albert H. Munsell in 1898, and the Munsell Color Company was formed shortly before his death in 1918. This system, like all color systems, originated from the need to describe colors in definite terms.

neutral color A color that has no hue or chroma; white, black, and the grays.

palette A selection of colors used for a particular purpose or series of similar purposes.

paraline drawing A drawing that uses parallel lines to create three-dimensional images. Isometric, dimetric, axonometric, and oblique drawings are all types of paraline drawing.

pastel A color stick made by combining dry pigment with a methylcellulose binder.

pastel "quickie" A color drawing created very quickly with the use of pastel.

patch A revised portion of a drawing applied directly over the original or over a reproduction of the original.

poché (n.) The shading of that part of an architectural drawing representing a section cut; (v.) to shade a section cut, usually with pencil or pen.

presentation drawing A drawing used to communicate design ideas in a presentation situation. In addition to communicating design content, presentation drawings are also prepared as compositions in their own right.

print A diazo reproduction of a drawing.

proportion The relationship between the various parts of a thing.

punch Visual impact in a drawing, usually created by value contrast.

reflection mass A group of objects reflected in a window or series of windows that are so dark as to appear in the reflection as a single mass.

refract To break white light into its component colors, usually by a prism or in a rainbow. The component colors of white light are red, orange, yellow, green, blue, indigo, and violet.

repetition A form of rhythm in which a characteristic is repeated throughout a drawing.

retrocolor The application of color to the back of a drawing on a translucent sheet, such as white tracing paper.

retrocolor hybrid A retrocolor drawing whose front-side image is created by both computer and hand drawing.

reversal An image in which the typical black-line-on-white-background is reversed, exhibiting white lines on a black background. A reversal is most easily made with the use of a color copier (most color copiers have a function to provide this kind of image). To produce the drawing surface for figures 4-76 through 4-78, the reversed image was again photocopied, using a black-and-white photocopier to transfer it to frosted mylar. The frosted mylar reversal was subsequently printed on blackline diazo paper, with the machine at *normal* speed.

rhythm Flow or apparent movement characterized by regular recurrence of elements or features. In color drawing, rhythm can be introduced with such things as gradations and repetition.

saturation The chroma of a color; its degree of purity, which can range from weak, or grayish, to strong or vivid.

setup An image that provides the basic guidelines for a drawing, usually a perspective view. Setups can be rough hand-drawn layouts, computer wireframes, real-life photographs, or photographs of models.

shade The diminished light on a surface as a result of its facing away from the source.

shadow The absence of direct light on a surface caused by an intervening object.

simultaneous contrast The effect created by placing complementary hues in proximity to each other. Each makes the other appear its most vivid. It can also mean the phenomenon whereby the eye conjures up the complement of a color it is seeing, even if that complement is not present.

sketch A quick, loose drawing used to depict an idea, usually preliminary in nature.

sketchpack A collection of exploratory design drawings that are assembled into a uniform, manageable size for subsequent review, usually 11" x 17". This term originated at CommArts.

source file A file of color photographs and clippings that is used as a reference for drawing elements, materials, and finishes.

spatial interest "The anticipated experience of a variety of spaces and vistas [seen in a drawing] which [promise to] become available as we move through the space" (from *Drawing as a Means to Architecture*, Revised Edition, by William Kirby Lockard. 1977. Tucson: Pepper Publishing).

spectrum value The value of a color when it is shown at its strongest chroma.

splice A revised portion of a drawing that is cut into the original or a reproduction of the original.

stipple The addition of small dots to a drawing, usually with pen or pencil, to create a texture.

subordinate That part of a color composition that does not possess the dominant qualities of the composition.

toned paper A paper that is not white, but has a gray or colored surface. The toned papers most commonly used for color design drawing are diazo print paper (run at a faster-than-usual speed through the machine), Canson paper, and white roll tracing paper backed with colored or kraft paper.

tooth See *grain.*

transfer The reproduction of a line drawing, usually by black-and-white photocopier, onto the final drawing surface.

transparency A transparent color film positive, the 35 mm version of which is also known as a "slide."

triad Any three hues that are approximately equidistant on a color wheel.

unity The quality of a composition whereby the various parts act together to form a single idea.

value The lightness or darkness of a color or colorless area.

value strategy Plan for arranging the major values of a drawing that best serves the ideas shown therein.

value study A small, quick study used to create and test possible arrangements of the major values for a presentation drawing. The chosen study is an effective guide in creating the final drawing.

values, major Large, contiguous areas of similar values in a drawing.

vellum A translucent drawing paper, heavier than white roll tracing paper, suitable for diazo printing. A common type is Clearprint 1000H.

vellum finish A lightly textured finish, characteristic of Bristol paper. Bristol can also be obtained in a very smooth "plate" finish, typically better suited for certain types of media such as graphite pencil.

visual mixture The color resulting from the blending by eye of several different colors (see also *medial mixture*).

warm gray A gray that is very slightly reddish.

warm hue A hue that is associated with warm temperatures. Red, yellow red, yellow, and green yellow are warm hues on the Munsell color wheel (see figure 6-2). Green and red purple form the boundary between warm and cool hues and can be made to be either warm or cool.

wash A coating of color, usually color pencil, but can also be created by marker or pastel.

xylene A fast-drying organic solvent used as a carrying agent for the aniline dye in markers. Markers containing xylene should be used in a well-ventilated place.

BIBLIOGRAPHY

Ackerman, Diane. 1991. *A Natural History of the Senses.* New York: Vintage.

Albers, Josef. 1963. *Interaction of Color.* New Haven, Conn.: Yale University Press.

American Society of Architectural Perspectivists. 1996. *Architecture in Perspective: 11th Annual International Competition of Architectural Illustration.* Rockport, N.Y.: Rockport Publishers.

Birren, Faber. 1965. *History of Color in Painting.* New York: Reinhold.

Birren, Faber. 1982. *Light, Color and Environment.* New York: Van Nostrand Reinhold.

Conran, Terence. 1993. *The Kitchen Book.* Woodstock, N.Y.: Overlook Press.

Doyle, Michael E. 1993. *Color Drawing.* Rev. ed. New York: John Wiley & Sons.

Drucker, Mindy, and Pierre Finkelstein. 1990. *Recipes for Surfaces.* New York: Fireside.

Feldman, Edmund Burke. 1987. *Varieties of Visual Experience.* New York: Abrams.

Goldstein, Nathan. 1977. *The Art of Responsive Drawing.* 2d ed. Englewood Cliffs, N.J.: Prentice-Hall.

Graham, Donald W. 1970. *Composing Pictures.* New York: Van Nostrand Reinhold.

Grice, Gordon, ed. 1997. *The Art of Architectural Illustration.* New York: McGraw-Hill.

Hale, Jonathan. 1994. *The Old Way of Seeing.* Boston: Houghton Mifflin.

Hope, Augustine, and Margaret Walch. 1990. *The Color Compendium.* New York: John Wiley & Sons.

Itten, Johannes. 1973. *The Art of Color.* New York: John Wiley & Sons.

Kautzky, Theodore. 1947. *Pencil Pictures: A Guide to Their Pleasing Arrangement.* New York: Van Nostrand Reinhold.

Lockard, William Kirby. 1977. *Drawing As A Means To Architecture.* Rev. ed. Tucson, Ariz.: Pepper.

Macbeth. 1996. *Munsell Color: The Universal Language* (brochure). New Windsor, N.Y.: Macbeth.

Neumeier, Marty. "Secrets of Design: Draftsmanship." *Critique* 6 (Autumn 1997): 18–27.

Simon, Hilda. 1980. *Color in Reproduction.* New York: Viking.

Spies, Werner. 1970. *Albers.* New York: Abrams.

Street-Porter, Tim. 1989. *Casa Mexicana.* New York: Stewart, Tabori & Chang.

The Editors of *Réalités.* 1973. *Impressionism.* Secaucus, N.J.: Chartwell Books.

DESIGN CREDITS

Fig. 1-2. After a photograph in *Casa Mexicana* by Tim Street-Porter. 1989. New York: Stewart, Tabori & Chang, Inc.

Fig. 1-3. After a photograph in *The Kitchen Book* by Terence Conran. 1993. Woodstock, New York: Overlook Press. The photograph is credited: "Rodney Hyett/Elizabeth Whiting and Associates (B. B. P. Architects, Melbourne, Australia)."

Fig. 1-8. Proposed modifications to Citywalk, Los Angeles. CommArts, designers, with Houston / Tyner, architects, for Universal Studios Hollywood.

Fig. 2-11. Park Meadows, Denver. CommArts, designers, with Anthony Belluschi Architects, for TrizecHahn.

Fig. 2-12. *The American Queen* (name originally proposed was *Belle of America*). CommArts, designers, for the Delta Queen Steamboat Company.

Fig. 2-13. Clark Street Improvements, St. Louis. CommArts, designers, for Judd Perkins.

Fig. 2-14. Plaza las Fuentes, Pasadena. CommArts, modification designers for Maguire Thomas Partners. Building architect was Moore Ruble Yudell.

Fig. 2-15. Houston Uptown, Houston. CommArts, designers, with Slaney Santana Group, landscape architects, for the Harris County Improvement District #1.

Fig. 2-16. St. Louis Union Station, St. Louis. CommArts, designers, with HOK, architects, for the Rouse Company.

Fig. 3-15. Ontario Mills, Los Angeles. CommArts, designers, with Feola Carli Archuleta, architects, for the Mills Corporation.

Fig. 3-16. Southwest Plaza, Denver. CommArts, designers, for Jordon Perlmutter Properties.

Fig. 3-17. Prestonwood, Dallas. CommArts, designers, with the Jerde Partnership, designers and architects, for TrizecHahn.

Fig. 3-18. Cineplex Odeon Theater at Citywalk, Los Angeles. CommArts, designers, with Houston / Tyner, architects, for Universal Studios Hollywood.

Figs. 3-22, 3-27, and 3-28. Fashion Place, Salt Lake City. CommArts, designers, with Feola Carli Archuleta, architects, for the Hahn Company.

Fig. 3-23. The Harvest Restaurant, Denver. CommArts, designers, for Jim and Paul Turley.

Fig. 3-24. Proposed modifications to stairway in the former location of the Angel's Flight funicular railway, Los Angeles. Stairway by Lawrence Halprin and Associates. Proposal for Maguire Thomas Partners.

Fig. 3-25. The Maxim Building, Boulder, Colorado. CommArts, designers, with the Hunter Group, architects, for 901 Walnut Street, L. L. C.

Fig. 3-26. Proposed modifications to Citywalk, Los Angeles. CommArts, designers, with Houston / Tyner, architects, for Universal Studios Hollywood.

Fig. 3-29. St. Louis Union Station, St. Louis. CommArts, designers, with HOK, architects, for the Rouse Company.

Fig. 3-30. St. Louis Union Station, St. Louis. CommArts, designers, with HOK, architects, for the Rouse Company.

Fig. 4-6. Pearlridge Mall, Honolulu. CommArts, designers, with Feola Carli Archuleta, architects, for Northwestern Mutual Life and E. Phillip Lyon Co.

Fig. 4-8. The Prudential Center, Boston. CommArts, designers, with Sikes, Jennings, Kelly and Brewer, architects, for the Prudential Property Company.

Fig. 4-10. Brothers Coffee, New York. CommArts, designers, for the Gloria Jean Coffee Company.

Fig. 4-46. Perimeter Mall, Atlanta. CommArts, designers, with D'Augustino, Izzo, Quirk, architects, for the Rouse Company.

Fig. 4-78. Pearlridge Mall, Honolulu. CommArts, designers, with Feola Carli Archuleta, architects, for Northwestern Mutual Life and E. Phillip Lyon Co.

Fig. 4-91. Houston Uptown, Houston. CommArts, designers, with Slaney Santana Group, landscape architects, for the Harris County Improvement District #1.

Fig. 4-120. Boulder County Courthouse Lawn Study, Boulder, Colorado. Comm Arts, designers, for Boulder County Commissioner Heath.

Fig. 4-135. The Maxim Building, Boulder, Colorado. CommArts, designers, with the Hunter Group, architects, for 901 Walnut Street, L.L.C.

Fig. 4-137. Westminster Promenade, Westminster, Colorado. CommArts, designers, with Martin and Martin Engineers, for the City of Westminster.

Fig. 5-1. Proposed modifications to Citywalk, Los Angeles. CommArts, designers, with Houston / Tyner, architects, for Universal Studios, Hollywood.

Fig. 5-2. Proposed modifications to the Uptown District of Houston. CommArts, designers, for Houston Metro.

Fig. 5-3. Hollywood Athletic Club, Los Angeles. Proposed modifications. CommArts, designers, for Hollywood Athletic Club.

Fig. 5-6. Brothers Coffee, New York. CommArts, designers, for the Gloria Jean Coffee Company.

Fig. 5-16. The Maxim Building, Boulder, Colorado. CommArts, designers, with the Hunter Group, architects, for 901 Walnut Street, L.L.C.

Fig. 6-1. The San Diego Exposition. Bertram Goodhue, architect. Illustration by Birch Burdette Long, from *Color in Sketching and Rendering* by Arthur Guptill. 1935 New York: Reinhold Publishing.

Fig. 6-3. The Seasons at Avon, Avon, Colorado. CommArts, designers, with Victor Mark Donaldson, architects, for the Gart Companies.

Fig. 6-8. United States Embassy Competition, Berlin. Moore Ruble Yudell Architects. Watercolor over pencil, 18" x 24". Illustration by Douglas E. Jamieson, 8271/2 Via de la Paz, Pacific Palisades, CA 90272 (310-573-1155).

Fig. 6-9. The United States Embassy, Cairo, Egypt. The Architects Collaborative (TAC), architects. Watercolor. Frank M. Costantino, illustrator. F. M. Costantino, Inc., 138 Pauline Street, Winthrop, MA 02152 (617-846-4766).

Fig. 6-10. Proposed Plaza, Olympics 2000, Istanbul, Turkey. Thomas W. Schaller, AIA, with Stang & Newdow / Atlanta. Watercolor, 36" x 24". Illustration by Thomas W. Schaller, Schaller Architectural Illustration, 2112 Broadway, Suite 407, New York, NY 10023 (212-362-5524).

Fig. 6-12. The Flamingo, Kansas City. CommArts, designers, with Gould Evans Goodman Associates, architects, for HHC / Development.

Fig. 6-13. The Maxim Building, Boulder, Colorado. CommArts, designers, with the Hunter Group, architects, for 901 Walnut Street, L.L.C.

Fig. 6-14. Teltow Housing Masterplan, Zeidler Roberts Partnership. Watercolor over pencil, 6½" x 8½". Illustration by Douglas E. Jamieson, 8271/2

Via de la Paz, Pacific Palisades, CA 90272 (310-573-1155).

Fig. 6-15. Art Museum, self-comissioned. Mixed media. Illustration by Ronald J. Love, Ronald J. Love Architectural Illustration, 3891 Bayridge Avenue, West Vancouver, BC V7V3J3, Canada (604-922-3033).

Fig. 6-16. From *The City.* Watercolor, 30" x 22". Illustration by Thomas W. Schaller, Schaller Architectural Illustration, 2112 Broadway, Suite 407, New York, NY 10023 (212-362-5524).

Fig. 6-17. Display window study for Gas Company Tower, Los Angeles. CommArts, window designers, for Maguire Thomas Partners.

Fig. 6-18. Proposed Hydroponics Research Center, Uruguay. Thomas W. Schaller, AIA, architect. Watercolor, 18" x 24". Illustration by Thomas W. Schaller, Schaller Architectural Illustration, 2112 Broadway, Suite 407, New York, NY 10023 (212-362-5524).

Fig. 6-19. Study for Old Orchard, Chicago. CommArts, designers, for Equity Properties.

Fig. 6-20. The Rattlesnake Club, Denver. CommArts, designers, for the Rattlesnake Club Associates.

Fig. 6-21. Naples Beachfront Cottages, Architectural Design Group, architects. Illustration by Curtis James Woodhouse, 3903 Loquat Avenue, Miami, FL 33133 (305-476-8098).

Fig. 6-22. Illustration by Edward Dixon McDonald, from *Color in Sketching and Rendering* by Arthur Guptill. 1935. New York: Reinhold Publishing.

Fig. 6-23. Park Meadows, Denver. CommArts, designers, with Anthony Belluschi Associates, architects, for TrizecHahn.

Fig. 7-12. Santa Monica Place (renovation), Santa Monica. CommArts, designers, with Ray Bailey Architects, for the Rouse Company.

Figs. 7-14, 7-15. Houston Uptown, Houston. CommArts, designers, with Slaney Santana, landscape architects, for Harris County Improvement District #1.

Fig. 7-16. Madison Square Garden, New York. CommArts, designers, with Gensler, architects, for Madison Square Garden.

Fig. 7-23. Perimeter Mall, Atlanta. CommArts, designers, with D'Augustino, Izzo, Quirk, architects, for the Rouse Company.

Fig. 7-30. Park Meadows, Denver. CommArts, designers, with Anthony Belluschi Architects, for TrizecHahn.

Figs. 7-38, 7-39. The Downtown Boulder Mall, Boulder, Colorado. CommArts, Everett / Zeigel Associates, and Sasaki Associates, Inc., design team, for the City of Boulder.

Fig. 7-40. Proposed modifications to Citywalk, Los Angeles. CommArts, designers, with Houston / Tyner, architects, for Universal Studios, Hollywood.

Fig. 7-47. World Trade Center, New York, Renovation Competition. CommArts, designers, with HOK New York, architects, for LCOR, Inc., and the Port Authority of New York and New Jersey.

Fig. 7-53. Madison Square Garden, New York. CommArts, designers, with Gensler, architects, for Madison Square Garden.

Figs. 7-60, 7-66. The Maxim Building, Boulder, Colorado. CommArts, designers, with the Hunter Group, architects, for 901 Walnut Street, L.L.C.

Fig. 7-67. Faneuil Hall Marketplace, Boston. Benjamin Thompson Associates for the Rouse Company.

Fig. 7-69. Proposed modifications to Citywalk, Los Angeles. CommArts, designers, with Houston / Tyner, architects, for Universal Studios, Hollywood.

Fig. 7-70. Mr. Steak, Denver. CommArts, designers, with Archiventure, architect, for Omnivest, Inc.

Fig. 7-71. Ontario Mills, Los Angeles. CommArts, designers, with Feola Carli Archuleta, architects, for the Mills Corporation.

Figs. 7-72, 7-78. Perimeter Mall, Atlanta. CommArts, designers, with D'Augustino, Izzo, Quirk, architects, for the Rouse Company.

Figs. 7-79, 7-83. The Maxim Building, Boulder, Colorado. CommArts, designers, with the Hunter Group, architects, for 901 Walnut Street, L.L.C.

Figs. 7-84, 7-86. Perimeter Mall, Atlanta. CommArts, designers, with D'Augustino, Izzo, Quirk, architects, for the Rouse Company.

Fig. 8-1. One Beaver Creek, Avon, Colorado. CommArts, designers, with Gwathmey Pratt Schultz, architects, for Vail Associates.

Fig. 8-2. Bridge for Buffalo Bayou, Houston Uptown District. CommArts, designers, for Houston Metro.

Fig. 8-3. Transit Stop Design, Houston Uptown District. CommArts, designers, for Houston Metro.

Fig. 8-5. Westin Hotel Ballroom Courtyard Study, Westminster, Colorado. CommArts, designers, for the City of Westminster.

Fig. 8-6. La Vega, Barcelona, Spain. CommArts, designers, with INGECO, engineering and coordination, for Jean Louis Solal, JLSI.

Fig. 8-7. International Terminal, JFK Airport, New York. CommArts, designers, with Skidmore, Owings and Merrill, architects, for LCOR, Inc., and the Port Authority of New York and New Jersey.

Fig. 8-18. La Vega, Barcelona, Spain. CommArts, designers, with INGECO, engineering and coordination, for Jean Louis Solal, JLSI.

Fig. 8-19. International Terminal, JFK Airport, New York. CommArts, designers, with Skidmore, Owings and Merrill, architects, for LCOR, Inc., and the Port Authority of New York and New Jersey.

Fig. 8-20. Ontario Mills, Los Angeles (above). CommArts, designers, with Feola Carli Archuleta, architects, for the Mills Corporation. Lake Forest, Lifestyle Cafe (below). CommArts, designers, for the Taubman Company.

INDEX